WORLD DRUG REPORT**2000**

United Nations Office
for Drug Control and Crime Prevention

OXFORD

UNIVERSITY PRESS

UNIVERSITY PRESS

Great Clarendon Street, Oxford OX2 6DP

Oxford University Press is a department of the University of Oxford It furthers the University's objective of excellence in research, scholarship, and education by publishing worldwide in

Oxford New York

Athens Auckland Bangkok Bogotá Buenos Aires
Calcutta Cape Town
Chennai Dar es Salaam Delhi Florence Hong Kong
Istanbul Karachi Kuala Lumpur Madrid Melbourne
Mexico City Mumbai Nairobi Paris São Paulo Shanghai
Singapore Taipei Tokyo Toronto Warsaw
with associated companies in Berlin Ibadan

Database right Oxford University Press (maker)

First published 2000

The maps in this publication are not intended to be exact representations. The designations on, and the presentation of, the maps does not imply the expression of any opinion whatsoever on the part of the United Nations concerning the legal status of any country, territory or area, or of its authorities, frontiers, or boundaries.

Design/Layout: WorldLinks, Vienna/ H. Kerstan

British Library Cataloguing in Publication Data
Data available
Library of Congress Cataloging in Publication Data
Data available

OUP ISBN: 0-19-829649-5 (pbk.)

The preparation of the World Drug Report 2000 was made possible thanks to financial contributions provided by the Governments of Italy and Sweden.

The opinions expressed in this publication do not necessarily represent the official policy of the United Nations International Drug Control Programme. The designations used do not imply the expression of any opinion whatsoever on the part of the United Nations concerning the legal status of any country, territory or area or of its authorities, frontiers or boundaries.

Printed in Great Britain by
The Bath Press Ltd., Bath

WORLD DRUG REPORT2000

United Nations Office
for Drug Control and Crime Prevention

Contents

LIST OF FIGURES

Chapter 2

LIST OF MAPS

LIST OF TABLES

WORLD DRUG REPORT 2000

Globalisation offers the human race unprecedented opportunities. Unfortunately, it also enables many anti-social activities to become "problems without passports." Among these are drug abuse, which brings misery to millions of families around the world every year, and drug trafficking which cynically promotes and exploits that misery for commercial gain. If the international community is to deserve its name, it must respond to this challenge.

Happily, it is beginning to do so. For decades we heard only reports of dramatic increases in drug production, drug trafficking and drug abuse. Such problems do not disappear overnight, but some of these trends are now changing, and even being reversed. Thanks to international cooperation, illicit production and manufacture of drugs like cocaine and heroin has stabilised, and in some cases declined. In some of the world's main markets, illicit drug *consumption* is now declining, too.

No less encouraging have been recent demonstrations of concerted political will. In 1998 the United Nations General Assembly held a Special Session on drugs, and established targets and deadlines to substantially reduce the world's drug problem by the year 2008. This year world leaders – gathered in larger numbers than ever before, at the Millennium Summit – have resolved to redouble their efforts to implement that commitment. Clearly, they share the belief that there are solutions to this global problem, *if* we all work together towards shared goals. We may be at a historic turning point.

The *World Drug Report* offers, as its name implies, a global overview of the drug issue. It contains information from many sources, which should help not only policy makers and scholars, but also the general public, to measure progress towards the ambitious goals that the General Assembly has set. This information suggests that, provided we do redouble our efforts, and do not relax our vigilance, we may at last be on our way to a world in which people can live their lives free from drug abuse, from drug trafficking, and from related crime and violence.

Kofi A. Annan
SECRETARY-GENERAL OF THE UNITED NATIONS

WORLD DRUG REPORT 2000

WORLD DRUG REPORT 2000

WORLD DRUG REPORT 2000

WORLD DRUG REPORT 2000

WORLD DRUG REPORT 2000

WORLD DRUG REPORT 2000

WORLD DRUG REPORT 2000

WORLD DRUG REPORT 2000

WORLD DRUG REPORT 2000

WORLD DRUG REPORT 2000

WORLD DRUG REPORT 2000

WORLD DRUG REPORT 2000

WORLD DRUG REPORT 2000

The time has come to change
the way we think about drugs. We must end the psychology of despair that has gripped the minds of a generation and would have us believe that nothing can be done to roll back, let alone stop, the consumption of drugs. Instead, we should focus on a pragmatic, integrated, long-term approach to addressing both supply and demand side issues. Through clear and concerted action we can indeed realize the twin objectives of substantially reducing the non-medical demand for drugs within eight years, and the eradication of coca and opium poppy production.

There are those who will scoff at such a view. Who argue that the tidal flow of addictive drugs is unstoppable and irreversible. Who believe that states and institutions are weak and will capitulate in the face of the organized criminal networks that are responsible for the production, trafficking and distribution of cocaine and heroin. Who can offer no way forward other than policy capitulation. Those unable to break out of this negative mindset should begin by considering a raft of recent and decidedly positive developments on the drugs front:

- Pakistan is virtually poppy free in the year 2000, production having all but been eradicated following the implementation of a 15-year programme.
- Bolivia has reduced the area under illicit coca cultivation by 78% in just three years, in line with its 'Dignity Plan', launched in 1997.
- Coca production in Peru, which rose steeply in the 1980s, has declined equally precipitously since 1992, with a 50% reduction in the supply of cocaine to the world market.
- Opium cultivation in Laos, the world's third largest producer, was cut by 30% over the last eighteen months, following an agreement between the President and myself.
- In Vietnam, cultivation of opium poppy was reduced by 90% in the 1990s.
- Opium poppy production in Thailand has fallen following the strong lead given by the country's king, with the support of local institutions and the

international community through the United Nations International Drug Control Programme (UNDCP), a part of ODCCP.

- The global area under opium poppy cultivation is at its lowest level since 1988, some 17% smaller in 1999 than 1990; similarly, the area under coca cultivation is at its lowest level since 1987, about 14% less in 1999 than in 1990.
- The profile of illegal drugs in the economies of the main producing countries has posted a decisive trend of decline. Even in countries where production levels have remained stubbornly high, the share of GDP has been falling, with drugs contributing some 2.5% of Colombia's economic output, down from a mid-1980s high of around 7%.
- During the 1990s consumption trends of the main problem drugs in the developed countries have been stable or declining; the abuse of cocaine fell in North America as compared to a decade earlier and heroin abuse was stable in Western Europe.

This good news belies the perception that the drugs problem can only get worse. It is no aberration. We need to remind ourselves that the history of addictive drugs is not one of a steady and inexorable deterioration. Rather, the past shows us fluctuating trends. Things can get worse, but they can also improve. For example, consider China, one of the states where comprehensive narcotics control strategies were first forged and implemented. China, for so long synonymous with the production and consumption of opium, succeeded in eradicating opium between 1949 and 1954, together with the organized crime, gambling and prostitution that was so much a feature of its recent past. We should remind ourselves that at the height of the problem China had about 20 million opium addicts, which is more than the approximately 14 million people worldwide addicted to opiates today.

The successful anti-opium drive in China was facilitated by attempts by the neighbouring state of India to control its opium production. Having commenced its strategy of control in the late 1940s, after 10 years, Delhi had brought the opium sector completely under control. Since then India has joined Australia as one of the world's leading licit exporters of opiates, with the poppy crop being used to supply much of the world's health needs for morphine. Turkey is a second country that, like India, has reduced and strictly controlled its output of opium since it switched from opium production as such, to the production of poppy straw in the early 1970s. Given the international drug control system in place and its improvements over the years, diversions from

licit production to illicit channels have been significantly reduced, so that they now play only a marginal role in the supply of the world's illegal drug markets.

The deterioration in the availability and consumption of drugs such as heroin or cocaine, is a more recent phenomenon, traceable to the late 1960s/early 1970s. Even over the last three decades, however, the story has been far from uniformly negative. While consumption of heroin in Western Europe increased in the 1970s and again in the late 1980s, it stabilized in the 1990s. Public health campaigns that warn about the dangers of drugs are beginning to have the same successes that those that identified the dangers posed by alcohol and cigarettes have already had. In the USA too, we have experienced positive trends. Demand for cocaine, as measured in national surveys on drug abuse, was some 70% lower in 1999 than in 1985.

THE PSYCHOLOGY OF DISEMPOWERMENT

If our experiences, both recent and distant, are far from being exclusively negative, then why is it that the conventional wisdom prevails that the spread of drugs cannot be faced down? After all, during the 1990s the world has responded with energy, purpose and determination to a host of global challenges of towering proportions, from environmental degradation, through world poverty to the spread of HIV. Surely, none of these are easier to beat than the threat from drugs.

I believe that there are three reasons why such a psychology of disempowerment has taken hold regarding drugs, especially among parts of the media in Europe. But these reasons, though understandable in the past, no longer apply.

First, it is a reflection of the accumulated demoralization and frustration that has grown up, flowing from the experiences of the 1970s and 1980s and the expansion in the availability and consumption of drugs. Concentrating on the trends of the 1990s, and hopefully into the future, should help us to escape this negative mindset.

Second, it is a function of the tendency to exaggerate the figures when discussing the issue of illegal drugs. The difficulty of generating solid and reliable statistics in a field dominated by illegality and marginality has meant that the

3

temptation to embellish figures in order to capture headlines has often proved irresistible. In this regard we need to see a disinflation of the figures, combined with a more rigorous and determined approach to estimating the magnitude of these problems. After all, we need to remember that only about 10% of the countries of the world have a reliable system in place for the collection of data relating to illegal drugs. There is therefore much room for improvement.

Third, it has been a product of the limited ability of the international community to forge effective cooperative strategies. For so long in the past, attempts to build international cooperative regimes foundered on the perception that countries were strictly differentiated into production, transit and consumption states. Moreover, cooperative ventures were paralysed for decades by an East-West and a North-South cleavage, especially within the United Nations body. Formal accords were routinely signed, but in practical terms action was limited, especially on the operational side.

The end of the Cold War and the emergence of real processes for peace in a number of hitherto insoluble conflicts have softened these tensions within the international system, making cooperation a more practical enterprise. Who, for example, could have envisaged UNDCP galvanizing a subregional drug control cooperation programme involving Egypt, Israel, Jordan and the Palestinian Authority, as occurred in February 1999, or India and Pakistan cooperating on drug control matters, under the auspices of UNDCP, as they have done in the late 1990s.

Furthermore, this apparently neat division among producer, transit and consumer states has clearly broken down since the late 1980s. Over the last decade we have witnessed an increasing globalization of drugs markets, which has enveloped parts of the developing world, especially with regard to heroin and cocaine. At least 134 countries and territories were faced with a drug abuse problem in the 1990s. Three quarters of all countries report abuse of heroin and two thirds abuse of cocaine. Authorities in Pakistan estimate that there could be some 1.5 million heroin addicts whereas in the early 1980s there were only a few. There are believed to be half a million heroin addicts in Iran. These figures increasingly mirror and even outstrip the so-called consumer countries in per capita terms. In the whole of Western Europe, there are some 1.2 million heroin addicts and about one million are found in the USA. Similarly, a number of Latin American countries – both coca producing countries and

neighbouring ones – are already faced with cocaine abuse problems that are at levels similar to Western Europe. Furthermore, developing countries have begun to be invaded by flows of synthetic drugs – notably of so-called Ecstasy-type drugs (MDMA, MDA MDME etc.) – produced in developed areas. Through these appalling developments, states across the globe have at least started showing more readiness to cooperate with one another against the scourge of drugs.

AN INFRASTRUCTURE FOR ACTION

It is against this backdrop of a new cooperative order that international society has set about forging an infrastructure for action over the last three years. A key point of departure was the Special Session on the international drug problem of the United Nations General Assembly, which took place on 8-10 June 1998, and in the holding of which Mexico played a pivotal role. In all, 185 states signed up to the declaration of the session, meaning that for the first time a response to the world drug problem was owned by virtually the entire global community. As I said in my closing remarks to the session, 'our meeting marks the start of a new chapter in global drug control. We have sent the world a message of hope this week'. In the two years that have elapsed since the meeting in New York I have had no reason to change or re-evaluate my conclusions.

While many good things sprang from the New York meeting, the most important outcome was the three objectives we set for ourselves, together with the clear but realistic target dates attached to them. The three significant objectives adopted at the session were:

*   All participants agreed to develop national strategies on illegal drugs, to be put in place by 2003;
*   All participants agreed to work for 'significant and measurable results' in reducing illegal drugs consumption by 2008, with a 50% reduction informally taken as an indicative target;
*   States where illegal production has taken place committed themselves to a total elimination of production, also by 2008. Alternative development was acknowledged as the only long-term solution to the problem of illicit narcotic cultivation.

WORLD DRUG REPORT 2000

The impact of the Special Session on Latin American states in particular was tremendous. Countries like Bolivia, Colombia and Peru, that have been ravaged by the effects of illegal drugs over the last three decades, could at last see that their national efforts were part of a global strategy. This gave a major boost to the morale of those engaged in the struggle against drugs in those countries, as well as softening some of the hemispheric tensions that had built up out of frustration at the persistence of drug production and trafficking in the continent. For states like Bolivia and Peru, that have resolutely committed themselves to the total eradication of coca production, the Special Session represented an occasion for recognition and for enhanced prestige, the international standing of these two Andean states having further grown with their achievements during the two years since the session. Furthermore, the general recognition of the efforts of La Paz and Lima has, in turn, increased the expectation and probability of economic benefits flowing from an end to coca cultivation, such as an eventual inflow of foreign direct investment. Thus economic incentives for the eradication of domestic production have continued to increase.

The momentum built up at the Special Session has been maintained and enhanced through further activity at the heart of the United Nations. In April 2000, for example, I was invited to brief the United Nations Security Council on the drugs situation in Afghanistan, the first time that narcotics has featured on the Council's agenda and evidence of the tangible way in which the world now sees drugs as a major security threat to all. The subsequent statement by the President of the Security Council placed the international spotlight on the production and trafficking of Afghan narcotics and its consequences for the continuation of the conflict in that country.

BIG CHALLENGE, BIG RESPONSE

Mention of Afghanistan of course reminds us that not all states have been as successful as Bolivia and Peru in combating drugs production over the last few years, even though progress was reported in 2000. As illicit opium production has been eliminated in several countries, so it has become increasingly concentrated in Afghanistan and, to a lesser extent, Myanmar. UNDCP's estimate, based on our annual opium poppy survey in Afghanistan, the world's largest producer of illegal opium, showed that approximately 91,000 hectares of opium poppy were cultivated in the country in 1999, an increase of more than 40% on the previous year.

In 2000 cultivation declined by some 10% to 82,000 hectares. However, we also note that the area under cultivation remains almost 30% higher than in 1998. A stronger fall was recorded in the opium output in 2000 from the 1999 record high of 4,565 tonnes. Some of the decline was due to eradication and alternative development efforts in the limited areas where UNDCP ran its project activities; most of the decline, however, had simply to do with unfavourable weather conditions – on which one cannot count in the future. Opium production in 2000 remained 22% above the 1998 levels. Though obviously such magnitudes of harvests continue to be of great concern, one should again resist the counsel of despair. One must remember that even in 1999, the year of the record harvest in Afghanistan, only 1.1% of arable land in Afghanistan was given over to opium poppy cultivation. The total value of the Afghan opium crop has been only around US$ 200 million a year, and slightly less than US$ 100 million at harvest time in 2000 (reflecting low prices due to large stocks built-up in 1999), which shows a potential for successful alternative development work once political conditions are conducive to do so. Moreover, results for 2000 – though far from satisfactory – show at least that even in Afghanistan opium production can go down.

Clearly Afghanistan remains the challenge for the global community in terms of curtailing opium production and hence the availability of heroin. Rising to this challenge will not be easy. We know too little about such basic building blocks as social and tribal structures in Afghanistan, the product of years of neglect and inaccessibility. Moreover, we also know little about the political structures of the country, the Taliban movement being one that rose without trace to take over some 90% of the territory of the country between 1995 and 1998. Since then the introspection of the Taliban and international concerns about issues of human and women's rights inside the country and the harbouring of suspected terrorists have greatly restricted interaction and hence the fostering of mutual understanding with Kabul. Most importantly perhaps the trauma, brutalization and displacement experienced by much of the population of the country over more than two decades have made it doubly difficult to predict developments in the country.

In Afghanistan a big challenge has required a big response. We have risen to that challenge by developing a Regional Action Plan for Afghanistan. This has been designed to build a coalition of countries on the border with Afghanistan. The aim of this coalition is to achieve an integrated strategy capable of delivering a reduction in opium production and trafficking from Afghanistan, while ensuring that these activities are not simply displaced to other adjacent areas. In short, the plan is really about eliminating opium completely from the region, rather than just from Afghanistan. The plan has a number of key components:

- **Prevent trafficking.** Owing to the problem of access to, and understanding of the particular case of Afghanistan, together with the inevitably long lead time involved in replacing opium cultivation inside the country, the first component of the plan has been to try to stop the drugs getting out. To this end, we have set about creating a security belt around Afghanistan which would ring fence the areas of opium cultivation in the south of the country, but also in parts of the north, which are controlled by the Afghan opposition, the Northern Alliance, and elsewhere.

- **Consolidate national institutions.** Many of the states of the region are either newly emerged, such as Kyrgyzstan and Tajikistan, or have struggled to rise to important challenges of development and identity. The United Nations Security Council meeting on Afghan drugs ended by urging Member States to increase their support for efforts aimed at strengthening the drug control capacities of states bordering Afghanistan. UNDCP has played its part by working closely with the Government of Tajikistan in particular, in order to establish a drug control agency capable of collecting accurate information, fighting organized crime and closing the Tajik bottleneck for drugs trafficking to the north. This enabled authorities in Tajikistan to increase heroin seizures over the January-July 2000 period by 450% to 789 kg, which is more than half the amount of heroin seized in the USA during all of 1998, and more than heroin seizures in Germany, Italy or Spain in 1998. The success was also made possible by the ongoing cooperation between the new agency and the Russian border guards along the frontier with Afghanistan. We feel that bolstering the Tajik effort is particularly important, because of the stockpiling of opium, morphine base and heroin, which we believe is taking place on the Afghan-Tajik border. Failure to take preventive measures today will prove potentially very costly in the future.

- **Prevent displacement.** Opium eradication is a big challenge, but it is clearly not the end of the story. A responsible supply side strategy simply cannot afford to disengage as soon as a country like Pakistan is declared to be poppy free. Only through careful monitoring, and a continuing commitment to alternative development strategies, can the absence of opium production be consolidated. Our commitment therefore needs to be a long term one. In partnership with the

European Space Agency, we are currently constructing a special programme for the monitoring of actual and potential areas of illicit cultivation worldwide.

- *Support country efforts.* Some of the countries bordering Afghanistan already have a proven track record of combating drugs trafficking. No country has a more exemplary record in this regard than Iran. The authorities in Tehran stamped out the domestic production of illicit opium after 1979. More recently, they have acted with vigorous political will in trying to stem the cross border trade in opium, which has fuelled their spiralling rates of domestic heroin addiction, much of which then continues westwards through Turkey and into Western Europe. Iran's share in global seizures of heroin and morphine has risen from 9% in 1987/88 to 42% in 1997/98. Maintaining such a valuable commitment has proved to be extremely costly for Iran, especially as 2,600 members of the security forces have been killed in anti-drug operations. With the cross border smugglers highly mobile and well equipped, the Iranian side has often found itself outgunned. UNDCP has looked for practical ways in which it can support Tehran in this dangerous task. With this in mind, a project to facilitate technical cooperation on both demand reduction and border control has been designed.

- *Implement alternative development.* This is a central pillar of our aim of phasing out poppy cultivation in Afghanistan over the next five years. It should be emphasized that alternative development is not the same as crop substitution. Finding replacement crops for opium farmers to grow can indeed be an important component of alternative development, but it is unlikely alone to result in the cessation of poppy growing. For alternative development to have a chance of being successful it needs to be much more holistic, spanning such areas as the provision of education and health facilities, and work outside the agricultural sector. A four-year UNDCP alternative development project in Qandahar and Nangarhar provinces has helped to pinpoint important areas of need in the future. These include:

  - the need to focus on itinerant harvesters in addition to farmers, both because of the importance of such cheap labour in the continuous weeding and harvesting of the crop, and the role of such casual labour in the spread of opium poppy cultivation. A programme of job creation might prove important in raising the price of labour and hence eroding the margins of opium cultivation.

9

- the need to address the problem of access to markets for farmers in Afghanistan, where it is estimated that nearly 60% of the road network has been eliminated as a result of the domestic conflict. In the absence of good market access, the willingness of middlemen to buy opium poppies at the farm gate represents a major incentive for farmers to cultivate the opium poppy crop.
- the need to address the problem of the lack of rural credit in Afghanistan, a problem that has got worse with the normative strictures against interest adopted over the past decade. Again the absence of cheap and both easily and widely available rural credit leaves the way open for middlemen, who will provide their own credit, conditional on the cultivation of opium, rather than the poppy's main crop alternative, wheat.

Though such an integrated, regional approach is of vital importance, the collaboration and cooperation that underlies it must extend beyond the specifics of the Regional Action Plan. Such a philosophy is being extended to levels of multinational, interstate and civil societal cooperation, in all of which UNDCP is involved. Examples of such cooperation are already multiplying. We are, for instance, cooperating fully with the 6 + 2 (border countries, plus Russia and the US) initiative on Afghanistan, to ensure that the issue of drugs is integrated into the diplomatic and mediation activities of that group. We are in close contact with subregional organizations like the Economic Cooperation Organization (ECO) on border control and illicit crop reduction strategies. We are also in the early stages of 'common programming' with other United Nations agencies and non-governmental organizations (NGOs) active in areas where opium production is particularly acute, with the province of Helmand, the centre of almost half of the poppy cultivation in Afghanistan in both 1999 and 2000, a top priority area. We believe that such careful, concerted and integrated approaches best expedite the aggregation of the efforts of us all in combating illegal drugs. They also provide a paradigmatic approach for supply-side responses elsewhere in the world.

HUMAN SECURITY

In the same way that there is a need for institutions working at different levels to cooperate together, we cannot afford not to locate the issue of illegal drugs in its broader context of failed, or failing states and human security. It is after all no coincidence that as the geographical orientation of plant-based drug

production contracts, it increasingly focuses either on the territory of failed states or geographically marginalized states. What one has to realize in this situation is not that such countries are somehow intrinsically wedded to the production of illegal drugs, but that drugs production has become a symptom of wider structural problems. It is from such areas, which display multiple associated problems that drugs have become most difficult to eradicate.

Failed or failing states refers to entities whose institutions are so weak or collapsed that they are unable to provide the most basic activities of states, namely non-partisan internal regulation (the rule of law) and external security. Often associated with such weakness is what one might call a moral shortfall, whereby states are regarded as unable or unwilling to act on behalf of their whole population. Such problems of state legitimacy are often the product of internal disputes about the nature, identity and orientation of the state. In the absence of strong and well-established political institutions, these disputes can easily degenerate into domestic conflict. It is indeed salutary that of an estimated 250 high and low intensity political conflicts afflicting the globe today, fewer than 30 involve old-style conventional inter-state conflicts. It has indeed been observed that the problem of war in international politics has been reduced primarily to the problem of state maintenance and state failures.

The emergence of failed or failing states also presents enhanced opportunities for organized criminal groupings. Against a backdrop of growing criminalization, the corruption of state institutions will tend to emerge, and the rule of law will be increasingly impaired. Once established, these criminal groups then have a strong vested interest in making sure that strong, effective and legitimate states are not rebuilt. Such criminal organizations are much less likely to be concerned about the basic human rights of the population than states themselves, which are at least subject to international treaty obligations, and can be made subject to the scrutiny of international organizations. Once states have collapsed, their reconstruction is inevitably a long, difficult and costly process, in terms of both institution building and instilling mutual trust among formerly warring communities.

Such facets of failed states are discernible in the decisions that individuals and groups make in drug-producing countries. At the individual and sectoral level, the cultivation of opium poppies in Afghanistan is the product of individual farmers seeking low risk means of ensuring survival in a high risk environment. In this context, the experience of Afghan society of protracted conflict, displacement, the threat from lethal weapons and regime instability are all material in an individual's decision to plant opium poppies. On a wider, political level, drugs production, or at least the 'tax' that is extracted from the producers and traffickers of drugs by local warlords, regionally based insurgent groups, such as the Revolutionary Armed Forces of Colombia (FARC), and others, is a means by which to generate a level of income necessary to sustain the activities of such groups and factions. In both cases, the poppy or coca production becomes an instrument of wider activities and objectives. One has to understand that in this way drugs production and trafficking often plays a role analogous to other similarly situated commodities, such as, most topically, the sale and trafficking of diamonds in the civil conflicts in Angola and Sierra Leone.

In order to combat the specific problem of drugs, one therefore has to be mindful of and active towards the overall context of poverty and displacement, internal strife and armed political conflict against which it takes place. The reality has to be acknowledged that the reduction and eradication of drugs production has to be accompanied by a range of other measures. These must include poverty reduction, the exploratory activities of two-track diplomacy, conflict resolution and mediation and, when circumstances eventually allow, institution building.

CONFRONTING UNCIVIL SOCIETY

Of course, it has to be appreciated that the related notion of human security is one that covers but also extends beyond that of civil conflicts. As far as the United Nations Office in Vienna is concerned, human security has to do with the physical insecurity of the individual caused by criminal and political violence, and, once removed, the deterioration in the quality of health resulting from the impact of illicit drugs. In the absence of proximate external threats to borders and states it is threats from within to the public space to which we are all most at risk. The preservation and expansion of human security involves defending society from such diverse threats as criminals, terrorists, street gangs, drugs dealers, arms smugglers, kidnappers, hostage takers, armed robbers and others endangering the well-being of our citizens.

Increasingly, international public opinion is demanding action on such matters. Unless all sources of profits of criminal organizations are attacked, it will be extremely difficult to dismantle such organizations. Similar considerations

in the field of drug control led to the expansion of the scope of international control to include all aspects of the drug trade, including money laundering and trade in precursor chemicals. But this is not enough. There is evidence that criminal networks, including those operating in the drug trade, can easily be used to engage in other criminal activities as well. By diversifying their activities, such organizations are able to overcome temporary setbacks caused by successful anti-drug operations without losing their capacity to continue operating. While international cooperation has already advanced in the field of drug control as such, other areas exploited by organized crime are still lacking a similarly coordinated response.

The United Nations Office for Drug Control and Crime Prevention (ODCCP) in Vienna, with its expanded remit to address the challenge of uncivil society, is well placed to play an important role in this realm. It offers a forum for debate and a context for formal treaties between states. It is also well placed to promote cooperation among criminal justice systems. In an era of globalization the United Nations has a special role to play, both in focusing the world's attention on international organized crime and in particular in highlighting the centrality of the human rights component of human security. For a more tangible expression of these general principles and practices made flesh I would highlight a key area of work that the United Nations has been involved in, namely coordinating the combating of transnational organized crime.

It is against such a backdrop that work has been moving ahead on the adoption of a United Nations Convention against Transnational Organized Crime, the very embodiment of the fight against uncivil society. Over 125 different states have been involved in the negotiations for the Convention, which is expected to be adopted by the United Nations General Assembly this November, to be followed by a signing conference in Palermo in December 2000. The main utility of the Convention will be that it will provide a single instrument through which to respond to the plethora of activities which fall under the rubric of transnational organized crime, and hence facilitate the harmonization of national legislation. The adoption of such an instrument will mark the passage of the fourth major international convention addressing issues related to illegal drugs and its associated threats to human security, following earlier conventions passed in 1961 (narcotic drugs), 1971 (psychotropic drugs) and 1988 (illicit trafficking, including money laundering).

WORLD DRUG REPORT 2000

The Convention is accompanied by three associated protocols on the illicit manufacturing and trafficking in firearms, the trafficking of persons – especially women and children – and the smuggling of migrants. Member States have been particularly welcoming of efforts in respect to the second of these draft protocols, and agreement has been relatively easy to achieve with regard to the core elements. The protocol represents the first attempt to address the problem of the trafficking in women and children in a comprehensive way. In an essentially balanced approach to the issue, it seeks both to prosecute and punish offenders while protecting the trafficked persons.

Important new aspects of the Convention and protocols include:

- a massive increase in the number of predicate offences covered by the accord;
- new provisions for the protection of victims and of witnesses, especially with regard to the vulnerability of women and children who have been trafficked and the crucial importance of their being prepared to come forward to give evidence;
- measures to shield legal processes from criminal activity, notably in the provision of public tenders;
- detailed provisions on the development of regulatory regimes to prevent and control money laundering and on the confiscation and sharing of criminal assets, which will help to minimize bank secrecy, while continuing to deliver bank confidentiality;
- the adoption of codes of conduct for relevant professional groups to prevent the misuse of expertise by organized criminal groups;
- an innovative implementation mechanism for the convention consisting of 'peer review' to monitor in a constructive way, the implementation of the convention by signatory states, and to ensure that developing countries receive the necessary technical assistance to facilitate its effective administration.

'A BALANCED APPROACH'

So far this introduction has been dominated by a discussion of supply side issues. This should in no way be interpreted as a reflection of the priorities or approach of UNDCP and its staff. It is of course true that until the last decade the demand side of the equation tended to have Cinderella status. There were unfortunate though understandable reasons for this. These included the practical difficulty

of data collection and the accuracy of the figures that were generated in trying to measure what was in fact a hidden population. Data sets, for example, were notoriously 'soft'. By contrast, collecting information on the supply side stretches back to the beginning of the twentieth century. Moreover, the three existing international conventions related to illicit drugs are well known for their imprecision on concerted demand side action. The drafters of these conventions were reluctant to set down rigid international standards on demand reduction, believing that individual states should be able to develop differing responses, depending on the nature and cultural context in which they were working.

It has now been some 30 years since governments began to make financial provision for action on the demand side of illegal drugs. However, it is really only with the political declaration of the Special Session of the General Assembly in June 1998 that the substance of 'a balanced approach between demand reduction and supply reduction, each reinforcing the other, in an integrated approach to solving the drug problem' has emerged. At the conference, Member States signed a declaration of principle on reducing demand, so that each country has agreed to tackle the problem in a systematic, coordinated way. Indeed, I would go so far as to say that if we have one main task in sight as a world community in addressing the threat of drugs it is on the demand side: to reduce addiction. Beyond that, we all have to realize that long-term prevention is surely the best, and certainly the cheapest, strategy.

Since the adoption of the political declaration in 1998, action has been concerted. It has been our goal to develop an action plan for each state through which to achieve the implementation of the goals of the declaration. Under the strategy, tasks have been ascribed to UNDCP and to individual states. Our first priority has been to try to facilitate the collection of reliable data in order to assess the extent of drug abuse across the world. To this end, a Global Assessment Programme (GAP) has been established, which has developed methodologies for use by states on the prevalence of drug consumption. Investment has also been made in the development of an early warning system to identify new trends in drug consumption among young people in particular, while a further aim of GAP is to point out the costs and consequences of illicit drug use, covering everything from the provision of treatment to the spread of HIV.

With the first step in the plan of action on data collection underway, we are in the process of planning and implementing step two. This is a flexible approach aimed at trying to decide what works and what does not in terms of demand reduction. Here, we are trying to develop a 'best practice' approach, but one which is especially sensitized to the opinions and views of young people themselves. We strongly believe that it is important to listen to the views of those who are rarely consulted, but who, owing to the nature of youth culture, are likely to be in closest proximity to the circulation of illegal drugs. To facilitate this bottom-up approach, UNDCP is making strenuous efforts to interact with NGOs and youth groups, which will in turn be extremely useful both in terms of disseminating best practice and as an antenna through which to detect rising trends. To facilitate the acquisition of this 'silent knowledge', a highly successful international meeting, for instance, was held in Banff in 1998, which resulted in the creation of a valuable international network in this field.

SPREAD OF SYNTHETIC STIMULANTS

The systematic analysis of data submitted to us by Member States, as well as working directly with young people have made us acutely aware of the shifts in drug consumption patterns. Nowhere has this been more evident than in the growing tendency towards the use of synthetic drugs, more specifically amphetamine-type stimulants (ATS) and within this group methylenedioxymethamphetamine (MDMA), better known by its street name, 'ecstasy'.

The United Nations has been at the forefront of pioneering work on synthetic drugs since they first emerged as major substances of abuse in a number of countries in the 1960s, and on a much broader scale, in the late 1980s and in the 1990s. By dint of their relatively recent emergence ('ecstasy', for instance, only emerged as a widespread substance of abuse in the late 1980s) and their changing chemical composition, the jury remains out on the long-term health consequences of synthetic drug use. Such kinds of systematic research into the long-term health impact has been seen, until recently as 'the missing link' between the diverging perceptions of synthetic drug use. Some recent research in this field, however, has yielded alarming results of apparent neurotoxicity (i.e. serious and possibly irrevocable damage to the brain, notably to its serotonine system) resulting from ecstasy use. This also confirms earlier results obtained through animal studies. There are some additional reasons to be concerned about the effect that ATS could have on our young people. These include:

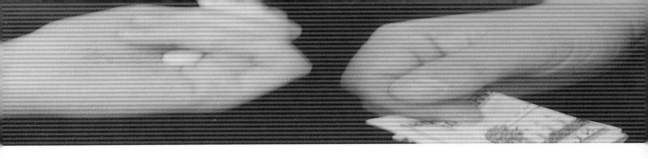

- **'Bingeing'.** The assumption on the part of many young people in Western Europe and North America that ATS do not cause lasting harm have helped to precipitate a high frequency of usage. It is not unusual to hear stories of young people taking ATS every night throughout a holiday, or routinely at weekends through large parts of the year. Such frequency of consumption has increased the cause for concern about long-term neurological dangers.

- **Polydrug use.** The broad range of different ATS and other drugs available, together with the evolving nature of such stimulants, makes the use of different combinations of drugs, licit and illicit, an increasingly common feature. This polydrug consumption is as typical among drugs users in a refugee camp in Peshawar or Afghanistan as it is among groups of young people in Western Europe. Such polydrug use makes it more difficult to check what combinations and under what circumstances such mixing might pose a particular health danger.

- **The 'Natural' fallacy.** Increasingly, healthy images are promoted in the marketing of ATS, such as the availability of so-called 'herbal ecstasy'. This represents an attempt to suggest that a particular drug is entirely plant-based rather than synthetic, that it is not illegal, that it is not a so-called 'hard drug', and that in fact it is completely safe. Though such drugs may include the addition of plant-based psychoactive substances, they are still synthesized in a laboratory, and usually involve off the shelf chemicals or precursors. The guarantee of their safety is anything but assured.

Beyond these particular health fears are a range of general trends and problems that are connected to synthetic drugs and their spread. Two in particular are worth mentioning here. The first is the widespread expansion of the consumption of ATS. It is already the case that ATS, notably methamphetamine and to a lesser extent MDMA, are being produced in growing volumes in South-East Asia, including Thailand, Myanmar and China, to service the rising demand across South-East and East Asia. The spread of Western-style youth culture, with the profile that ATS enjoys within it, to such parts of the world is likely to accelerate the attractiveness of ATS accordingly, in turn stimulating the supply side.

The second is the tendency for the production and distribution of synthetic drugs increasingly to be structured and integrated into international organized criminal activities. With a rapidly expanding market and wide profit margins criminal networks are likely to be increasingly attracted to such activities. Of particular worry are the suspicions that ATS and heroin may be manufactured in the same laboratories and circulated through the same distribution channels. It raises the sinister possibility of criminal market makers trying to turn their heroin clients into additional users of ATS and their ATS clients into additional consumers of heroin.

UNDCP: THE 'SOFTWARE' OF THE SYSTEM

This introduction began by suggesting that there has been much good news in the advance against illegal drugs, especially in the last few years. We need to maintain this momentum in order that Bolivia and Peru can join Pakistan in being free of cultivated plant-based drugs. Beyond that, we have to ring fence the chronic coca and opium producer states, notably Afghanistan and Colombia. We need to support the extraordinary effort the current President of Colombia, Andres Pastrana, has made which is aimed at bringing peace to the country through a strategy involving both a peace process and the elimination of illicit coca cultivation. Then we can prepare the way for the big push designed to squeeze the cultivation out of these two countries and hence out of global markets. If these trends continue in coca and opium production we look forward to the day when the defeatism of the past, which has so often bordered on prejudice, will also be squeezed out.

This introduction has also accepted that, in spite of this good news, there are many challenges that still face us. We here at UNDCP are mindful of this and are forever reevaluating our own mission and activities to see how we can enhance and expand our contribution. In doing so, we should neither replicate what Member States are or should be doing. Instead, we must be clear about where our comparative advantage lies. This may be refined into seven key elements:

- *Providing a global view.* In the same way that we cannot do what states do, no single state can have the global view of UNDCP. As the June 1998 session in New York has shown, only action under the United Nations auspices is capable of taking a genuinely global look at the challenge of drugs. In turn, only under the United Nations umbrella can the entire international community be co-opted behind a broad-based, integrated, long-term strategy. And only through united action can criminal activities be driven out of

the system. With the ideological impediments of the past largely removed, the prospect of further effective multilateral action against drugs is one that is both an exciting and empowering prospect.

- *Providing quality data and analysis.* The main reason behind the original idea to publish a United Nations World Drug Report was the need to have a sober and neutral set of data and analysis about drugs in the world. Today, we are increasingly confident that we know what we say we know, and know what we need to know. We believe that our low key but highly effective on the ground research in Afghanistan, working in a context of great difficulties, has been invaluable in terms of helping to build up a better picture as to the dynamics of opium poppy cultivation in that country. UNDCP remains strongly committed to trying to improve the information base on which the drugs strategies and policies of the world are based. To facilitate that end, we have expanded our own in-house research staff, as well as establishing a new money laundering monitoring unit.

- *Establishing priorities.* The history of action against illegal drugs has been blighted by the politicization of debates, policies and priorities surrounding the subject. This has continued to be the case up to the present, as a range of continuing arguments about different national approaches to demand strategies illustrates. We here at UNDCP regard the politicization of such issues as deeply undesirable. They lead to gesture politics, grandstanding and short termism, which in turn tend to be the enemies of the sort of quiet, integrated, longer term strategies that are actually more likely to have a chance of success. The best way to depoliticize future responses to drugs and to adopt priorities on a sound basis is by letting the United Nations take the lead. We believe that the events of the last two years show that hard and diligent work undertaken in a pragmatic, problem-solving spirit is the best way to set about establishing priorities and targets for action.

- *Innovative initiatives.* UNDCP has a concentration of some of the best minds working in the area of combating illegal drugs and organized crime. These professionals are in turn increasingly well networked to the best technical know-how in different branches of national governments, among national and international NGO communities and in universities and research institutions across the globe. This insider informed and global view makes us uniquely well placed to develop innovative, dynamic yet realistic initiatives for future action, as epitomized by the outcome of the 1998 meeting of the United Nations General Assembly.

- *Planning and coordination.* The strategic response to drugs requires that everyone play their part. It also requires that those contributions fit into a pre-planned framework and that the efforts of individual states, strong and weaker alike, be coordinated and monitored. In this respect one might think of an orchestra: everyone has to play their own instruments, but the music improves if everyone is playing together. Only through such means can a well meaning but otherwise patchy response be turned into an integrated and effective one. UNDCP sees one of its main roles as being to provide a context in which the efforts of states can be maximized through the provision of good planning and a coordinated follow-up.

- *Providing technical cooperation.* Some countries lack the resources or expertise to play their part fully in this concerted global effort. UNDCP operates a technical cooperation programme to assist them in four thematic areas: i) support for the basic structures of policy, legislation and advocacy, primarily through the provision of advisory services; ii) assistance to demand reduction programmes, targeting high priority prevention, treatment and rehabilitation initiatives; iii) the strengthening of law enforcement capacities along major trafficking routes; and iv) support to alternative development programmes in the main illicit crop production zones. Technical cooperation activities are structured at national, regional and global levels, enabling a careful targeting in geographical as well as functional terms.

- *Maintaining focus.* States are concerned with a multitude of different tasks and issues. It is therefore easy for national governments, in spite of good intentions, to become deflected from a constant engagement even with such a pressing and serious issue as illegal drugs. It is at times when other subjects have grabbed the headlines and the public policy agenda has moved elsewhere, that UNDCP has a further role to play. That is in maintaining the spotlight on the issue of drugs and its associated phenomena of corruption, state failure, the breakdown of the rule of law and money laundering.

But it is not sufficient for us merely to do what we have done before. We too must change and grow. Since I took over the helm, UNDCP has already down-sized the Vienna administration and shifted resources into the field. We have developed and seen endorsed in June 1998 a bold strategy for a global response to illegal drugs. Since then we have been implementing this strategy with vim and vigour and increasing success. We believe that the 300 person staff of UNDCP provides very good value indeed for the US$ 70 million budget that we have at our disposal.

In the future we feel that we can do even more. We need to be more flexible than in the past. In particular, we need to build our capacity to be able to face fast-moving trends and emergencies. Of course this will necessitate more funds, but we believe that the track record of the organization is one that merits additional financial support. Moreover, we believe that there is a popular mandate the world over for the effective use of targeted funds to combat the dangers of drugs. To use an analogy, we need to be the software of the system to the hardware of the Member States; we need to play the role of a merchant bank to the commercial banks of the Member States. Working in close and complementary relations, there is every prospect that Member States and the United Nations organization together can strengthen and deepen the positive trends beginning to emerge in the area of drugs in the 21st century.

Pino Arlacchi
EXECUTIVE DIRECTOR OF ODCCP

CHAPTER **1**
RECENT TRENDS IN PRODUCTION,
TRAFFICKING AND CONSUMPTION:
AN OVERVIEW

The present chapter provides an overview of broad global trends in illicit drug production, trafficking and consumption[a]. Despite the well-known difficulties associated with measuring the size of a hidden population and the magnitude of an illicit activity, the statistics that follow go a long way towards documenting the international drug problem, and how it changes over time.

1.1. PRODUCTION

Opium and coca leaf

Throughout the latter half of the 1990s, global illicit production of opium, the raw material for heroin, remained stable, and the production of coca leaf, the raw material for cocaine, declined. This trend is in marked contrast to the two previous decades when both opium and coca leaf production increased steadily (see Figures 1 and 2).

Despite a record harvest of Afghan *opium* in 1999[1] which increased global production sharply (to some 5,800 tonnes, more than the 1994-99 average of about 4,900 tonnes), the increase in the 1990s turned out to be far more moderate than in the 1980s when output tripled. *Coca leaf production* estimates suggest that global output declined over the last few years – an even stronger contrast to the tripling of coca leaf production, and the quadrupling of cocaine manufacture in the 1980s.

a) The United Nations International Drug Control Programme (UNDCP) gathers much of its information on the supply and demand of illicit drugs from its Member States through the UNDCP Annual Reports Questionnaire (ARQ). The ARQ is a comprehensive survey designed to provide information on a country's drug problems and steps taken to address them. Parties to the three international drug control Conventions (1961, 1971 and 1988) are required to submit the questionnaire annually; nevertheless the questionnaire is sent to most countries in the world, and is also submitted by many countries not party to the Conventions. However, as the consistency, regularity and comprehensiveness of the countries' responses to the ARQs vary considerably from year to year, there are significant gaps in the data. These gaps are filled by extrapolation, qualitative evidence, scientific studies and drug-related data published by several governments and organizations. The resulting database, UNDCP DELTA (Database for Estimates and Long-term Trends Analysis) is the source of all the data in this *Report*, unless otherwise cited. Statistics drawn from DELTA are also published annually by UNDCP, the latest version of which is *Global Illicit Drug Trends 2000* (Vienna, 2000).

Fig. 1: Global illicit production of opium

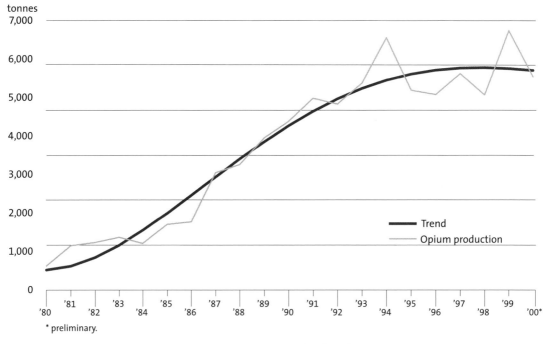

* preliminary.

Source: UNDCP, Database for Estimates and Long-term Trends Analysis (DELTA).

Fig. 2: Global illicit production of (dry) coca leaf

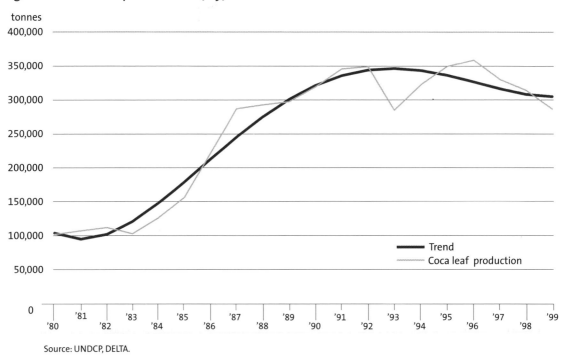

Source: UNDCP, DELTA.

24

Fig. 3: Areas under cultivation of opium poppy and coca bush (in hectares)

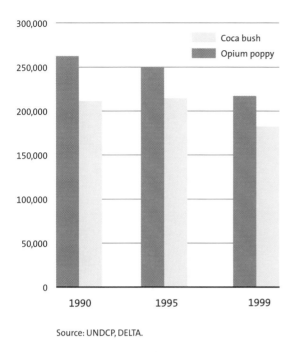

Source: UNDCP, DELTA.

Fig. 4: Opium production

tonnes

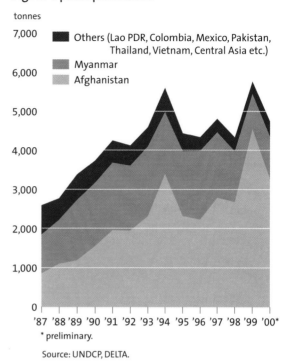

* preliminary.

Source: UNDCP, DELTA.

The global area under opium poppy cultivation is at its lowest level since 1988, some 17% smaller in 1999 than in 1990. Similarly, the area under coca cultivation is at its lowest level since 1987 and about 14% less in 1999 than in 1990 (see Figure 3). All of this suggests that alternative development, eradication, intensified law enforcement activities, and the effort of governments concerned to reduce levels of cultivation, have led to positive results. Such results would also have appeared if demand was static, but, as argued below, this does not appear to have been the case at the global level. The success achieved in the 1990s, and notably over the last few years, to reverse the massive upward trend seen in the 1980s, would have been even more pronounced if better yields per hectare had not offset the progress made in reducing the areas under cultivation.

The total area under opium poppy (estimated at 217,000 hectares in 1999) or coca bush cultivation (estimated at 183,000 hectares in 1999) is not really large by global standards. Together, the total areas under opium poppy or coca bush are, for example, just a quarter of the size of Puerto Rico, and two to three times the size of cities such New York or Berlin. Even in the main drug producing countries, the total areas under opium poppy or coca bush represent only about 1% of arable land.[b] Yet if just 1% of arable land in a few medium-sized countries is needed to guarantee global supply of heroin and cocaine, there remains a constant danger of displacement: production shifting to other areas in response to eradication.

In contrast to popular perception, the extent of illicit crop cultivation is fairly small and

---

b) For instance, in Afghanistan, the world's largest producer of opium, the total area under opium cultivation amounted to 90,600 ha in 1999, equivalent to 0.1% of the total size of the country or 1.1% of arable land. In Myanmar the total area under opium cultivation was 89,500 ha in 1999, equivalent to 0.1% of the size of the country or 0.9% of arable land. The picture is similar in the coca leaf producing countries. In the three main producer countries, the areas under coca bush cultivation do not exceed 0.1% of the size of the country.

Map 1. Global illicit opium poppy cultivation in the 1990s

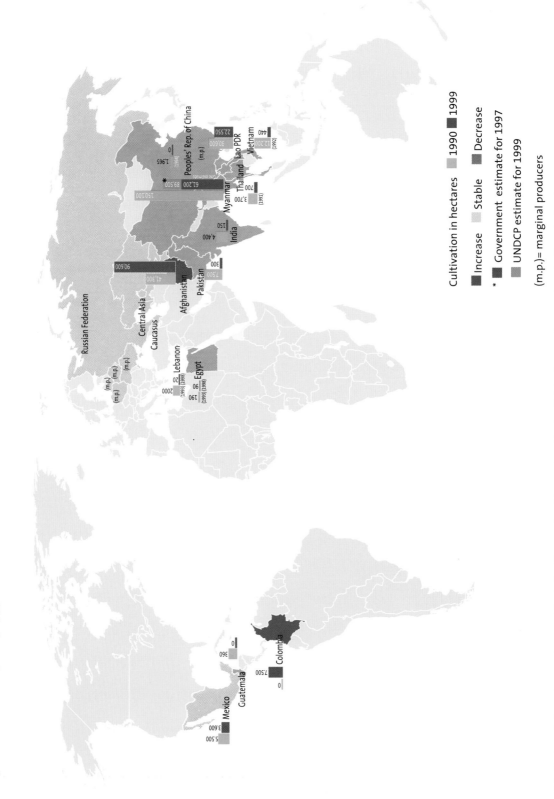

Cultivation in hectares 1990 1999

Increase Stable Decrease

* Government estimate for 1997

UNDCP estimate for 1999

(m.p.) = marginal producers

Note: The boundaries and names shown and the designations used on this map do not imply official endorsement or acceptance by the United Nations.
Routes shown are not necessarily documented actual routes, but are rather general indications of the directions of illicit drug flows.

Map 2. Global illicit coca cultivation in the 1990s

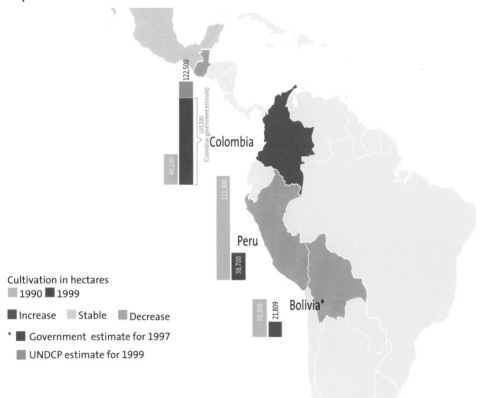

Cultivation in hectares
1990 1999

■ Increase ■ Stable ■ Decrease

* ■ Government estimate for 1997
■ UNDCP estimate for 1999

Colombia

122,500

103,500 (Colombian government estimate)

40,100

Peru

121,300

38,700

Bolivia*

50,300 21,809

declining; so is the overall income that cultivation generates for farmers. Globally aggregated income of farmers from opium poppy and coca leaf cultivation (without further processing) was approximately US$ 1.1 billion in1999.[2] This may seem like a big sum but it is a very small proportion of global drug sales of a few hundred billion dollars a year[3] or the tremendous economic costs resulting from drug abuse of several hundred billion dollars a year. In the USA alone, annual economic costs related to drug abuse were estimated to be US$ 110 billion a year (1.5% of GDP)[4] in the mid-1990s.

Despite some limitations, existing data are robust enough to track some significant shifts in the production/distribution pattern over the last decade. Throughout the 1990s the production of illicit opium and coca leaf became concentrated in fewer countries (see Maps 1 and 2). While a few decades ago, opium was produced in a large number of countries for both licit and illicit purposes, illicit *opium production* is now concentrated in just two countries: **Afghanistan and Myanmar** (see Figure 4). Together they accounted for about 90% of global illicit opium production over the last few years and nearly 95% in 1999. More than 75% of global opium production in 1999 occurred in Afghanistan alone. In 2000, the combination of drought and some successful programmes in Afghanistan, reduced opium production by nearly 30%, thereby lowering global production to some 4,800 tonnes (preliminary estimates).

Afghanistan however is the main source of opium, morphine and heroin in neighbouring countries (Iran, Pakistan, India and Central Asia) and of heroin in Europe (both Eastern and Western Europe). It is also the main source of heroin found in some countries along the Arabian peninsula and Eastern Africa.

Fig. 5: Coca leaf production in 1990
         (total: 319,200 tonnes)

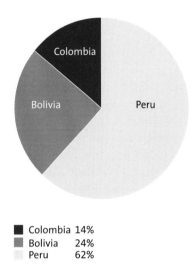

■	Colombia	14%
■	Bolivia	24%
□	Peru	62%

Source: UNDCP, DELTA.

Fig. 6: Coca leaf production in 1999
         (total: 287,000 tonnes)

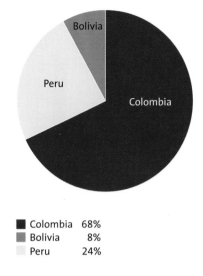

■	Colombia	68%
■	Bolivia	8%
□	Peru	24%

Source: UNDCP, DELTA.

Fig. 7: World potential* cocaine manufacture**

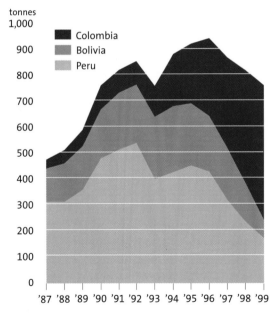

* 'Potential' refers to the amount of cocaine that could be manufactured from domestic coca; 'actual' manufacture was larger
  than 'potential' manufacture in Colombia but smaller in Peru and
  Bolivia. In contrast to 'potential' manufacture, 'actual' manufacture grew in Peru and Bolivia in much of the 1990s – though
  from low levels.
** Estimates based on conservative assumptions; actual cocaine
  manufacture could be higher (by up to one third).

Source: UNDCP, DELTA.

Fig. 8: Price of coca leaf in Peru and Bolivia

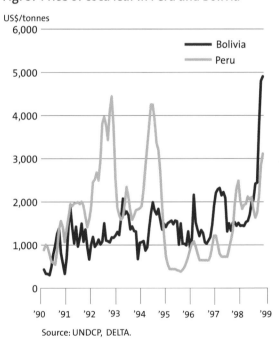

Source: UNDCP, DELTA.

Following Afghanistan and Myanmar the next largest producers of opium are the Lao PDR, Colombia and Mexico. Opium production in Latin America is mainly destined for the US heroin market.[5] While Mexican opium has traditionally gone to the USA for decades, Central American countries, such as Guatemala, virtually disappeared as significant producers of opium in the 1990s.[6] During this same period, Colombia emerged as a supplier of heroin, produced from domestically grown opium poppy. Neighbouring countries such as Peru and Venezuela have reported some small-scale production of opium, and this potential threat will have to be watched in the future. Although Colombia's opium production is small by global standards, it is important regionally, replacing some of the South-East Asian heroin, which had previously dominated the US market. In the late 1990s, 65% of the heroin seized in the USA was from Colombia.[7]

Paradoxically, increasing heroin addiction throughout East and South-East Asia went hand in hand with a sharp decline of opium production in these countries in the late 1990s and the loss of market share of South-East Asian heroin in the USA. During the same period, former large-scale producers of opium, such as Thailand or Pakistan achieved substantial reductions in output. Thus, domestically produced opium from these countries lost significance in supplying international drug markets. Both countries are now net importers of opiates. The same is true for Lebanon and Iran. Opium cultivation was successfully eliminated in the early 1990s in Lebanon, and in Iran a decade earlier. Though Turkey has remained an important drug transit country, the shift in production from illicit to licit opium production in the 1970s resulted in the *de facto* elimination of illegal Turkish opium from international drug markets. The re-emergence of opium poppy production in Egypt in the second half of the 1990s was successfully curtailed at an early stage. The same is true for China, the largest producer of opium in the interwar period from 1919-1939. Attempts to expand poppy cultivation across the borders of Myanmar to China in the mid-1990s were not successful. Also, though there is a potential threat, large-scale opium cultivation has not appeared in the Central Asian countries.

More than 98% of global coca leaf cultivation is concentrated in the three Andean countries: Colombia, Peru and Bolivia. Within these countries, there has been a marked shift in production over the last decade, from Peru and Bolivia to Colombia (see Figures 5 & 6). Historically, Colombia was the largest manufacturer of cocaine hydrochloride (HCL) in the region – importing the necessary cocaine base from Peru, and to a lesser extent from Bolivia. In terms of coca leaf cultivation, however, Colombia used to be the smallest producer among the three Andean countries. This changed during the 1990s. By 1997 Colombia's production was at par with that of Peru and by 1999, two thirds of all coca leaf was produced in Colombia. During the same period, coca leaf production declined in Peru and in Bolivia.

The shift can be attributed to a number of factors (see Figure 7). In the early 1990s, a fungus destroyed significant amounts of the domestic coca harvest in Peru. Secondly, clandestine flights have been successfully curtailed. In the second half of the 1990s the 'air corridor', which was used to transport coca leaf/base from Peru to cocaine laboratories in Colombia was closed. Farm gate prices of coca collapsed in Peru[8] (see Figure 8). As clandestine producers in Colombia were barred from easy access to coca in Peru, they looked to other sources of supply – and found these in Colombia itself.[9] The dismantling of some of the large Colombian drug cartels (Medellin and Cali) may have also played a part. The successor organizations did not have the kind of infrastructure that would have allowed them to organize the logistics to transport large amounts of coca leaf, paste or base from neighbouring countries to Colombia. Colombia's ongoing civil conflict was also a factor in the domestic expansion of coca leaf production. Though the Colombian Government has stepped up eradication efforts in recent years, and actually has the most eradication worldwide, the government does not exercise control over all coca-growing regions. With some of the guerilla and the paramilitary groups benefiting from the drug trade, political instability indirectly promotes the spread of coca cultivation in the country.[10]

While Colombia's 'potential' manufacture (cocaine produced from domestic sources) increased strongly in the 1990s, the increase was less significant in terms of 'actual' manufacture as Colombia was already responsible for the bulk of cocaine manufacture in the Andean region. Thus, despite a new record high in 'potential' manufacture in 1999, there are no indications that the flow of cocaine out of Colombia actually increased.[c] In other words, domestic production of coca leaf in Colombia seems to substitute, rather than complement coca leaf or base imports.

Improved control and alternative development efforts in Peru and Bolivia have helped to reduce coca leaf production significantly in the 1990s, more than offsetting increases in Colombia. Systematic interventions to break the air bridge from Peru to Colombia[11] brought coca leaf prices below US$ 1,500 per tonne. (Prices below US$ 1,500 per tonne of coca leaf usually inhibit the expansion of production while prices below US$ 1,000 per tonne usually lead to the voluntary abandonment of existing fields, as happened over the 1995-98 period). Prices in Bolivia were less affected by these interventions as alternative outlets were found in Brazil and Chile (see Figure 8).

One displacement effect of better control efforts was, however, the creation of domestic cocaine processing capacities in Peru and Bolivia. Cocaine seizures reflected this trend. Despite a strong decline in coca leaf production in the 1990s in both Peru and Bolivia, seizures of cocaine HCL actually quintupled between the periods 1991/92 and 1998/99 in both countries. Hardly any cocaine HCL seizures were reported in Peru and Bolivia up to the mid-1980s. By 1999, cocaine HCL seizures accounted for 35% of all cocaine-related seizures in Peru, reflecting an increase in domestic cocaine processing capabilities. These, however, are still small compared to Colombia, which represented 90% of all cocaine HCL seizures in the Andean region in 1998/99.

In response to substantial eradication in Bolivia and some increase in European and Latin American demand, farm gate prices for coca leaf increased strongly all across the Andean countries in 1999. Prices also recovered as trafficking groups in Peru and Bolivia, denied access to Colombia, began to transform coca-leaf into cocaine HCL themselves, and began to create new routes to ship the end product directly to consumer markets.

Despite the increase in coca leaf farm gate prices in 1999, eradication in Bolivia and Peru prevented a net increase in coca leaf production. Yet declining production in Peru and Bolivia will have to be sustained by dismantling the new cocaine manufacturing facilities and closing the new trafficking routes. Otherwise there is a danger that the rise in farm gate prices may stimulate the rehabilitation of abandoned coca fields, particularly in Peru.

Cannabis
In marked contrast to coca bush and opium poppy, cannabis is grown across the globe and in

---

c) Cocaine HCL seizures in Colombia rose from 21.5 tonnes in 1995 to 54.7 tonnes in 1998, but fell back to 22.7 tonnes by 1999; cocaine HCL and base seizures taken together rose from 41 tonnes in 1995 to 84 tonnes in 1998 but fell back to 31.7 tonnes by 1999, the lowest such figure in the 1990s. (Bureau of International Narcotics and Law Enforcement Affairs, *International Narcotics Control Strategy Report 1999,* Washington, March 2000). As the decline in seizures in 1999 went hand in hand with increased efforts by the Colombian authorities, it can be assumed that actual cocaine manufacture in Colombia did not increase further in 1999. A shortage in one key precursor chemical – *potassium permanganate* – for the processing of cocaine, created by means of better international cooperation among law enforcement authorities ("Operation Purple"), following the UN 1998 Special Session, led to the halting and seizing of 32 suspicious shipments in 1999 (2,226 tonnes of *potassium permanganate*).(International Potassium Permanganate Monitoring Initiative, Operation Purple, Phase 1, Final Report, 2000). The resulting shortage of potassium permanganate could not stop manufacture, but apparently contributed to the decline in Colombia's cocaine output, despite a record harvest in coca leaf.

almost all geographic locations. Over the last decade, 120 countries reported illicit cultivation of cannabis in their territory.[12] Interpol identifies 67 'source countries' for cannabis through seizures made in 1998. Of these, 22 countries were in Africa, 15 in Asia, 15 in Europe and 13 in the Americas.[13]

Estimating the extent of illicit cannabis cultivation, production and trafficking is much more difficult than for other plant-based drugs because of the significant amounts of wild cannabis growth, the diverse nature of cultivation and the sheer magnitude of trafficking. In contrast to other plant-based narcotic drugs, illicit cannabis products can originate from three qualitatively distinct sources of supply: outdoor illicit cultivation; naturalized cannabis plant populations (wild growing cannabis); and plants cultivated indoors by means of sophisticated growing technology. While outdoor illicit cultivation has traditionally been the primary source of cannabis, the importance of wild growing cannabis and indoor-cultivated cannabis as sources for illicit markets has been growing.

The largest areas under wild growth are in the states of the Commonwealth of Independent States (CIS) notably the Russian Federation and Kazakhstan. Authorities estimate that about one million hectares might be under wild cannabis in the Russian Federation. The extent of wild cannabis growth does not correlate with cannabis production or exports. In Kazakhstan for instance, two surveys in 1998 and 1999 found about 400,000 hectares under wild growth; only a minute part of this, some 2,300 hectares, appear to have been used for actual cannabis production and export. Kazakhstan therefore lags behind countries such as *Morocco* (50,000 ha according to the ministry of interior), the world's largest producer of cannabis resin (hashish), and the major producers of cannabis herb (marijuana): *Colombia* (5,000 ha in 1999) or *Mexico* (3,700 ha in 1999),[14] and it is not mentioned among the major source countries at the global level.

The largest source countries of cannabis, as identified by Interpol, are Morocco, Afghanistan and Pakistan for hashish; Colombia, Mexico, Nigeria and South Africa for marijuana; and Jamaica for cannabis oil.

Indoor cannabis cultivation continues to develop in Europe and in North America, especially in the Netherlands, Canada and the United States and, to a lesser extent in the United Kingdom, Germany, the Scandinavian countries and Eastern Europe.[15] This method of cultivation appears to have increased the average THC level of the plant from 3% to 7% before 1990, to levels ranging from 10% to 30% in the 1990s.

Tentative estimates suggest that in the late 1990s about a quarter of all cannabis herb in Western Europe and the United States was cultivated domestically (both outdoor and hydroponically). In the Netherlands there are estimates that over half of cannabis is cultivated domestically; in monetary terms, cannabis exports exceeded imports[16] as domestically grown cannabis is characterized by higher THC levels and thus commands a higher price.

Available cultivation and production estimates are not sufficient to determine whether production at the global level has increased or decreased in recent years. There are, however, indications that cannabis cultivation in Latin America is now lower than a decade ago; but it apparently increased in Europe, Central Asia, South-East Asia and Africa.[17] The large number of countries reporting an increase in cannabis consumption (two thirds of all countries reporting drug abuse trends in 1999) would suggest that overall production must have increased; but this is only partly confirmed by seizure data. Cannabis seizures (plant, herb and resin) were higher in 1998 than in 1990, but they have not increased since the mid-1990s. It is difficult to judge whether this is a reflection of either particular national policies shifting priorities and resources to the interdiction of other drugs, or if there has in fact been a real stabilization of global production and trafficking.

31

Seizures Afghanistan Tajikistan border
© Stefano Zardini

Cultivation estimates (including wild growth), based on reports from Member States in the 1990s, range from 670,000 hectares (three times the extent of opium poppy or four times that of global coca cultivation) to 1,850,000 hectares (eight times the area under opium-poppy or 10 times the area under coca). Production estimates vary by a factor of 30, from 10,000 tonnes to 300,000 tonnes. Linking production and consumption estimates, UNDCP estimates world wide cannabis production to be at about 30,000 tonnes.[18]

1.2. TRAFFICKING

The utility of seizure statistics

Seizures and related data are the most readily available indicator of illicit drug supply, and have been collected since the beginning of the twentieth century by the United Nations[d] and its predecessor, the League of Nations.

Seizure data can be used to *identify the global spread* of drug trafficking. In 1980-81, one hundred and twenty countries and territories reported drug

---

d) UNDCP collects seizure data as part of its "Annual Reports Questionnaire", which the Member States who are party to the drug conventions are obliged to return every year. These and related seizure data are then complemented and cross-checked with similar information collected by other international organisations, such as ICPO/Interpol, the World Customs Organisation, and regional organisations, such as CICAD or Europol. All of this information is then collated in UNDCP's database (DELTA).

seizures. By 1987-88, this number had increased to 144. Over the next decade, it again increased substantially, to 170 in 1997-98 (See Figure 9). Though the total number of countries in the world also increased during the period, this is still unequivocal evidence of the fact that drug trafficking is now a truly global phenomenon. (See Maps 3 to 7, which show trafficking patterns and trends in the 1990s, and Maps 13 to 16, which link trafficking and abuse patterns).

Heroin and cocaine are – at the global level – the most significant illicit drugs in terms of treatment demand, hospitalization, overdose, drug related mortality, involvement of organized crime and drug related violence, including violence against the state. The most widely trafficked drug, however, is cannabis. Figure 10 shows that 98% of all countries and territories which had seizures in 1997/98 reported seizures of cannabis products. This was a higher proportion than for opiates (91%), coca-type substances (79%) amphetamine-type stimulants (48% including ecstasy) or depressants (36%). Trafficking in LSD (29%) and methaqualone (12%) concern only a minority of countries, and are not shown in the figure.

Seizure statistics provide some indication of the *extent of trafficking*. In 1998, Member States reported 963,000 drug seizure cases; more than half of these were cannabis-related. Cannabis is also, in terms of volume, the largest of the illicit drugs that are seized. Within this, cannabis herb is much more voluminous than cannabis resin (see Figure 11). The pattern becomes clearer in view of the fact that cannabis is the most widely abused illicit drug worldwide.[19]

With regard to cocaine and heroin, the volume of cocaine trafficked internationally is much larger than heroin. In 1998, total potential production of cocaine was 824 tonnes, and opiates (in terms of heroin equivalent) was 435 tonnes.[20] Seizures, however, do not appear in the same ratio as production. In the same year, 380 tonnes of cocaine were seized, compared to 75 tonnes of opiates.[21] In production terms, cocaine was about double the opiates; in seizure

terms, it was five times more. The principal explanation of this was noted in the discussion on interception rates above: cocaine supply and demand are more concentrated geographically, and it is trafficked in bulky consignments, often by container ship. Thus, in 1998, the average amount of cocaine per seizure was eleven times larger than the average heroin seizure.

The ATS do not appear significantly in seizure statistics because they are usually produced in, or close to, areas of consumption. They are not trafficked across long distances, and thus possibilities of interdiction are limited. The consequent low interception rate is unique to ATS and precludes seizures being used as an indicator of supply as directly as with cocaine and heroin. The total number of reported ATS seizure cases exceeds those of heroin; but the average volume per ATS seizure was only a third of that for heroin in 1998. Long-distance trafficking occurs more frequently with precursor chemicals. Thus higher volumes of ATS precursor chemicals have been intercepted than ATS end-products. If one considers the total amount of ATS precursors, which were prevented from diversion into illicit trade, it exceeded total seizures of opiates in 1998.

Seizures leave important tracks and they enable the mapping of *trafficking patterns* and *trafficking routes*. In general terms, the pattern shows the following concentration of trafficking: cocaine in the Americas; cannabis herb in the Americas and Africa; opiates in Asia and Europe; cannabis resin in Europe, North Africa and South-West Asia; and ATS in South-East Asia, Europe and North America. Within this general pattern a number of key *drug trafficking routes* can be identified:[22]

- *opiates* from Afghanistan *via* Pakistan, Iran, Turkey and the Balkan route (and its various branches) to countries of the European Union and the European Free Trade Association;
- *cocaine* from the Andean countries to North America, notably the United States, either directly, or *via* Mexico and the Caribbean region;
- *cannabis herb* from Mexico to the USA;

Fig. 9: Number of countries and territories reporting drug seizures

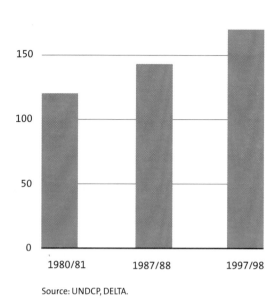

Source: UNDCP, DELTA.

Fig. 10: Countries and territories reporting seizures in 1997/98 (N=170) – main drug groups

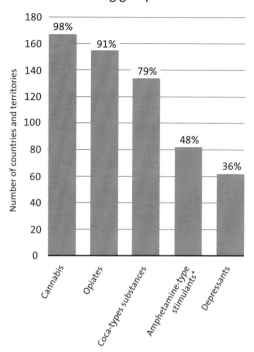

* including substances of the ecstasy group

Source: UNDCP, DELTA.

Fig. 11: Seizures in 1998 (in tonnes)

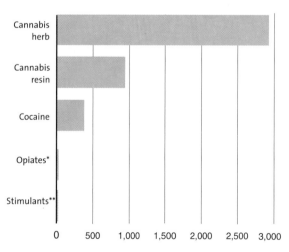

* Opiates: heroin, morphine and opium in heroin
  equivalents (1 gram morphine assumed to equivalent
  to 1 gram heroin; 1 gram opium to be equivalent to
  0.1 gram of heroin
** Amphetamine-type stimulants, excluding ecstasy,
  reported in kg, litres and in units (1 unit assumed to be
  equivalent to 10 mg, 1 litre equivalent to 1 kg)

Fig. 12: Average annual growth of drug seizures in the 1990s (1990/91-1997/98)

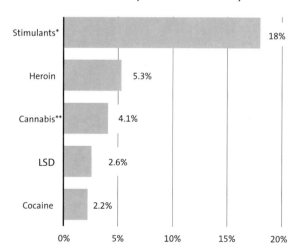

* Amphetamine-type stimulants, excluding ecstasy
** Cannabis herb and cannabis resin

Source: UNDCP, DELTA.

Source: UNDCP, DELTA.

- *cannabis resin* from Morocco *via* Spain to other European countries.

There has been, over the last decade, a certain *diffusion* of the principal trafficking routes:

- *Opiates* from Afghanistan *via* Central Asia to Europe;
- *Cocaine* from the Andean countries: *via* Central America to Mexico and the USA; *via* the Pacific coast to North America, *via* Venezuela and/or the Caribbean to Europe; from Peru and Bolivia to Brazil and *via* western or southern Africa to Europe;
- *Opiates* from Colombia (now an important opium producing country in Latin America) along new trafficking routes – often parallel to those already in existence for cocaine – to the USA;
- *Opiates* from Myanmar *via* China (including Hong Kong SAR and Taiwan, Province of China) to North America (complementing and partly replacing the traditional route via Thailand and Hong Kong SAR);
- National mail and commercial courier services are now used more frequently for smuggling drugs to final destinations;
- Various African countries are increasingly linked into trafficking routes for transshipment purposes.

The two main *cannabis resin* trafficking routes are from Morocco via Spain to other countries in Western Europe, and from South-West Asia to Europe. The principal trafficking routes for *cannabis herb* are from Mexico and Colombia to the USA, though increasing levels of high-quality cannabis production in North America are expected to diminish the importance of these routes. Some of the Colombian cannabis herb has already been re-directed to markets in western Europe, where it competes with cannabis herb from Sub-Saharan Africa, South-East Asia, and, in recent years, from Albania.[23] Moreover, domestically-grown hydroponic cannabis has gained importance in Europe as well.

East and South-East Asia, Europe and North America have seen a considerable increase in trafficking of *amphetamine-type stimulants*, particularly methamphetamine. Trafficking in ATS continues to be more limited in geographical terms than heroin or cocaine as production and consumption usually take place within the same region. The only exception in this regard are the '*ecstasy*' substances (MDMA, MDA MDME etc). Originating mostly in Europe, ecstasy is shipped all across the world, to North America, East and South-East Asia, West Asia, North and South America, and southern Africa.[24]

Seizure statistics also show an interesting pattern in the *concentration* of drug trafficking. Although a large number of countries report seizures, the bulk of trafficking is concentrated in a very small number of countries. Three-quarters of total seizures of all drugs, on average, take place in just five countries (see Table 1).

Finally, seizure statistics enable the identification of drug *trafficking trends*. Through the 1990s (from 1990/91 to 1997/98), seizures of stimulants (ATS including ecstasy) grew the strongest. They grew in volume terms by an annual average of 18%, compared to 5% for heroin, 4% for cannabis and 2% for cocaine (see Figure 12).

Table 1. Concentration of Drug Trafficking 1997/98

Drug	% age of total seizures in five largest countries	Five largest countries
Cannabis herb	71%	Mexico, USA, South Africa, Colombia, India
Cannabis resin	76%	Spain, UK, Pakistan, Netherlands, Morocco
Cocaine	68%	USA, Colombia, Mexico, Spain, Panama
Opiates (heroin/morphine)	74%	Islamic Rep. of Iran, People's Rep. of China, Turkey, Pakistan, UK
Stimulants	75%	UK, Thailand, USA, China, Netherlands
Unweighted Average	73%	

BOX 1A: Following the tracks: Using seizures to identify trends.

In the foregoing discussion, seizures have been interpreted as a direct indicator of underlying drug trafficking activities. Is such an interpretation correct? Or are seizures, in reality, no more than an indicator for the activities and the performance of law enforcement agencies?

Seizures are, in fact, a reflection of both the success of enforcement agencies and of the visible tip of a much larger iceberg of drug supply and trafficking. This 'double nature' of seizures regularly creates confusion in the interpretation of such statistics for the identification of trafficking trends. The principal question is whether increases in seizures indicate more trafficking.

Short-term changes in seizures (for example, on a yearly basis) in any particular country without additional information (such as development of prices, purities, changes in law enforcement priorities etc.) are, in general, not a reliable indicator for changes in trafficking activities. Large seizures in a country may reflect a larger volume of drugs in circulation; but they can also reflect the opposite: because the large seizure, in itself, would have reduced the amount of drugs available for trafficking. A number of other factors – such as changes in the level of police activities, changes of priorities, of funds made available for investigations, length of investigations, changes in the judicial system and random chance (the 'luck factor') of law enforcement institutions in a particular year influence the outcome, and can offset underlying trafficking trends. In the absence of such detailed additional information, price data can help to gain some clarity as drug markets – in many respects – behave similarly to licit markets. Rising seizures going hand in hand with falling prices are an indication of growing drug supply. If rising seizures go hand in hand with rising prices, data point to a law-enforcement-induced contraction of the market.[e]

Over *longer periods*, and using broader geographical units (regional or global level) as a basis for investigation, as well as some simple smoothing techniques (e.g. two-year or three-year averages to avoid statistical noise), trends in seizures do tend to correlate positively with a number of other drug indicators that are linked to trafficking.

For instance, drug supply and trafficking are closely correlated. Thus, if seizures are a good indicator for trafficking trends, seizures and supply should correlate as well. This seems to be the case. The correlation coefficient for opium production and heroin seizures (based on a 3 year moving average) and the correlation coefficient for coca leaf production and cocaine seizures (3 year moving average) over the 1980-1998 period were found to be close to 0.95. (A value of 1.00 would signal a perfect fit (see Figures 13 and 14)).

Changes in demand, in general, also correlate with trafficking, irrespective of whether the drug market is considered to be demand- or supply-driven. (The larger the demand for drugs, the more drugs will be trafficked; or the larger the supply, the more drugs are likely to be consumed and thus trafficked.) If variations in seizures are to reflect underlying changes in trafficking activities, changes in demand indicators can be expected to correlate with seizures as well (except for transit countries).

Some empirical evidence points in this direction. For instance, data for the European Union (the largest heroin market in economic terms, characterized by low levels of transit trade[f]), show that there is a strong correlation between the number of acute drug-related deaths (which are mostly linked to opiate abuse) and heroin seizures (Correlation coefficient of R = 0.97 over the 1985-1997 period; see Figure 15). In other words, the larger the supply of heroin, the better are the chances to seize it; but the overall risk of death from heroin abuse is also greater. Similarly, in the world's largest marijuana market (the USA, also characterized by low levels of transit trade), cannabis herb seizures and cannabis use among high-school students, were found to correlate strongly.[g] (Correlation coefficient of R= 0.96 over the 1978-1998 period; see Figure 16).

All of this suggests that seizure statistics – even without additional information – are a relatively good indicator for the identification of trafficking trends once longer periods are investigated.

---

e) This is true unless there are indications that the price hike was caused by a massive short-term increase in demand. In general, however, demand for drugs moves up or down gradually. The implication is that in the short run, the demand side can be considered to be almost constant. Short-term price changes are thus the result of changes on the supply side: increases in supply as trafficking networks extend their operations, or contractions of the market due to seizures and dismantling of criminal groups.

f) Drug transit trade is important in EU countries, if considered from a purely national perspective: most drugs seized are actually in transit for final destination in a neighbouring country. However, from a broader EU perspective, transit trade is almost negligible. Drugs entering the EU are usually for consumption within the EU.

How can this positive correlation be explained? One obvious cause was already noted. If more drugs are in circulation, the likelihood of seizures increases as well, i.e. if trafficking increases, seizures, over time, are likely to rise as well.[h]

Moreover, many of the factors influencing the extent of seizures in the short term (law enforcement budgets, priorities and know-how, cooperation with partners abroad, etc.) are positively correlated with trafficking activities in the long run. In many countries, larger budgets for enforcement institutions, for instance, have been the result of negative effects of drug trafficking, such as spill-overs from transit traffic into domestic markets; increased drug related morbidity and mortality; reduction in the age of initiation; increasing levels of violence and drug related crime. The transmission mechanism from such negative effects to increases in drug control budgets frequently works *via* the media. As public pressure builds, the political system reacts and more priority is given to the drug problem. More funds will be eventually dedicated to drug control activities (on both the supply and the demand sides) in order to secure public support. In some of the transit countries that are not immediately confronted with the negative effects of trafficking, the transmission mechanism often works through development assistance funds earmarked for enforcement. Such funds enable the police to make more seizures. Similarly, a constant decline in trafficking activities would make it difficult for policy makers to defend an ever larger share of scarce resources being spent on interdiction. Falling budgets may accelerate an already existing trend of declining seizures, but – except under special conditions – are unlikely to 'create' such a trend in the first place.

To sum up, whatever the problems with the interpretation of seizure data in the short-term, trafficking activities remain the key underlying parameter to explain changes of seizure data in the long run. Both theoretical considerations and empirical evidence support this view. Several parameters, responsible for short-term changes in seizures, are influenced by changes in underlying trafficking activities. Though there may be time-lags between increases in trafficking and increases in seizures, which may distort the picture in the short run, time-lags are not significant once longer periods are considered and data are smoothed to reduce the possibility of accidental shifts in particular years (the 'luck factor'). The existence of a number of reinforcing factors suggest that changes in seizures could over-estimate actual increases, or decreases, of trafficking in the short-term. If considered over any prolonged period of time, however, seizures will systematically show the underlying trafficking trend.[i]

---

g) Seizures are actually linked to 'consumption' (amounts consumed) rather than to 'prevalence' (number of people consuming). In most cases the differentiation is of only academic interest as prevalence rates and consumption move in parallel. There are, however, cases in which the differentiation does play a role. For instance, no positive correlation can be found between cocaine seizures and cocaine prevalence rates in the USA for the last two decades; rising cocaine seizures in the 1980s went hand in hand with falling prevalence rates. At the same time, however, a number of indirect 'consumption indicators', such as cocaine related emergency room visits, treatment demand for cocaine abuse, etc. continued rising in the 1980s – parallel to increases in seizures. As the bulk of cocaine is consumed by a small number of heavy users (whose number has not declined), a fall in the prevalence rate of cocaine use had no impact on overall consumption, and seizures (reflecting the supply side) continued rising.

h) The link between changes in seizures and prevalence rates at the national level is usually less strong because much of the seizures are drugs in transit. Once the analysis is shifted from the national to the regional level where transit trade plays less of a role, long-term seizures trends do reflect changes in drug consumption. Although this is not necessarily identical with changes in prevalence rates. Even if prevalence rates decline consumption may remain high and continue rising for a number of years as hard-core drug addicts tend to consume ever larger amounts and a number of casual users become hard-core addicts.

i) Exceptions to this rule can be only expected in countries where strongly increasing trafficking and high levels of drug addiction are dwarfed by even greater social problems affecting the population at large.

Fig. 13: Global production of opium and global heroin seizures*: 1980-98

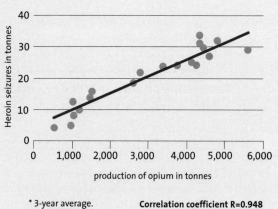

* 3-year average.   **Correlation coefficient R=0.948**
Source: UNDCP, DELTA.

Fig. 14: Global production of coca leaf and global cocaine seizures*: 1980-98

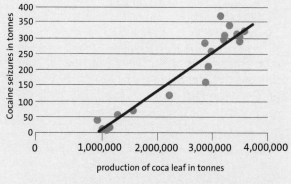

* 3-year average.   **Correlation coefficient R=0.954**
Source: UNDCP, DELTA.

Fig. 15: Heroin seizures* and acute drug-related deaths in the European Union: 1985-97

Fig. 16: Cannabis herb seizures* and cannabis use among 12th graders (past month) in the USA: 1978-98

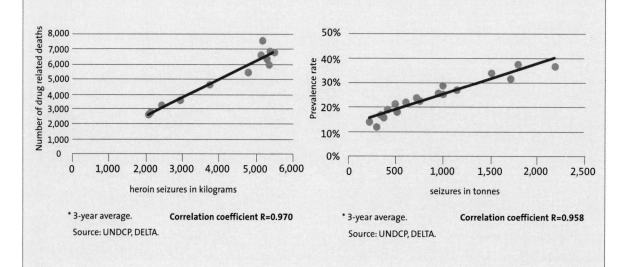

* 3-year average.   **Correlation coefficient R=0.970**
Source: UNDCP, DELTA.

* 3-year average.   **Correlation coefficient R=0.958**
Source: UNDCP, DELTA.

Heroin

Though heroin trafficking showed an upward trend over the last three decades, it grew less rapidly in the 1990s than in the 1980s (Map 3 shows patterns and trends in the 1990s). Average annual growth in heroin seizures amounted to 25% per annum in the 1980s and fell to 5% over the 1990-98 period (see Figure 17).

Most regions of the world were affected by increasing levels of trafficking in opiates over the last decade. Seizures of heroin and morphine combined almost tripled, to 54.8 tonnes p.a. in 1997/98 reflecting greater interdiction efforts in countries along the main trafficking routes.

Figure 18 shows a clear geographical concentration of heroin and morphine trafficking. More than 70% of all seizures of heroin and morphine continue to be made in Asia. This is followed by Europe (23%), and the Americas (4%).

Despite a proliferation of opiate trafficking routes from Afghanistan, more than half of world heroin and morphine seizures in 1997/98 were made in South-West Asia, notably in the Islamic Republic of Iran, whose share in global seizures rose from 9% in 1987/88 to 42% in 1997/98. In 1999, seizures of heroin more than doubled, and overall heroin/morphine seizures in Iran grew by a quarter over the 1997/98 average, reflecting the massive increase of opium production in neighbouring Afghanistan, the increasing use of Iranian territory by drug trafficking organizations, and the priority given by the Iranian authorities to drug interdiction.

Europe accounted for 23% of all opiate seizures in 1997/98. Most of these took place in Western Europe, including Turkey, accounting for about 20% of global total. Seizures in the European Union doubled over the last decade, though the EU's share in global seizures has been falling with the stabilization of the West

Fig. 17: Global heroin seizures in tonnes

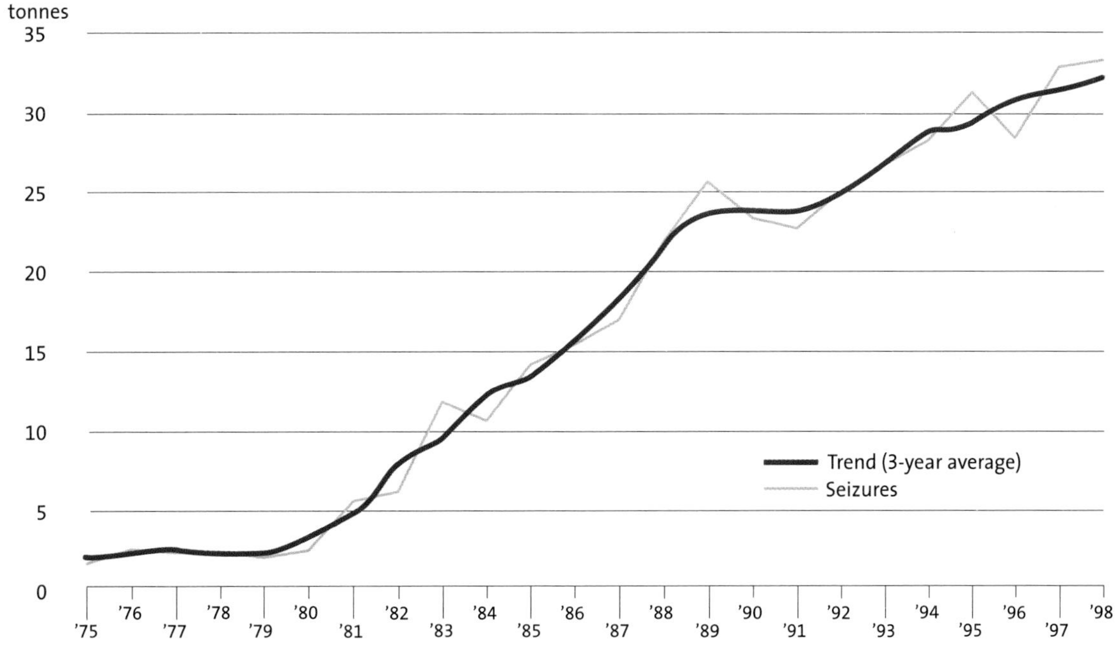

Source: UNDCP, DELTA.

Map 3. Patterns and trends in heroin and morphine trafficking in the 1990s

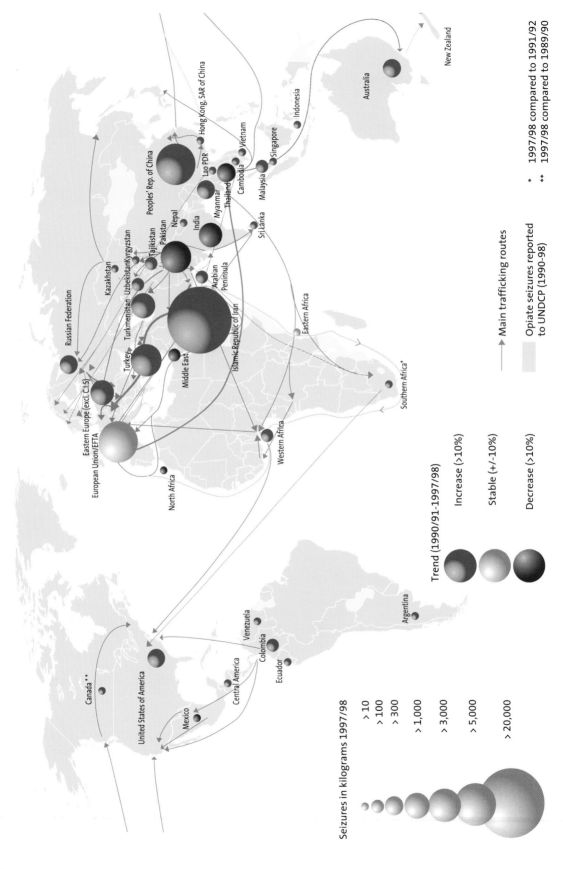

* 1997/98 compared to 1991/92
** 1997/98 compared to 1989/90

Main trafficking routes

Opiate seizures reported to UNDCP (1990-98)

Trend (1990/91-1997/98)

Increase (>10%)

Stable (+/-10%)

Decrease (>10%)

Seizures in kilograms 1997/98

> 10
> 100
> 300
> 1,000
> 3,000
> 5,000
> 20,000

Note: The boundaries and names shown and the designations used on this map do not imply official endorsement or acceptance by the United Nations.

40

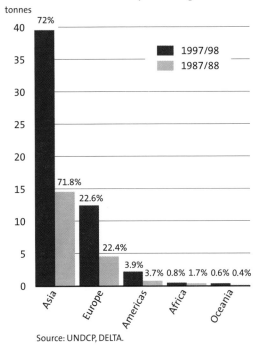

Fig. 18: Heroin and morphine seizures:
in tonnes and as a percentage of total

Source: UNDCP, DELTA.

European heroin market in the late 1990s. Within the EU, seizures in the UK increased by more than 80% in 1999.[25] This is significant because the UK already accounted for almost a third of all heroin/morphine seizures of the EU in 1997/98, more than the Netherlands (one fifth) and Germany (one eighth).

Over the last decade, heroin and morphine seizures tripled in Turkey. The country also emerged as a final destination and transit territory for one of heroin's main precursor chemicals, *acetic anhydride*, produced in Europe and trafficked to South-West Asia.[26] Most of the morphine/heroin crossing *Turkey* is shipped along the Balkan route – identified as the transit route for over 80% of heroin seized in Europe in 1999[27] – to final destinations in the countries of the European Union and the European Free Trade Association. Markets in Eastern Europe are developing as well,[28] and an ever increasing part of total heroin shipments are actually consumed in countries along the main trafficking routes. This is par-

ticularly true for Iran, Pakistan, the Central Asian countries, parts of the Russian Federation, as well as some countries along the Balkan route, notably Bulgaria.[29]

Seizures in *Pakistan*, on the eastern border of Afghanistan, accounted for 9% of global heroin/morphine seizures in 1997/98, i.e. almost as much as all seizures in the countries of the European Union. In contrast to rapidly rising seizures in Iran and Turkey over the last decade, seizures in *Pakistan* declined between 1987/88 and 1997/98 by about a fifth, and only rose again strongly in 1999 as traffickers – following Afghanistan's bumper harvest[30] – used all available routes to ship opium, morphine and heroin out of the region. The decline before 1999 may be explained by the sharp reduction in domestic opium supply in Pakistan and a reorientation of Afghan trafficking activities to the Islamic Republic of Iran and to the Central Asian countries. Seizures in the five Central Asian Republics rose from negligible levels a few years ago to 3% of global seizures in 1997/98.[31]

Seizures of heroin and morphine in *India* have fallen by more than 60% over the last decade, leading to a decline in the overall share of South Asia, in global seizures of opiates, to only 2% in 1997/98. Some of the decline may be due to improved controls over licit opium production – India is the world's largest licit opium producer – which reduced diversions into illegal markets.

The second largest concentration of trafficking in Asia takes place in the countries of *South-East Asia* (about 16% of global seizures) where some marked changes in the trafficking patterns have occurred. Traditionally, the main outlet of heroin was the so called Golden Triangle. *Thailand* accounted for almost 60% of all seizures of opiates in South-East Asia in the late 1980s; by 1997/98 this proportion had fallen to just 5%. In parallel, seizures in *the People's Republic of China* (excluding Hong Kong SAR) rose from 4% in 1987/88 to 77% in 1997/98, equivalent to 12% of global seizures. Much of this heroin was smuggled directly from *Myanmar* to China, for re-export to North America (often via Hong Kong SAR and Taiwan Province of China) but increasingly for domestic consumption in China itself.[32] In 1999, however, the strong decline of opium production in the region due to poor weather conditions led to a fall in trafficking, reflected in falling seizures of opiates. Heroin seizures in Myanmar fell by one third in 1999, those in China fell – from a record level in 1998 – almost 30% in 1999 and seizures in the countries of South-East Asia, excluding China, declined by more than 15% on a year earlier.[33]

In *North America,* which accounted for about 3% of global seizures in heroin and morphine in 1997/98, the main sources of supply have changed significantly in recent years. Until the mid-1990s, the US market was dominated by heroin from South-East Asia. As of the mid-1990s, however, high quality Colombian heroin began to take over the US market,[34] notably the

cities of the east coast which have the largest heroin consumption in the country. With lower quality, but cheaper, Mexican heroin in the south-west, more than 60% of the heroin seized in the USA was found to have originated in Latin America over the 1995-99 period.[35]

Cocaine
Cocaine trafficking followed a trend similar to heroin: strong growth in the 1980s, slowing considerably in the 1990s (Map 4 shows patterns and trends in the 1990s). Seizures of cocaine rose by 38% p.a. in the 1980s and by just 3% p.a. over the 1990-98 period following the stabilization of cocaine output (see Figure 19).

The highest growth rates over the decade 1987/88 to 1997/98 were reported by countries in Eastern Europe (77% p.a.) and Africa (59% p.a.), reflecting both low baseline levels and the proliferation of trafficking routes from the Andean countries to Europe and rising levels

Fig. 19: Global cocaine seizures in tonnes

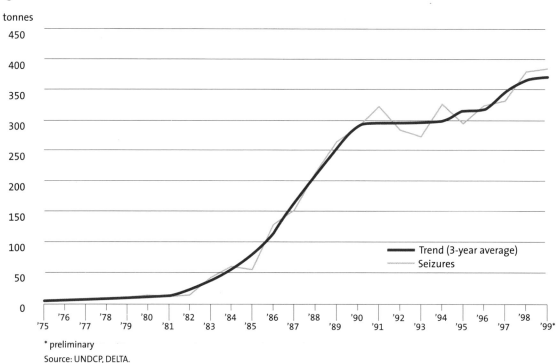

* preliminary
Source: UNDCP, DELTA.

Map 4. Patterns and trends in cocaine trafficking in the 1990s

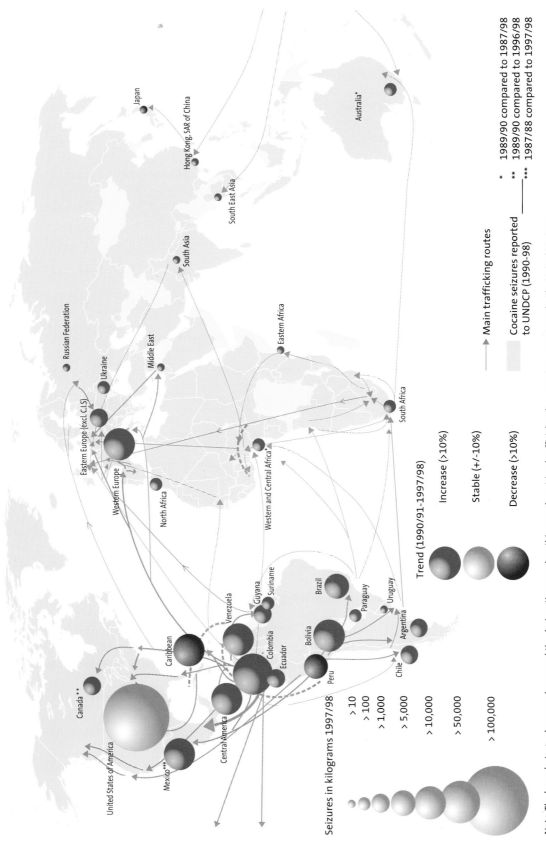

Seizures in kilograms 1997/98

> 10
> 100
> 1,000
> 5,000
> 10,000
> 50,000
> 100,000

Trend (1990/91-1997/98)

Increase (>10%)

Stable (+/-10%)

Decrease (>10%)

→ Main trafficking routes

Cocaine seizures reported to UNDCP (1990-98)

*   1989/90 compared to 1987/98
**   1989/90 compared to 1996/98
***   1987/88 compared to 1997/98

Note: The boundaries and names shown and the designations used on this map do not imply official endorsement or acceptance by the United Nations.
Routes shown are not necessarily documented actual routes, but are rather general indications of the directions of illicit drug flows.

43

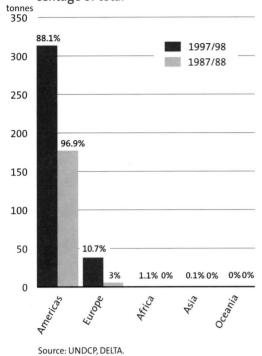

Fig. 20: Cocaine seizures: in tonnes and as percentage of total

Source: UNDCP, DELTA.

1999, as important points of entry and centres of cocaine consumption in Europe. Moreover, large cocaine seizures in 1999 were reported from seaports in the Nordic and the Baltic countries as well as by countries in south-eastern Europe as criminal groups, already involved in heroin and cannabis trafficking, expanded into cocaine as well.[36]

In contrast to North America, the European cocaine trade is not a well organized one. Distribution is still in pockets, rather than linked in chains of professional dealers. As cocaine abuse spreads, however, the involvement of organized crime increases. There is evidence from Interpol of Albanian and Nigerian criminal groups being associated with the cocaine trade.[37] The traditional links between Colombian cocaine suppliers and the Italian mafia[38] as well as Russian criminal groups also point towards a more organized cocaine trade emerging in Europe.[39]

The large portion of cocaine trafficking continues to take place in the Americas where 88% of all cocaine seizures were made in 1997/98 (see Figure 20). The USA is still the world's largest market for cocaine and responsible for almost a third of all cocaine seizures worldwide (31% in 1997/98), ahead of Colombia (21%), the world's largest producer of cocaine, and Mexico (8%). Among the Andean countries Colombia accounts for almost 80% of all cocaine seizures, reflecting the efforts by the Colombian authorities against drug trafficking and high levels of manufacture in the country. (According to Interpol, almost 80 per cent of the world's cocaine is refined in Colombia).[40]

The strongest growth rates in cocaine seizures over the last decade in the Americas, with the exception of Canada, were reported by countries neighbouring the main cocaine manufacturing centres in the Andean region, Chile, Ecuador, the countries of Central America, Venezuela and Paraguay. The increase reflects a general trend toward less direct trafficking (by air) from the production centres to the main

of consumption along these routes. Cocaine seizures in the Republic of South Africa, for instance, rose by 77% p.a. over the decade.

Ninety seven per cent of all European cocaine seizures still take place in Western Europe (1997/98). The bulk of these shipments are trafficked from the Andean region via the Caribbean or via a few other South American countries such as Brazil, Argentina, Ecuador, Venezuela and Paraguay. The proportion of global cocaine seizures being made in Europe rose from 3% (1987/88) to 11% (1997/98), equivalent to an average annual growth rate of 21%, and a record number of seizures in 1999.

The largest cocaine seizures in Europe over the last few years took place in Spain and the Netherlands, the two main points of entry for cocaine. These two countries accounted for 63% of all European cocaine seizures in 1997/98. In addition, the UK, Germany, Italy, Belgium, France and Switzerland have emerged, particularly in consumer markets, with neighbouring countries increasingly being used to circumvent stricter controls in the countries of final destination. In 1998/99 Venezuela and Brazil both experienced an increase in trafficking, by maritime containers and by air.

Another trend has been a certain shift in trafficking from the Caribbean region to Mexico following the creation of the North American Free Trade Association and of the temporary void created by the dismantling of some of the Colombian drug cartels in the first half of the 1990s. Colombian groups, in general, seem to prefer shipping the cocaine by air from Colombia (or neighbouring countries) to the USA – or by boat *via* the Caribbean region. The Mexican groups – first on behalf of Colombian groups but increasingly independent from them – market cocaine *via* the south-western states of the USA. As a result, groups operating from Mexico now largely control much of the wholesale cocaine distribution in the West and midwest of the USA. Mexico's cocaine seizures, which used to be of the same size as those reported by the Caribbean countries a decade ago (1987/88) were more than twice as large in 1997/98,[41] making Mexico one of the main cocaine transit countries in the world.

In *per capita* terms, cocaine seizures in the Caribbean region are still larger than those of Mexico, underlining the Caribbean's continuing significance as a major transit point of cocaine destined for the United States, and increasingly for Western Europe.[42] Indeed, it is mainly as a consequence of rising cocaine trafficking to Western Europe that the Caribbean region has regained importance in more recent years.

Rising levels of cocaine trafficking within Latin America, and the use of countries neighbouring the Andean ones for trans-shipment purposes, has led to the emergence of important cocaine consumer markets in Central and South America. By contrast, the spread of cocaine abuse among the general population in the USA fell over the last decade,[43] and cocaine seizures in the USA, despite a large and rapidly growing budget for drug-related law enforcement activities,[44] grew by just 3% p.a. over the 1987/88-1997/98 period, and generally stabilized in the 1990s.

Cocaine trafficking does take place outside the America-Africa-Europe triangle and seizures even grew over the last decade. Nonetheless, the amounts trafficked are still modest, and there are no indications of an important cocaine market emerging in Asia. The situation is slightly different in Australia where rising levels in trafficking went hand in hand with rising levels of cocaine use over the last few years.[45] The largest seizures outside the main cocaine trafficking regions have been made in recent years in Hong Kong SAR, Australia, Israel and Lebanon.

Cannabis herb
The largest seizures, both in terms of volume and number of cases worldwide are reported for cannabis. At the global level, cannabis herb (marijuana) is trafficked mainly in the Americas and Africa and cannabis resin is trafficked mainly in Europe, northern Africa and South-West Asia.[46]

Trafficking in cannabis herb is more widespread than trafficking in any other substance (see Map 5). Following strong increases in the 1960s and 1970s, it showed a marked downward trend in the 1980s. This was mainly related to the strong decline of marijuana consumption in the world's largest marijuana market, the USA[47] and the strong eradication efforts in Latin America. Rapidly rising demand in Europe[48] caused trafficking in cannabis herb to pick up again in the first half of the 1990s but in the second half of the decade, seizures remained stable (see Figure 21).

The Americas accounted for 72% of all cannabis herb seizures in 1997/98 (see Figure 22). More than 60% of global seizures were made in North America, including Mexico. The largest

Map 5. Patterns and trends in cannabis herb trafficking in the 1990s

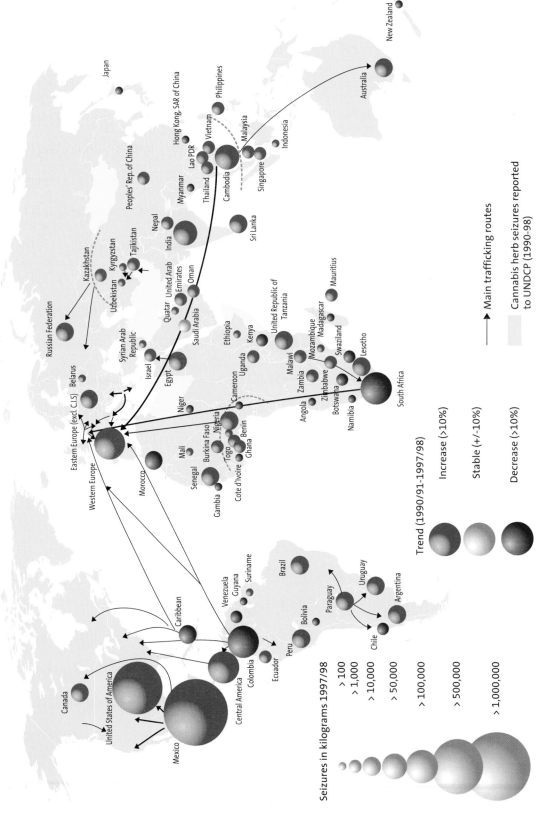

Seizures in kilograms 1997/98

> 100
> 1,000
> 10,000
> 50,000
> 100,000
> 500,000
> 1,000,000

Trend (1990/91-1997/98)

Increase (>10%)

Stable (+/-10%)

Decrease (>10%)

→ Main trafficking routes

Cannabis herb seizures reported to UNDCP (1990-98)

Note: The boundaries and names shown and the designations used on this map do not imply official endorsement or acceptance by the United Nations.
Routes shown are not necessarily documented actual routes, but are rather general indications of the directions of illicit drug flows.

46

Fig. 21: Cannabis herb seizures in tonnes

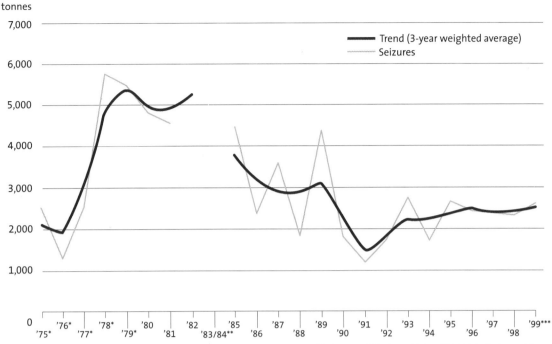

* Data for 1975-79, include seizures of cannabis plants;   ** No comparable data available for 1983/84;   *** 1999: Preliminary data.
Source: UNDCP, DELTA.

Fig. 22: Seizures of cannabis herb in tonnes and as a percentage of total

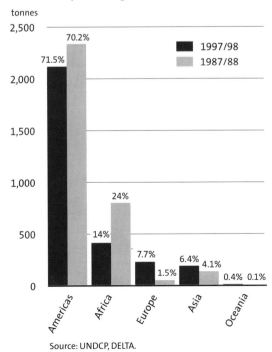

Source: UNDCP, DELTA.

seizures in the Americas have been reported by Mexico (35% of all seizures in 1997/98), the United States (25%) and Colombia (3.5%).[49] Mexico continues to be the main source of herbal cannabis in the USA and over half the total amount seized in the USA in 1999 was along the south-west border with Mexico.[50]

Over the last decade cannabis herb seizures have increased significantly in Mexico, the Central American countries, Brazil and Paraguay; but they fell strongly in Colombia and in the Caribbean region. As a result, overall seizures of cannabis herb in Latin America declined (-2.6% p.a. over the last decade). By contrast, they increased slightly in the USA and Canada (2.7% p.a.), reflecting *inter alia* the growing importance of domestically grown cannabis, (and exports from Canada to the USA).[51] A growing proportion of cannabis produced in South America is consumed within the region, though not necessarily within the same country. Paraguay, for instance, has emerged as an important production site for cannabis herb consumed in neighbouring countries.

Overall seizures of cannabis herb in Africa (14% of the total in 1997/98) are twice as large as those reported from Europe. The largest seizures were reported from Egypt, Ghana, Kenya, Lesotho, Malawi, Mauritius, Morocco, Nigeria, Republic of South Africa, Senegal, Swaziland and the United Republic of Tanzania.[52]

In southern Africa, large-scale eradication of cannabis in the South African Republic in the mid-1990s meant that overall cannabis herb seizures are down from a decade ago. The Republic of South Africa continues to report the third largest seizures of cannabis herb worldwide after Mexico and the USA, and a significant proportion of domestic production continues to be exported.[53] Individual seizure statistics show that in 1998 South Africa was the third largest source of cannabis herb in North America and the second largest source of such substances seized in Western Europe in 1999. High growth rates in cannabis herb seizures over the last decade were also reported by countries in Central and Western Africa (14% p.a.) and in Eastern Africa (13% p.a.) reflecting increasing domestic production, consumption and exports, mainly to markets in Western Europe. Most of the West African cannabis herb seized in Europe in 1998 and 1999 was identified to have originated in Ghana and, to a lesser degree, Senegal.[54]

The strongest growth rates in cannabis trafficking in the 1990s, in line with strong increases in cannabis use among youth, were seen in Europe: they grew 16% p.a. between 1987/88 and 1997/98. Though the bulk of cannabis trafficking affects Western Europe, growth has been strongest in Eastern Europe (28% p.a.) The largest seizures in 1997/98 were reported from the Netherlands (though cannabis sales within Netherlands are *de facto* decriminalized at the retail level), Italy, the UK (which has Europe's highest prevalence rate of cannabis use) and the Russian Federation. Much of the rise in

herbal cannabis traffic in Western Europe in recent years was linked to cannabis grown in Albania which was trafficked to Greece and to Italy for further distribution throughout Europe.[55] Individual seizure statistics show that Albania was the main source of cannabis seized in Western Europe in 1998 and 1999.[56]

Cannabis herb seizures in Asia (6% of the total) rose throughout the 1990s (3% p.a.). Increased trafficking was notable in Central Asia (mostly for trafficking to the Russian Federation)[57] and in South-East Asia (mostly directed towards Western Europe). Cambodia emerged as a major new exporter of cannabis herb in the 1990s.[58] For South Asia, traditionally the largest production, trafficking and consumption region for cannabis herb in Asia,[59] trends are less clear. Reported cannabis herb seizures reached a record high in Nepal in 1987, in Sri Lanka in 1993 and in India in 1994. Overall seizures in South Asia in 1997/98 turned out to be lower compared to a decade earlier, higher compared to the early 1990s (1990/91) and again lower if compared to the peak in 1993/94.

Cannabis herb seizures in Oceania grew by an average 9% p.a. between 1987/88 and 1997/98, the second highest growth rate after Europe. Though seizures are not particularly large in absolute terms, they are almost 30% higher than in Europe, in per capita terms, with 96% taking place in Australia.[60]

Cannabis resin

Trafficking in cannabis resin has shown an upward trend throughout the last three decades: though seizures growth fell from 14% p.a. in the 1980s (1980-90) to an average 5% p.a. in the 1990s (1990-98). This was still twice the growth rate for cannabis herb seizures (see Map 6 and Figure 23).

Much of the global increase in cannabis resin trafficking was due to a rapidly growing market in Europe. Seizures in Europe grew over the 1987/88-1997/98 period by 14% p.a., twice as

Fig. 23: Cannabis resin seizures in tonnes

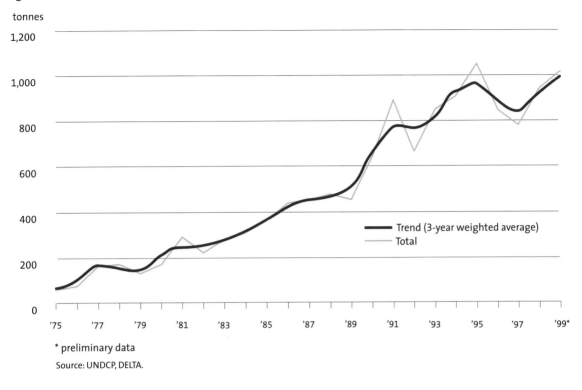

* preliminary data
Source: UNDCP, DELTA.

Fig. 24: Seizures of cannabis resin in tonnes and as a percentage of total

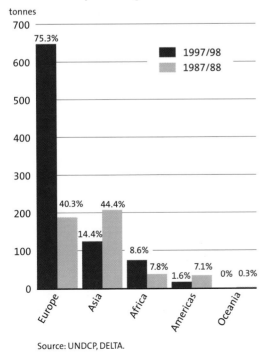

Source: UNDCP, DELTA.

fast as at the global level (7% p.a.). The bulk of all cannabis resin is now seized in Europe (75% of total in 1997/98; (see Figure 24), mostly in Spain (41% of total), the UK (11%), the Netherlands (8%) and France (6%). In comparison, cannabis resin seizure in the USA accounts for just 0.1% of total seizures.[61] In contrast to other drugs, which are trafficked into Europe by many non-European criminal groups, hashish is to a large extent, smuggled in by various European criminal groups.[62]

Large cannabis resin seizures outside Europe take place only in the main countries of origin, Morocco (7%) and Pakistan (9%). Morocco accounts for more than 85% of all cannabis resin seizures in Africa, and Pakistan for almost 70% of all cannabis resin seized in Asia.[63] Most of the resin seized in Pakistan is of either domestic or Afghan origin. Afghan hashish is collected in Pakistan and transported by sea to Europe, North America, the Persian Gulf and Australia;[64] some of it goes overland, through

Map 6. Patterns and trends in cannabis resin trafficking in the 1990s

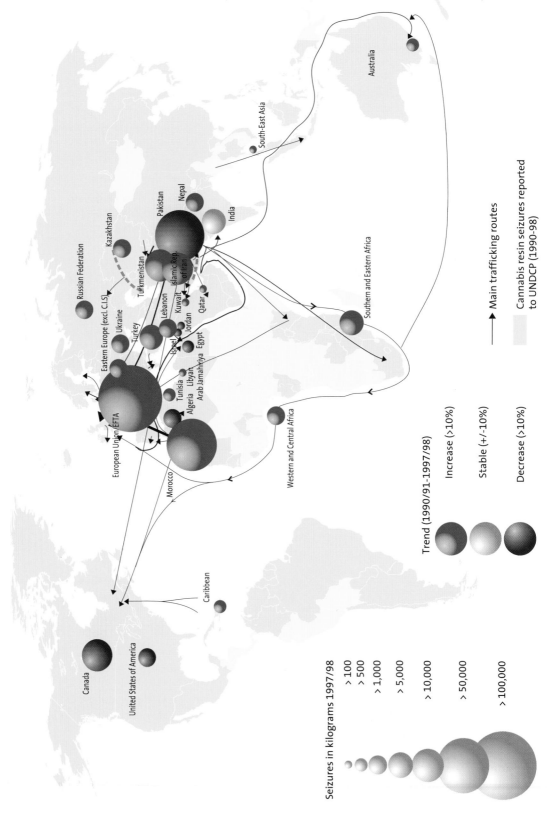

Seizures in kilograms 1997/98

> 100
> 500
> 1,000
> 5,000
> 10,000
> 50,000
> 100,000

Trend (1990/91-1997/98)

Increase (>10%)

Stable (+/-10%)

Decrease (>10%)

→ Main trafficking routes

Cannabis resin seizures reported to UNDCP (1990-98)

Canada
United States of America
Caribbean
Morocco
European Union/EFTA
Eastern Europe (excl. C.I.S)
Ukraine
Turkey
Israel
Tunisia
Algeria
Libyan Arab Jamahriya
Egypt
Jordan
Lebanon
Kuwait
Qatar
Islamic Rep. of Iran
Turkmenistan
Kazakhstan
Russian Federation
Pakistan
Nepal
India
South-East Asia
Australia
Southern and Eastern Africa
Western and Central Africa

Note: The boundaries and names shown and the designations used on this map do not imply official endorsement or acceptance by the United Nations.

Iran and Turkey, to the main market in Europe. The next largest seizures take place in Central Asia (1.5% of total), which is the main source of cannabis resin for the Commonwealth of Independent States' countries, and which is increasingly used to trans-ship Afghan hashish.[65]

Overall cannabis resin seizures in Asia showed a marked decline over the last decade (-5% p.a.), mainly due to falling seizures in Pakistan. Cannabis resin seizures in the other countries of South Asia also fell over the 1987/88-97/98 period, though they remained basically stable in the 1990s, and at significantly lower levels than those reported from Pakistan. The decline in seizures in the Middle East (-17% p.a.) can be directly linked to successful eradication in the Bekaa Valley of Lebanon in the early 1990s.[66]

Cannabis resin seizures grew in Africa by 7% p.a. over the last decade, with seizures in Morocco rising by 22% p.a. Morocco was an important supplier of hashish to Europe throughout the 1980s, but emerged as the main supplier in the 1990s.[67] In 1999, Interpol reported that over 90% of traceable seizures of cannabis resin in Europe originated in Morocco.[68]

The more moderate growth of cannabis resin seizures in North Africa as a whole (6% p.a.) is also linked to supply reduction in the Middle East. Seizures in Egypt, which in 1987/88 were the fourth largest worldwide, declined markedly in the 1990s. The decline has generally been seen as a reflection of reduced exports from Lebanon. Egypt was traditionally one of the main markets for hashish and was among the first countries to restrict its use, and bring it under international control.[69]

Amphetamine-type stimulants
Trafficking in amphetamine-type stimulants (ATS) grew more strongly than that of any other drug category over the last decade. ATS seizures, excluding ecstasy, quadrupled over the 1990-98 period, while seizures of heroin or cocaine rose by less than 50%.

ATS seizures increased from 12% p.a. in the 1980s to 19% p.a. in the 1990s (see Figure 25 and Map 7). If substances of the 'ecstasy' group (MDMA, MDA, MDME. etc.) were included, growth in ATS seizures would have been even larger. Under current reporting practices, however, ecstasy is put under the category of 'other hallucinogens,' and thus is not included in statistics on ATS.

Increases in ATS trafficking in the 1980s were limited to a few regions (North America and a few countries in East and South-East Asia, the Middle East and West Africa). They were of a local nature, and interestingly occurred across very diverse social groups: biker gangs in the USA; fishermen, truck drivers and sex workers in East and South-East Asia, and students in Europe and the Americas. This changed in the 1990s when ATS consumption began to proliferate among youth in general, through recreational use in the music, dance and rave subculture.[70] Unlike most previous drug epidemics, this was not confined to a marginal population but spread among mainstream youth from all social classes and backgrounds.[71] In the 1990s, the ATS became what cocaine had been in the previous decade: the key growth sector in the global drug market. This was reflected in both seizure statistics and consumption data.

In the late 1990s, there were some signs of slowing growth in some of the main consumer markets of Western Europe and North America. This has been, however, offset by an acceleration of trafficking in previously less developed ATS markets.[72]

ATS trafficking is concentrated in three regions: East and South-East Asia (41% of total ATS seizures in 1997/98), Western Europe (38%) and North America (16%). In addition, Australia (1.5%) is an important market for ATS in the Oceania region (see Figure 26).

The UK is the main ATS market in Europe, representing 20% of global seizures in 1997/98.

Fig. 25: Trafficking trends: Global seizures: Index: 1990=100

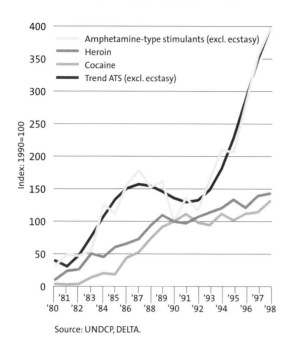

Source: UNDCP, DELTA.

Fig. 26: Amphetamine-type stimulant seizures*

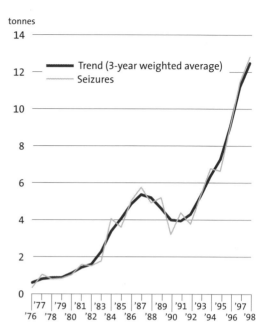

* Seizures in weight terms (grams), volume terms (litres)
and units transformed at 1g=1ml; 1unit=10mg;
excluding seizures of substances of the 'ecstasy' group.

Source: UNDCP, DELTA.

Fig. 27: Seizure of amphetamine-type stimulants* in tonnes and as a percentage of total

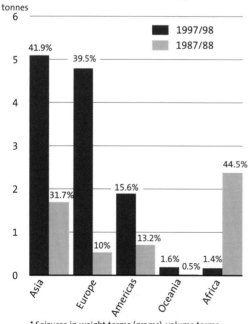

* Seizures in weight terms (grams), volume terms
(litres) and units transformed at 1g=1m;
1unit=10mg; excluding seizures of substances
of the 'ecstasy' group.

Source: UNDCP, DELTA.

A concentration of trafficking, given the size and population of the countries, is found in the Benelux countries (13%), notably in the Netherlands (11%) which is an important manufacturing site for these substances. Smaller though still important markets are in the Nordic countries (3%), Germany (2%), France (1.5%) and Spain (1%). Close to two thirds of all European seizures in 1998/99, in which origin of the ATS could be determined, were traced back to the Netherlands, 15% to manufacture in Poland and 12% to manufacture in Belgium.[73]

The North American ATS market is dominated by the USA, which represents 14% of global seizures. There is a concentration of manufacture, trafficking and abuse of methamphetamine in south-western states of the country although over the last few years this has been spreading towards the centre and the east of the country as well.[74]

Map 7. Patterns and trends in amphetamine-type stimulants trafficking in the 1990s

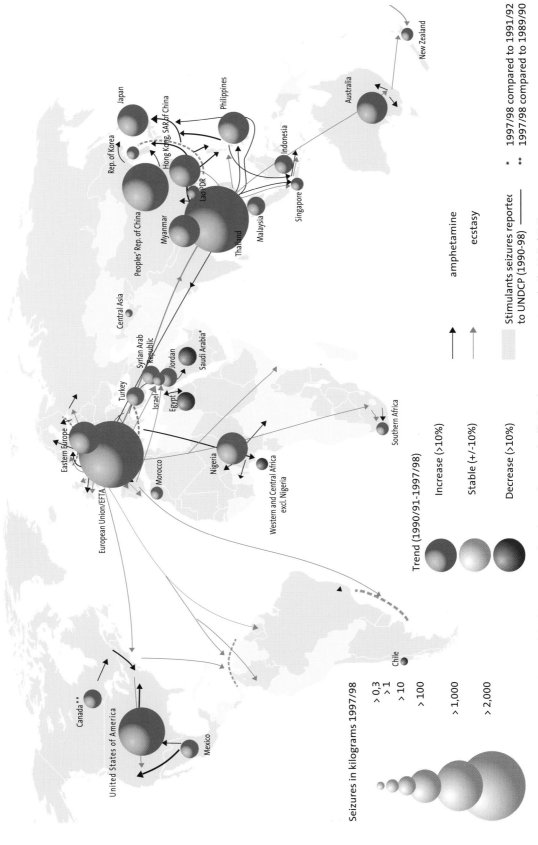

Seizures in kilograms 1997/98

> 0,3
> 1
> 10
> 100
> 1,000
> 2,000

Trend (1990/91-1997/98)

Increase (>10%)

Stable (+/-10%)

Decrease (>10%)

amphetamine

ecstasy

Stimulants seizures reported
to UNDCP (1990-98)

*   1997/98 compared to 1991/92
**   1997/98 compared to 1989/90

Note: The boundaries and names shown and the designations used on this map do not imply official endorsement or acceptance by the United Nations.
Routes shown are not necessarily documented actual routes, but are rather general indications of the directions of illicit drug flows.

53

Establishing the relative size of markets in East and South-East Asia is difficult because seizures tend to fluctuate strongly from year to year. In 1997/98, Thailand reported the largest amounts seized (19% of global seizures), followed by the People's Republic of China (11%), the Philippines (3%), Japan (3%), Special Administrative Region of Hong Kong, (1%) and Myanmar (1%).[75] Other important locations for ATS trafficking are Taiwan, Province of China, and the Republic of Korea.

While methamphetamine is the main ATS in the East and South-East Asia and North America, amphetamine and ecstasy dominate the European market. Trafficking in methamphetamine is still very limited in Europe, except for the Czech Republic where it is produced, trafficked and consumed under the name of 'pervitin'. Much of the trafficking in East Asia and Hawaii is 'ice' (high-purity methamphetamine that is smoked). The methamphetamine trafficked in S.E. Asia is lower-purity, and mixed with other products in tablet form. Methamphetamine in the USA is frequently injected.[76]

Methcathinone (locally known as 'ephedrone') is frequently trafficked in the countries of the former Soviet Union. By contrast, the ATS consumed in South America are usually not trafficked; they are mostly anorectics (weight-loss drugs), sold in pharmacies often without proper prescriptions.[77] This explains the high prevalence of ATS use, the high demand for 'licit' ATS, as well as the very low amounts seized. ATS trafficked and consumed in the countries of the Middle East are usually fenetylline (sold under the name of captagon) which in the past was legally produced in Europe. Though legal production has stopped, there are still clandestine stocks and probably some clandestine production to supply the markets in the Middle East, notably Saudi Arabia, Syria and Jordan.[78] Fenetylline seizures in Turkey are mainly shipments for the Middle East.[79] In Egypt, the main ATS trafficked is Maxiton Forte, originally dexamfetamine, a pharmaceutical drug produced in Europe. The brand name remained but the product was changed, and is now probably methamphetamine, produced in clandestine laboratories within the country.[80] However, its production, and thus seizures, declined strongly in the 1990s. Many of the ATS found in the parallel drug markets in West Africa (amphetamine, ephedrine and pemoline) are usually diverted from licit sources. Nigeria has emerged as a major re-distribution centre for such ATS in the region.

The strongest growth rates of ATS seizures over the last decade (1987/88-1997/98) were in Europe (25% p.a.), Oceania (21% p.a.) and East and South-East Asia (12% p.a.). These regions also saw the strongest increases in ATS consumption in the 1990s. Declines in ATS seizures were confined to South America, Africa and some countries in the Middle East. In all of these cases, the bulk of ATS are diverted to the illicit market from licit sources. Improved controls of licit manufacture and distribution of ATS in the 1990s contributed to a reduction of such diversions, and subsequently to seizures.

By contrast, in North America, Europe, Australia and the East and South-East Asia, the bulk of illegal ATS are from clandestine manufacture. Precursor chemicals are diverted from licit into illicit channels in order to manufacture ATS in clandestine laboratories.[81] While the control systems for ATS end-products are now well established in a large number of countries, precursor control is less developed and at an early stage in most countries. Because many precursor chemicals have a large range of legitimate uses, the development and implementation of a comprehensive system to monitor their trade is extremely complicated and will continue to challenge many nations.

Clandestine manufacture of ATS has been taking place in the United States and Western Europe since the 1960s, and spread to East Asia (the Republic of Korea, the Philippines, Taiwan, Province of China and Hong Kong SAR) in the 1980s.[82] In the 1990s, significant expansion of

ATS manufacture took place in almost all regions. Production capacities in South-East Asia expanded rapidly, notably in the People's Republic of China, and in more recent years in Thailand and Myanmar where a number of heroin manufacture and trafficking organizations diversified their activities to include methamphetamine. During the same period, clandestine manufacture in Western Europe, notably in the Netherlands and in the UK, expanded from small-scale kitchen laboratories to more established facilities. Parallel to this, ATS production capacities in the Baltic States, Bulgaria, the Czech Republic, Mexico, Poland, and USA also expanded significantly.

While trafficking in most drugs is inter-regional, trafficking in ATS is largely intra-regional; i.e. production and consumption are usually within the same region, often within the same country.

Ecstasy is the exception to this. Most of the ecstasy is still produced in Europe: often in the Netherlands, though there is also significant production in Germany and Belgium, and a spread of production to Eastern Europe. Production is also spreading, to Israel, South Africa, Australia, South America and Thailand.[83] Originally, ecstasy was almost exclusively destined for consumption within Europe, and Europe continues to remain the principal area for trafficking and consumption. However, in the second half of the 1990s, there were huge increases in trafficking of ecstasy from Europe to North America, Australia/New Zealand, South Africa, and various Asian countries, as well as from the Middle East to the Far East. In 1999, the USA had the largest ecstasy seizures worldwide; most of it was of European origin.[84] Though the volumes were not large, an inter-regional pattern of ecstasy trafficking is emerging.

1.3. CONSUMPTION

1.3.1. THE GEOGRAPHICAL SPREAD OF DRUG ABUSE

Drug abuse is a global phenomenon. There is hardly any country in which it does not take place. While the extent and characteristics of the problem obviously differ from country to country, abuse trends, especially among youth, show same signs of convergence over the last few decades.

According to replies to UNDCP's Annual Reports Questionnaire at least 134 countries and territories were faced with a drug abuse problem (defined in the following section of this Chapter) in the 1990s. The overall number of countries in which drug abuse takes place is higher.

Figure 28 shows that the most frequently mentioned substances, reflecting the geographic spread of consumption, are still the plant-based drugs: cannabis (consumed in 96% of all countries reporting a drug abuse problem), the opiates (87%) and the cocaine-type substances (81%). They are followed by the synthetic drugs, i.e. by amphetamine-type stimulants (73%), benzodiazepines (69%) and various volatile substances or inhalants (69%) (Table 2 shows these data by region). Three quarters of all countries report abuse of heroin and two thirds abuse of cocaine. Both abuse of heroin and of cocaine are more widespread than abuse of their respective intermediate products – opium/ morphine or coca leaf/coca paste which are usually consumed close to the areas of production.

The most widely consumed drug is cannabis. It is used either in the form of cannabis herb (marijuana) or cannabis resin (hashish) in almost all countries across the globe.

By contrast, the abuse of the opiates is concentrated in Asia and Europe, and of cocaine in the Americas, and to a lesser extent in Europe.[85] Abuse of synthetic drugs, notably ampheta-

Fig. 28: Countries and territories reporting an abuse problem in the 1990s – for most commonly mentioned substances as a percentage of all countries reporting on drug abuse (N=134)

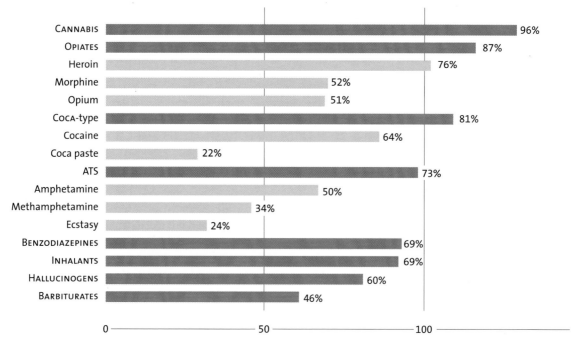

Number of countries and territories
Source: UNDCP, DELTA.

mine-type stimulants (ATS) and benzodiazepines, is concentrated in Europe. Within the group of ATS, amphetamine and methamphetamine are the most abused substances worldwide, followed by the ecstasy substances. While methamphetamine is the dominant ATS in North America and East and South-East Asia, amphetamine is the most widely abused ATS in Europe. Consumption of the various substances of the ecstasy group is concentrated in Europe, though spreading to other regions as well.

Barbiturates, which a couple of decades ago constituted a major problem, are now mentioned by less than half of all reporting countries, reflecting better controls to prevent diversion and a shift towards the use of the slightly less addictive benzodiazepines instead. Benzodiazepines

and barbiturates – in contrast to cannabis, opiates or cocaine-type substances – are usually obtained from licit sources, either through over-prescriptions or direct purchase in pharmacies or parallel markets in countries lacking adequate control systems.

The overall ranking of drug abuse in geographical terms (except for benzodiazepines and inhalants), is very similar to the ranking of countries reporting seizures, indicating that countries with drug trafficking eventually face a drug abuse problem.

1.3.2. MAIN PROBLEM DRUGS
The definition of a problem drug relates to the extent to which use of a certain drug leads to treatment demand[j], emergency room visits

---

j) In order to establish a pattern, the relative proportions of treatment demand for each specific drug in each country or city for which data was available, were calculated. These proportions were subsequently averaged to arrive at a regional average, which is the basis for the present discussion on problem drugs.

(often due to overdose), drug related morbidity (including HIV/AIDS, hepatitis etc.), mortality and other drug-related social ills, such as drug-related crime and violence. The term problem drug does not relate to the size of the population consuming it. Cannabis, for example, is the most widely consumed illegal substance worldwide; it is not, however, the main problem drug in terms of the adverse health and social consequences described above. (There are indications that it does play a role as a 'gateway drug' to the use of other substances. Most cannabis users do not, and will not, move on to other drugs; but almost all available studies show that most users of other drugs, such as heroin or cocaine, have used cannabis at some earlier stage in their drug careers.) The main 'problem drugs' in the 1990s were the opiates, primarily heroin, and cocaine (see Map 8).

EUROPE AND OCEANIA

Opiates
Opiates are the main problem drugs in Europe (both Western and Eastern), in most parts of Asia and Oceania notably Australia. On average, opiates account for three quarters of all treatment demand in both Europe[86] and Asia[87] and two thirds in Australia. They are also responsible for the large majority of drug-related mortality and morbidity cases.

Amphetamine-type stimulants
The overall proportion of methamphetamine abusers in treatment in Asia (12%) exceeds the proportion of ATS abusers in treatment in Europe (8%) and in North America (5%). Australia has a high share of treatment admissions (13%) for abuse of both amphetamine and methamphetamine.

Table 2. Spread of drug abuse – Regional concentration of countries and territories reporting drug abuse in the 1990s

	Regions					Global (average)
	EUROPE	ASIA	AMERICAS	AFRICA	OCEANIA	ALL
Number of countries & territories reporting drug abuse to UNDCP, of which	41	37	27	22	7	134
Cannabis	100%	95%	92%	95%	100%	96%
Opiates	**100%**	**100%**	56%	86%	57%	87%
* Heroin	**88%**	81%	42%	82%	29%	76%
* Morphine	59%	**62%**	48%	36%	29%	51%
* Opium	44%	**81%**	19%	36%	29%	51%
Amphetamine-type stimulants (ATS)	**93%**	62%	63%	59%	43%	73%
Benzodiazepines	76%	62%	69%	68%	14%	69%
Inhalants (volatile substances)	76%	62%	74%	64%	57%	69%
Cocaine	73%	32%	**85%**	64%	43%	64%
Barbiturates	51%	43%	42%	36%	14%	46%

close to global average: black
above global average (> 10%): red
clearly below global average (< 30%): light blue

Source: UNDCP, DELTA (Replies to Annual Reports Questionnaires).

Map 8. Main problem drugs (as reflected in treatment demand) in the late 1990s

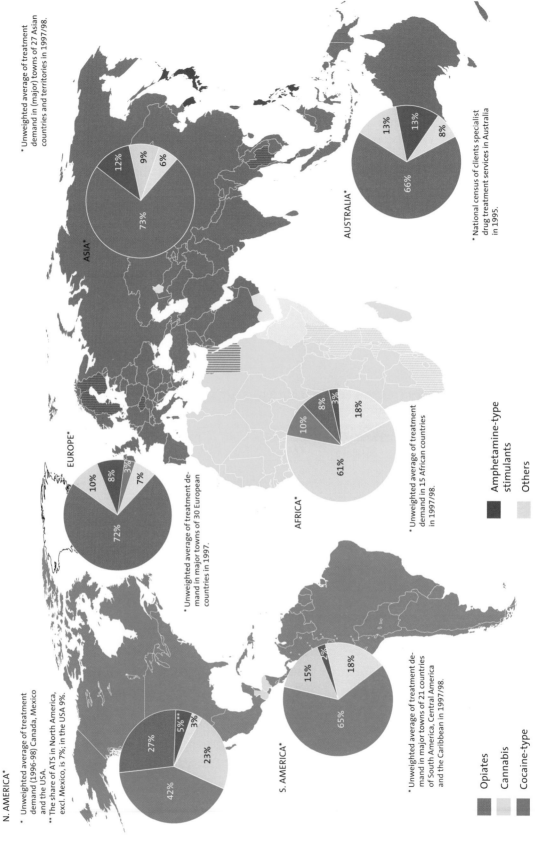

N. AMERICA*

* Unweighted average of treatment demand (1996-98) Canada, Mexico and the USA.
** The share of ATS in North America, excl. Mexico, is 7%; in the USA 9%.

ASIA*

* Unweighted average of treatment demand in (major) towns of 27 Asian countries and territories in 1997/98.

AUSTRALIA*

* National census of clients specialist drug treatment services in Australia in 1995.

EUROPE*

* Unweighted average of treatment demand in major towns of 30 European countries in 1997.

AFRICA*

* Unweighted average of treatment demand in 15 African countries in 1997/98.

S. AMERICA*

* Unweighted average of treatment demand in major towns of 21 countries of South America, Central America and the Caribbean in 1997/98.

Legend:
- Opiates
- Cannabis
- Cocaine-type
- Amphetamine-type stimulants
- Others

Sources: Asian Multicity Epidemiology Working Group; CCSA; CICAD; Council of Europe (Pompidou Group); EMCDDA; SACENDU; SAMHSA; UNDCP
Note: The boundaries and names shown and the designations used on this map do not imply official endorsement or acceptance by the United Nations.

In several countries of *East Asia*, notably Japan, the Philippines, and the Republic of Korea, *methamphetamine* is the main problem drug, accounting for 90% or more of treatment demand.[88] Though opiates are the dominant problem drug in South-East Asia, rapidly rising levels of methamphetamine-related treatment cases have been reported from this subregion in recent years, particularly from Thailand,[89] where methamphetamine users already exceed the number of heroin users.

In *Europe*, only the Czech Republic reports high levels of methamphetamine-related treatment, which accounts for almost half of all treatment cases in Prague.[90] Relatively high amphetamine-related treatment demand has been also reported from Finland and Sweden.[91]

Cannabis

Nine per cent of treatment in Asia is related to cannabis, a similar percentage as in Europe, but less than in Australia (13%), the Americas (16%) or Africa (61%). The latter proportions reflect the strong demand for opiate treatment rather than low levels of cannabis abuse. High proportions for *cannabis* in treatment in Asia have been reported by the Maldives, the countries of central Asia, the Philippines, Nepal, South India; in Europe by Cyprus and within the EU by the Netherlands, notably the city of Amsterdam (21%) where cannabis consumption is *de facto* decriminalized.[92]

Cocaine

Cocaine is hardly mentioned at all in the admission reports of Asian treatment centres and its spread appears to be limited in Europe. Only 3% of total treatment demand in *Europe* was related to cocaine abuse. Within Europe, treatment demand is below 1% in Eastern Europe, but above 5% in the countries of the European Union.[93] In Amsterdam, cocaine accounts for 32% of all treatment demand, reflecting its geographic proximity to Rotterdam, one of the main entry points of cocaine to Europe.[94]

AMERICAS

Cocaine-type substances, i.e. cocaine hydrochloride, crack-cocaine, and related cocaine-type products such as basuco (an intermediate product in the cocaine manufacturing process) are, the main problem drugs in the Americas. They are responsible for an average 61% of treatment demand and most drug-related crime and violence. The next most frequently mentioned substances in treatment centres are cannabis (16%) and inhalants (7%).[95]

South America, including Central America and the Caribbean

The proportion of *cocaine* and related products is highest in the countries of *South America* where about two thirds of all treatment demand is cocaine-related. Most of the rest is accounted for by *tranquilizers and inhalants,* which make up the bulk of the relatively large category of 'other drugs', and by *cannabis*.

Cannabis abuse is spread all across the Americas, but its role as a problem drug is mainly concentrated in Central America and the Caribbean. Opiates, by contrast, are not very important as a problem drug in this region; they are not even mentioned in most treatment centres.[96]

North America

In *North America* (Canada, Mexico, USA), *cocaine* is still the main problem drug, responsible for more than 40% of treatment cases on average. Though the USA now has the lowest proportion among all North American countries, in absolute terms the total number of people in treatment for cocaine abuse is still by far the highest worldwide.[97] But the numbers are falling: 222,000 people were treated for cocaine abuse in 1997 (29% of all treatment cases, excluding alcohol), as compared to 267,000 persons (43% of treatment cases) in 1992.[98] Three quarters of all cocaine abuse related treatment in the USA is linked to crack-cocaine (see Table 3).

Table 3. Relative risks of drug abuse – as revealed in US data on substance abuse and treatment admissions (1997)

Drug category	Estimated number of users according to national household survey (annual prevalence) 1997	Treatment admissions according to primary substance of abuse 1997	Annual treatment admissions per 1,000 users
Heroin*	597,000	217,868	365
Crack-cocaine	1,375,000	163,211	119
Methamphetamine**	802,364	53,006	66
Cocaine (all)*	4,169,000	222,001	53
Amphetamine-type stimulants***	1,687,000	67,137	40
Cannabis	19,446,000	191,724	10
All drugs (incl. others)	24,189,000	764,142	32
Memo:			
Alcohol (incl. use of drugs)	138,500,000	713,739	5
Alcohol (excl. use of drugs)	138,500,000	401,961	3

* Broader US estimates provided by ONDCP, which aim at including marginalized groups not living in households, saw the number of hardcore heroin users at 935,000 in 1997; this would lower the ratio to 233 treatment admissions per 1,000 heroin users; the comparable ONDCP's estimate on the number of hard-core cocaine users was 3,503,000, equivalent to 63 treatment admissions per 1,000 cocaine users ('hardcore' being defined as weekly users). If hardcore and occasional users are taken together, the respective ratios of treatment admissions per 1,000 users would be 142 for heroin and 32 for cocaine.

** Estimate for annual prevalence based on available life-time prevalence data and relationship between life-time and annual prevalence for the broader group of ATS.

*** ATS excluding ecstasy.

Sources: SAMHSA, US National Household Survey (1998); SAMHSA, Treatment Episode Data Set (TEDS), 1992-97; ONDCP, The National Drug Control Strategy : 2000, Annual Report.

Opiates account for slightly more than a quarter of all treatment demand in North America. This is a high proportion given the low levels of heroin use among the general population. The number of people in treatment for cocaine abuse, for example, was equivalent to 5% of the estimated number of annual cocaine users as revealed in the national household survey on drug abuse (or 12% for crack-cocaine users). The number of heroin treatment cases was equivalent to 36% of the number of annual heroin users. The corresponding proportions for amphetamine-type stimulants and cannabis were 4% and 1% respectively.

The overall proportion of *cannabis* in treatment demand is, nonetheless, fairly high in the USA (25% for the USA; 23% for North America as a whole). The high proportion is related to two important factors: the higher levels of THC in domestically grown cannabis in the USA and Canada, which has made cannabis consumption more risky; and the fact that in some circumstances cannabis users are required by law to seek treatment. The latter accounts for about half of all cannabis related treatment in the USA.[99]

Amphetamines, mostly in the form of *methamphetamine* (80% of all treatment for ATS is related to methamphetamine abuse) account for 9% of all treatment in the USA[100] – i.e. a slightly higher proportion than ATS in Europe (8%), though if the unweighted average for the three North American countries is calculated, the proportion falls to 5%, due to the low level of methamphetamine-related treatment cases in Mexico.[101]

AFRICA

Cannabis

Only in Africa and a few countries of Central America does *cannabis* appear as the main problem drug in treatment demand. However, even in these countries where treatment demand is high, cannabis-related mortality and crime are low. On average, some 60% of treatment demand in Africa in the late 1990s was related to long-term abuse of cannabis. This statement, however, needs to be qualified. Currently available data for many countries in Africa are not very robust. The number of people who have actually been treated in hospitals and specialized treatment facilities is very small. This is not necessarily a reflection of low levels of drug abuse but of a poor treatment infrastructure and, in many cases, the social stigma attached to the use of such facilities. People are often treated outside the formal system and consequently do not register in the data set.

Other drugs in Africa

Treatment data do show that various *psychotropic* substances (mostly in Western Africa) but also opiates and in more recent years cocaine, have made inroads into Africa, and their abuse is growing.

In Egypt, for instance, despite a tradition of cannabis consumption and abuse, with hashish having been the main problem drug until the 1970s, *opiates* emerged in the 1990s as the main problem drug (45% of all cases in treatment centres in 1999), followed by benzodiazepines (32%).[102] Opiates are also showing up in treatment demand in several countries along the eastern coast of Africa, down to South Africa.

Cocaine abuse is manifested in treatment demand in Western Africa and increasingly in some of the countries of Southern Africa. In the Republic of South Africa it accounts for 15% of all treatment demand, as compared to 3% for abuse of opiates.[103] The main problem drug-combination in South Africa, however, is a mixture of *methaqualone* (known as Mandrax) and *cannabis*, which is also found in some of the other African countries along the Indian Ocean.[104] In the horn of Africa, large-scale khat consumption is reflected in treatment demand.[105]

1.3.3. TRENDS IN DRUG ABUSE

Once a drug abuse problem is identified, its development and dynamics have to be charted.[k] Drug abuse continued spreading in the 1990s particularly in countries located along the main trafficking routes. The overall spread, however, was less dramatic than in the 1980s. In 1997/98 less than half the countries reporting on drug abuse trends saw an increase in drug abuse, a third saw a stabilization and more than a quarter experienced a decline.[l] Among the countries reporting an increase, less than half experienced a strong increase (see Figure 29).

---

k) Trend data should ideally be based on sound epidemiological studies. International standard-setting for such work, however, has only developed gradually. In the '*Declaration on the guiding principles of drug demand reduction*', passed at the Special Session of the General Assembly in June 1998, it was categorically established for the first time that programmes had to be based 'on a regular assessment of the nature and magnitude of drug use and abuse and drug-related problems in the population' and that this was 'imperative for the identification of any emerging trends' (see Chapter II in the present *Report*). Though a number of countries have started to develop comprehensive drug monitoring systems, most countries still lack them. In the absence of consistent and comprehensive epidemiological surveys, the available trend data reflect observations by professionals in treatment institutions or health authorities. While one cannot exclude bias in individual expert opinions, there is no evidence of any systematic bias.

l) In the UNDCP Annual Reports Questionnaire, countries note their perception of abuse trends for different drug categories. Assuming that in a particular country, the abuse of some drugs increases, of others it remains stable, and of others it declines, the distribution would be equal: 33.3% each for increase, stable and decline. Any deviation from this pattern is measured and reflected in these trend data.

Fig. 29: Drug abuse trends* in 1997/98: all drugs

Fig. 30: Drug abuse trends* in 1992-98: all drugs

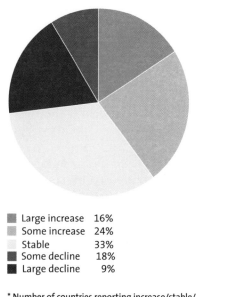

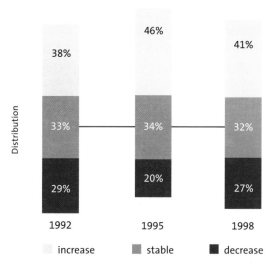

■ Large increase   16%
■ Some increase   24%
□ Stable   33%
■ Some decline   18%
■ Large decline   9%

□ increase   ■ stable   ■ decrease

* Number of countries reporting increase/stable/
decrease; N=96

* Countries and territories reporting increase/stable/
decline in drug abuse as a proportion of all countries
and territories reporting trends.

Source: UNDCP, DELTA.

Source: UNDCP, DELTA.

Fig. 31: Substance abuse trends*: selected drugs (1992/1998)

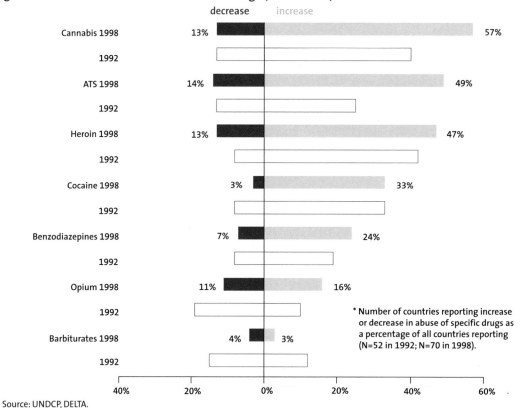

Source: UNDCP, DELTA.

Drug abuse at the global level was still expanding in the early 1990s, but this expansion lost momentum in the second half of the decade. Between 1995 and 1998 the number of countries reporting an increase in drug abuse fell while the number of countries reporting a decline in drug abuse rose. The fact that some of the stabilization or decline in drug abuse was reported in the main consumer countries makes it unlikely that overall abuse, in terms of absolute numbers, is expanding even though it may continue spreading in geographic terms.

For all of the major drug types, the number of countries and territories reporting an increase in abuse continues to outnumber those reporting a decline (see Figure 30). The strongest overall spread of drug abuse in the 1990s was for the *amphetamine-type stimulants (ATS) and cannabis* (see Figure 31). The most 'dynamic' drugs were the ATS. The number of countries and territories reporting an increase in ATS abuse almost tripled between 1992 and 1998 (see Figure 31).

More than half of all countries reported increases in cannabis use in 1998. The ongoing spread of cannabis consumption is problematic for the medium term. In many countries, the level of cannabis consumption correlates positively with the level of consumption of major problem drugs. Thus, with cannabis consumption spreading, one might expect the consumption of problem drugs to escalate once a proportion of the cannabis users 'advances' to other drugs.

Increases in the abuse of other drugs, including heroin and cocaine, were by far less significant in the 1990s. While half of all countries in 1998 saw an increase in ATS, only one third reported an increase in cocaine abuse. Although there was a spread in cocaine abuse, the number of countries reporting an increase stagnated over the 1992-98 period. It is also interesting to note that throughout the 1990s more countries reported an increase in heroin than in cocaine abuse – which conforms to the production trends of opium and coca leaf.

Opiates

Abuse trend data for the opiates (heroin, morphine, opium) for the late 1990s (1998 or previous years) reveal the following patterns (see Map 9):

- an increase, in drug transit countries, notably *Central Asia and East European countries along the Balkan route, Southern and Eastern Africa,* and in some of the countries of Northern Africa; by contrast, there were signs of decline in some of the Western African countries, after having grown rapidly in previous years;
- a stabilization or decline in the main consumer markets of *Western Europe* (except for the UK, and – though starting from low levels – some Nordic countries), in some countries of central Europe, and in the *USA,* following a period of strong increases in previous years; increases in opiate abuse, however, continued in both Canada and Mexico;
- an increase in *South America,* particularly Colombia, linked to the increase in the domestic production of opium and heroin, some of its neighbouring countries (Venezuela and Ecuador), and Argentina; in Brazil, Bolivia and Paraguay, by contrast, opiate abuse remained stable;
- increases in practically all countries of Asia, with the exception of Myanmar, which reported a decline in 1998; and
- an increase in Australia.

Compared to the first half the 1990s (1994 or previous years), the most striking features appear to be:

- declining levels of abuse in Western Europe;
- the apparent end of the 'heroin chic' in the USA, which had started in the first half of the decade and was related to the emergence of high quality heroin on the US market; and
- the increasing abuse problem in drug transit countries.

Cocaine-type drugs

Abuse trend data for cocaine in the late 1990s (1998 or previous years) reveal the following tendencies (see Map 10):

Map 9. Changes in abuse of heroin and other opiates, 1994 (or latest year available)

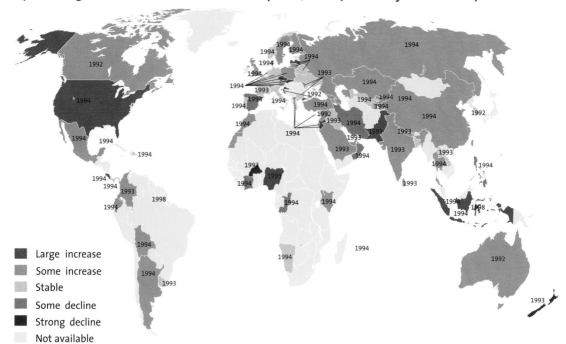

Large increase
Some increase
Stable
Some decline
Strong decline
Not available

Changes in abuse of heroin and other opiates, 1998 (or latest year available)

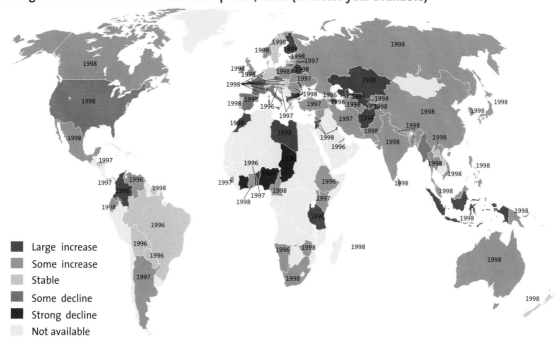

Large increase
Some increase
Stable
Some decline
Strong decline
Not available

Sources: UNDCP Annual Reports Questionnaires data; Asian Multicity Epidemiology Workgroup; Bundeskriminalamt (BKA) and other Law Enforcement Reports; Comisión Interamericana para el Control del Abuso de Drogas (CICAD); Council of Europe (Pompidou Group); PHARE, Summary Reports on the Drug Situation in Central and Eastern European Countries; SACENDU (South African Community Epidemiology Network; United States Department of State, *International Narcotics Control Strategy Report*.
Note: The boundaries and names shown and the designations used on this map do not imply official endorsement or acceptance by the United Nations.

- a decline in cocaine consumption in the USA, the world's largest cocaine market;
- increases in cocaine consumption in South America, Central America, Europe (primarily Western Europe), Southern Africa and Australia; and
- very limited abuse in Asia.

Compared to the mid-1990s, the most striking features appear to be:

- the intensification of abuse throughout Latin America, Western Europe and Australia; and
- the emergence of a cocaine abuse problem in the countries of Southern Africa, after they became trafficking transit countries; Western Africa showed mixed results with cocaine abuse apparently shifting to countries where it did not exist before, and declining in others.

Cannabis

The following trends can be observed for cannabis abuse in the 1990s (see Map 11):

- stable consumption in North America, the world's largest market for marijuana;
- decline in cannabis abuse in most Asian countries, except for Kazakhstan and a few countries in East and South-East Asia;
- increase in cannabis abuse in Europe, both Eastern and Western (except for a few countries, including the UK and Ireland, which already have the highest levels of cannabis consumption in Europe);
- increases in cannabis abuse in both South America and Central America;
- increases in several countries of Southern Africa, Central Africa, Northern and Western Africa ;
- increases in most countries in the Oceania region.

The most striking changes compared to the mid-1990s were the decline in cannabis consumption in much of Asia, and the increase in Europe.

Amphetamine-type stimulants

Consumption of amphetamine-type stimulants (ATS) increased throughout the 1990s, notably in Europe (both amphetamine and ecstasy), and if methamphetamine is considered, in East and South-East Asia and North America. Though still most frequent in Europe, 'ecstasy' abuse has increased across all continents.

The years 1994 and 1998 have been chosen as the basis for comparison of drug abuse trends because the two years, on the whole, are typical years for the first and the second half of the decade, for opiates, cocaine and cannabis (see Maps 9, 10 and 11). They are, however, less representative, when it comes to consumption of amphetamine-type stimulants. The increase in ATS use was most pronounced after 1994 and prior to 1998. Almost all countries reported increases in ATS abuse over the 1995-97 period (see Map 12).

By 1998, a number of countries in Europe, North America and East and South-East Asia, including the USA, the UK, Spain and Japan, saw stabilization or decline in ATS abuse for the first time in years. Nonetheless, overall abuse continued increasing in the late 1990s, in South-East Asia (particularly Thailand), and some European countries, including the Nordic countries and countries such as France or Italy which had started out from lower levels.

A mixed picture emerges for countries in Latin America in the late 1990s. While Mexico, Colombia and Brazil reported rising ATS consumption, there was a decline in the south of the continent in Chile and Argentina. This is linked to better controls of licit ATS, which are still the main source of supply in this part of the world. However, there have been some signs that consumption could shift from ATS to cocaine as the latter becomes more easily available.

ATS abuse is fairly widespread in Africa, but, in contrast to other regions, there are no indications of an increase. ATS in Africa, like in South America, are still mostly licit medicines that

Map 10. Changes in abuse of cocaine, 1994 (or the previous year(s))

- Large increase
- Some increase
- Stable
- Some decline
- Strong decline
- Not available

Changes in abuse of cocaine, 1998 (or latest year available)

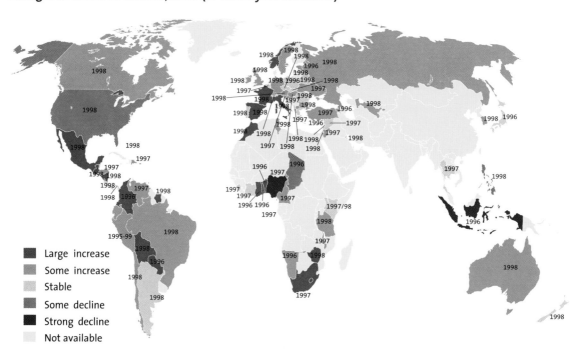

- Large increase
- Some increase
- Stable
- Some decline
- Strong decline
- Not available

Sources: UNDCP Annual Reports Questionnaires data; Asian Multicity Epidemiology Workgroup; Bundeskriminalamt (BKA) and other Law Enforcement Reports; Comisión Interamericana para el Control del Abuso de Drogas (CICAD); Council of Europe (Pompidou Group); PHARE, Summary Reports on the Drug Situation in Central and Eastern European Countries; SACENDU (South African Community Epidemiology Network; United States Department of State, *International Narcotics Control Strategy Report.*
Note: The boundaries and names shown and the designations used on this map do not imply official endorsement or acceptance by the United Nations.

Map 11. Changes in abuse of cannabis, 1994 (or the previous year(s))

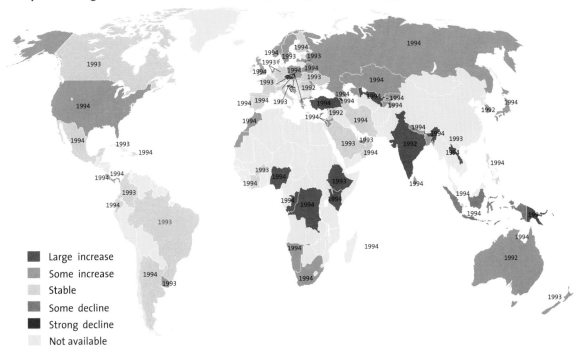

Large increase
Some increase
Stable
Some decline
Strong decline
Not available

Changes in abuse of canabis, 1998 (or latest year available)

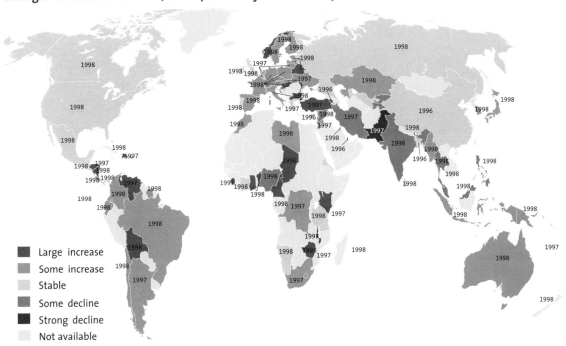

Large increase
Some increase
Stable
Some decline
Strong decline
Not available

Sources: UNDCP Annual Reports Questionnaires data; Asian Multicity Epidemiology Workgroup; Bundeskriminalamt (BKA) and other Law Enforcement Reports; Comisión Interamericana para el Control del Abuso de Drogas (CICAD); Council of Europe (Pompidou Group); PHARE, Summary Reports on the Drug Situation in Central and Eastern European Countries; SACENDU (South African Community Epidemiology Network; United States Department of State, *International Narcotics Control Strategy Report*.
Note: The boundaries and names shown and the designations used on this map do not imply official endorsement or acceptance by the United Nations.

Map 12. Changes in abuse of amphetamine-type stimulants, 1994 (or the previous year(s))

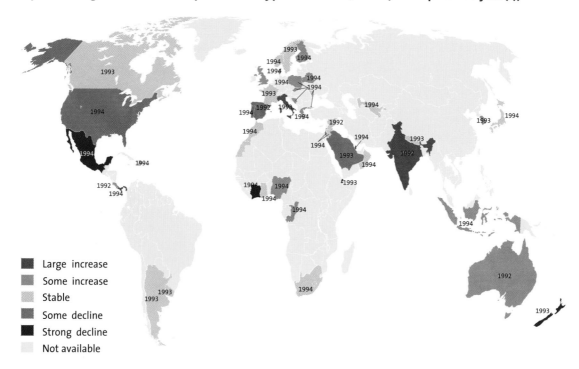

Large increase
Some increase
Stable
Some decline
Strong decline
Not available

Changes in abuse of amphetamine-type stimulants, 1998 (or latest year available)

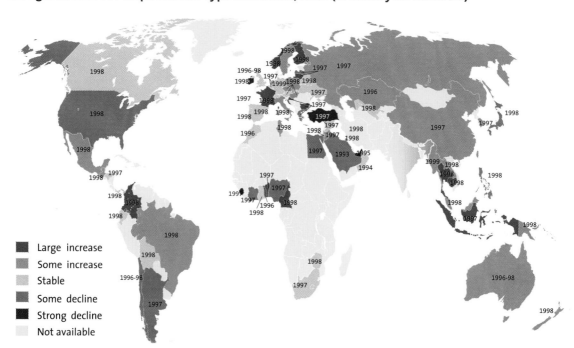

Large increase
Some increase
Stable
Some decline
Strong decline
Not available

Sources: UNDCP Annual Reports Questionnaires data; Asian Multicity Epidemiology Workgroup; Bundeskriminalamt (BKA) and other Law Enforcement Reports; Comisión Interamericana para el Control del Abuso de Drogas (CICAD); Council of Europe (Pompidou Group); PHARE, Summary Reports on the Drug Situation in Central and Eastern European Countries; SACENDU (South African Community Epidemiology Network; United States Department of State, *International Narcotics Control Strategy Report*.
Note: The boundaries and names shown and the designations used on this map do not imply official endorsement or acceptance by the United Nations.

68

have been diverted into illicit channels. Better controls of licit manufacture and trade at the global level limited diversion into illicit channels during the 1990s.

1.3.4. THE EXTENT OF DRUG ABUSE

Assessing the extent of drug abuse (the number of drug abusers) is a particularly difficult undertaking because it involves measuring the size of a hidden population. Margins of error are thus considerable, and tend to multiply as the scale of estimation is raised, from local to country, regional and global levels.

110 countries provided UNDCP with estimates on the level of drug abuse in the 1990s (79 countries in 1997/98). These estimates are very heterogeneous, in terms of quality and reliability. They are, in general, difficult to compare. Detailed information is available from countries in North America, a number of countries in Europe (mostly Western Europe), some countries in South and Central America, a few countries in the Oceania region, and a limited number of countries in Asia and in Africa. For several other countries, available qualitative information on the drug abuse situation allows for making some 'guesstimates'.[m] In the case of complete data gaps for individual countries, it was assumed that drug abuse was likely to be close to the respective subregional average, unless other available indicators suggested that abuse levels were likely to be above or below such average.

Even in cases where detailed information exists, there is considerable divergence in definitions used, as well as time and place of the studies in question: general population versus specific surveys of groups in terms of age, profession or special settings (such as hospitals and prisons); lifetime, annual or monthly prevalence; frequent use, problematic use, registered use etc.). All of this limits comparability. In order to reduce the error from simply adding up such diverse estimates, an attempt was made to 'standardize' the very heterogeneous data set as far as possible. Thus, all available estimates were transformed into one single indicator – annual prevalence among the general population aged 15 and above, using transformation ratios derived from analysis of the situation in neighbouring countries, and if such data were not available, on estimates from the USA, the most studied country with regard to drug abuse.

Comparability also suffers as the methodologies for estimation differ from country to country; moreover, the utility of particular methodological approaches differs from drug to drug. Indeed, the methodology chosen may have as much of an impact on final results as underlying differences in the drug problem.[n] In order

---

m) UNDCP, for instance, has undertaken a number of rapid assessment studies in developing countries. They usually do not provide precise quantitative information on the overall extent of the problem, but they describe the country-specific drug abuse problem rather well, and thus provide some basis for rough estimates. cf. *Bulletin on Narcotics*, Special Issue on Rapid Assessment of Drug Abuse, Vol. 48, 1996.

n) Household surveys, for instance, have been shown to provide, in general, good results with regard to the overall level of drug abuse or the abuse level of a widely used substance such as cannabis, but less so for typical 'problem drugs' concentrated among marginalized sections of society. According to data of the US National Household Survey, for instance, 3.8 million people consumed cocaine in 1998 (annual prevalence), which is 1.7% of the population age 12 and above. However, once the drug taking habits of marginalized groups (homeless, people in prison, etc) have been properly taken into account, the US Office of National Drug Control Policy (ONDCP) estimated the total number of cocaine users at 6.5 million people or 3% of the population age 12 and above (3.3 million hardcore and 3.2 million occasional users), suggesting that by means of a household survey only some 60% of the total number of cocaine users could be identified. Differences were found to be even larger for heroin. While the US National Household Survey estimated the number of heroin users (annual prevalence) at 253,000 people in 1998 (0.1% of the population age 12 and above), ONDCP estimates – including marginalized groups – arrived at an estimate of 1.2 million people (of which 980,000 were hardcore users). In other words, only some 20% of the total number of heroin users could be identified by means of a household survey in 1998. (On average, the share fluctuated around 30% in the 1990s.) Similar differences are also found in Europe. In Germany, for instance, the estimated number of problematic drug users (mostly opiate users) based on data of a national household survey, was only 20% to 30% of the estimates made by using various multiplier methods based on police and treatment data or combinations of capture-recapture estimates and multivariate indicator calculations. Even if household survey data are excluded, differences of scientifically valid estimates may still be significant. Estimates of problematic drug use for Italy, based on different data sets (police data, treatment data, HIV/AIDs data, death data) and multipliers can lead to results that may deviate by up to 100% from one another. In the UK, the highest estimate for problematic drug use (based on the use of multivariate indicators) deviated by as much as 300% from the lowest estimate (based on the mortality multiplier approach).

Table 4. Estimated number of drug abusers (annual prevalence) in the late 1990s – World

	Illicit drugs of which:	Cannabis	Amphetamine-type stimulants*	Cocaine	Opiates	of which heroin
Global (million people)	180.0	144.1	28.7	14.0	13.5	9.2
in % of global population	3.0%	2.4%	0.5%	0.2%	0.2%	0.15%
in % of global population age 15 and above	4.2%	3.4%	0.7%	0.3%	0.3%	0.22%

* Amphetamines (methamphetamine and amphetamine) and substances of the ecstasy group.

Source: UNDCP, DELTA (including UNDCP estimates).

to minimize the potential error from the use of different methodological approaches, all available estimates for the same country were taken into consideration and – unless methodological considerations suggested a clear superiority of one method over another – the mean of the various estimates was calculated and used as UNDCP's country estimate.

All of this – pooling of national results, standardization and extrapolation from sub-regional results in the case of data gaps – does not guarantee an accurate picture, but it should be sufficient to arrive at reasonable orders of magnitude about the likely extent of drug abuse. Based on such calculations, UNDCP estimates that in the late 1990s there were some 144 million people taking cannabis, some 29 million taking amphetamine-type stimulants°, 14 million taking cocaine and 13.5 million taking opiates (of whom some 9 million were taking heroin.) The total number of drug users is estimated to be some 180 million people, equivalent to 3% of global population or 4.2% of the population age 15 and above. As drug users frequently take more than one substance, the total is not identical with the sum of the individual drug categories (see Table 4).

These estimates largely confirm previous ones of the abuse situation in the mid-1990s, published in the 1997 World Drug Report. Deviations from the previous aggregate estimates (such as for amphetamine-type stimulants and for opiates) are in many cases the result of improved data quality rather than of actual increases or decreases in the number of abusers, and thus direct comparisons should not be made. As far as comparison between the mid-1990s and the late 1990s is feasible, data largely confirm the abuse trends reported to UNDCP by Member States.

Most countries for which data were available showed minor increases in *cannabis* abuse. With regard to the *amphetamine-type stimulants*, prevalence data show strong increases in East and South-East Asia and Australia. In Europe the picture is mixed with some of the larger ATS markets showing signs of saturation and even decline while in many of the smaller markets (those of Eastern Europe) ATS abuse is still

o) Users of amphetamines (methamphetamine, amphetamine) and of substances of the ecstasy group (MDMA, MDA, MDME etc.); in many countries ATS use is still a relatively recent phenomenon and there are indications of significant under-reporting. This bias has been partly offset by simply adding users of amphetamines and of ecstasy, even though there is some overlap between the two.

Map 13. Abuse and trafficking of cannabis

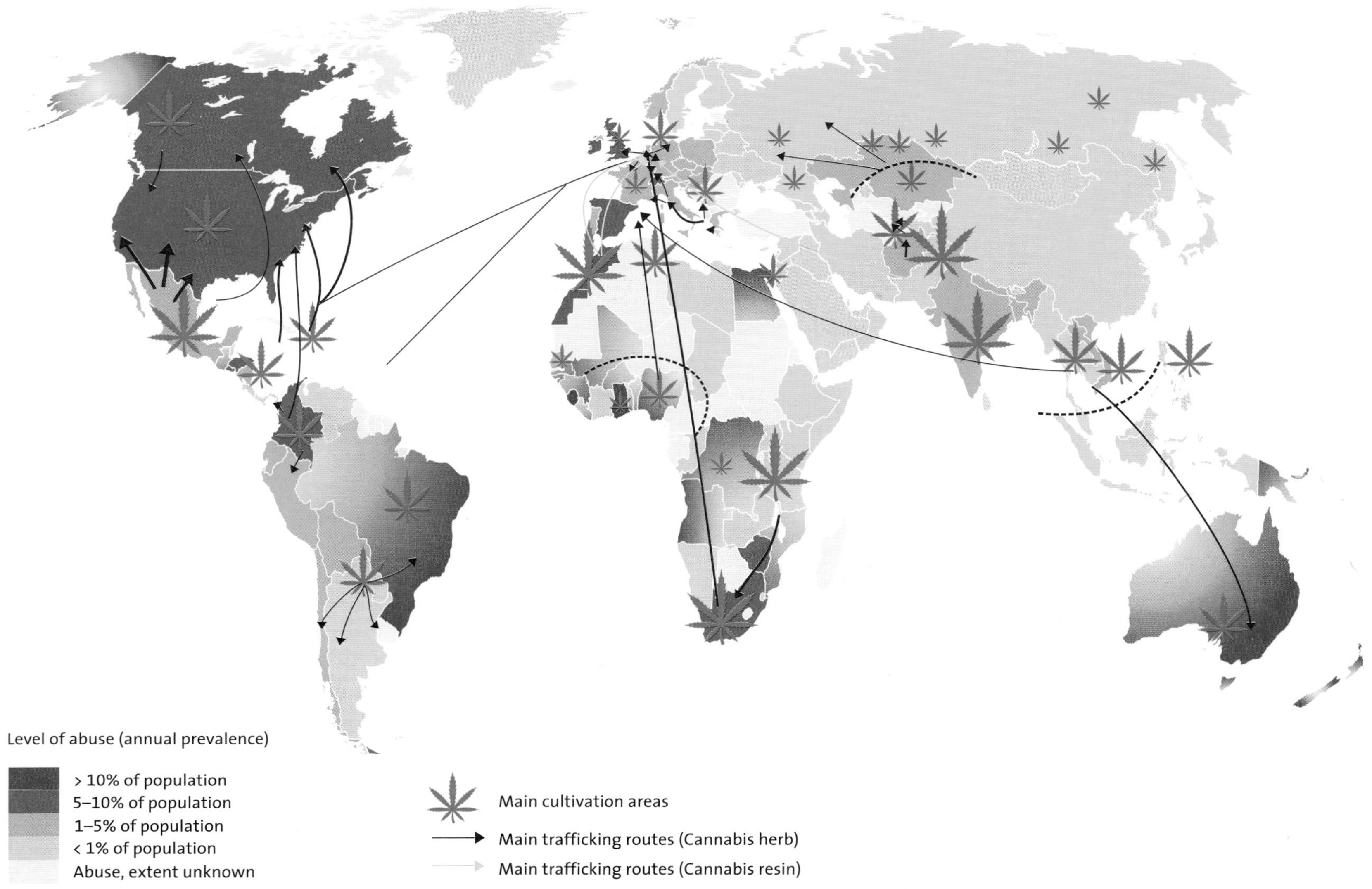

Level of abuse (annual prevalence)

- > 10% of population
- 5–10% of population
- 1–5% of population
- < 1% of population
- Abuse, extent unknown

Main cultivation areas

Main trafficking routes (Cannabis herb)

Main trafficking routes (Cannabis resin)

Note: The boundaries and names shown and the designations used on this map do not imply official endorsement or acceptance by the United Nations. Routes shown are not necessarily documented actual routes, but are rather general indications of the directions of illicit drug flows.

71

rising. By contrast, in the USA and a number of Latin American countries overall abuse of ATS appears to have declined even though there are indications that *ecstasy* use – as in many other parts of the world – is still on the rise. Data also point to an increase in the number of *cocaine* abusers in Latin America, Europe, Australia and Africa, going hand in hand with a stabilization in the USA; a stabilization/decline of *heroin* abuse in Western Europe, parallel with an increase in many other parts of the world, including countries neighbouring Afghanistan, those along the Balkan route, and – though starting from comparatively lower levels – North America and China.

The regional breakdown of prevalence estimates (see Map 13 and Table 5) shows that the highest rates for *cannabis* abuse are found in the Oceania region (with many countries reporting double digit figures), followed by the Americas (both North and South) and Africa, particularly Western and Southern Africa. Though growing in Eastern Europe cannabis abuse is still most widespread in Western Europe (5.5%). According to the 1998 British Crime Survey[106] it appears to be particularly strong in the UK (9% of those aged 16-59 years), a similar level as in the USA (8.6% of those aged 12 years and above according to the 1998 US household survey).[107] Comparatively low levels of cannabis use in Asia (2%) are mainly due to low levels reported from China and Japan. Nonetheless, more than a third of the world's cannabis users are to be found in the highly populated Asia region, more than in the Americas or in Africa.

About 29 million people are estimated to be taking ATS, which is twice as many as those who were taking cocaine or opiates. The bulk of this

Table 5. Estimated number of cannabis abusers (annual prevalence)

	Number of people (in million)	in % of population age 15 and above
Oceania	4.5	19.3
North America	22.2	7.2
South America	14.7	5.3
Americas	36.9	6.3
Africa	27.2	5.8
Western Europe	17.4	5.4
Eastern Europe	4.7	1.5
Europe	22.1	3.5
Asia	53.5	2.1
Global	144.1	3.4

above global average*
close to global average:
below global average**

* at least double the global prevalence rate.
** less than half the global prevalence rate.

Source: UNDCP, DELTA (including UNDCP estimates).

Table 6. Estimated number of amphetamines abusers (annual prevalence)

	Number of people (in million)	in % of population age 15 and above
Oceania	0.6	2.9
Western Europe	3.1	0.8
Eastern Europe	1.0	0.4
Europe	4.1	0.7
North America	2.1	0.7
South America	2.2	0.8
Americas	4.3	0.7
Asia	12.6	0.5
Africa	2.5	0.5
Global	24.2	0.6

above global average*
close to global average:
below global average**

* at least double the global prevalence rate.
** less than half the global prevalence rate.

Source: UNDCP, DELTA (including UNDCP estimates).

Map 14. Abuse and trafficking of amphetamine-type stimulants

Level of abuse (annual prevalence)

> 1.5% of population
> 1–1.5% of population
> 0.5–1% of population
> 0.1–0.5% of population
> 0.1% of population

Main manufacturing areas

Main trafficking routes (amphetamines)

Main trafficking routes (ecstasy)

Note: The boundaries and names shown and the designations used on this map do not imply official endorsement or acceptance by the United Nations. Routes shown are not necessarily documented actual routes, but are rather general indications of the directions of illicit drug flows.

is amphetamine and methamphetamine, consumed by some 24 million people (0.6% the population aged 15 years and above) worldwide. ATS are the second most widely abused substance after cannabis, notably in Oceania, Europe, Africa and East and South-East Asia (see Map 14 and Table 6).

Overall inter-regional differences in the spread of ATS, except in Oceania, are minor, though intra-regional differences remain important. High levels of ATS abuse in the Oceania region are mainly found in Australia, which reported a prevalence rate for *amphetamines* of 3.6% in 1998.[108] This is several times the global average and exceeds the figures reported from the UK (3% in 1998),[109] Europe's largest market for ATS.[110] Such high figures do point to high levels of consumption; but they may also have to do with the specific social and legal context in which studies take place. This results in the case of Australia (and some other countries with a long tradition of social research) in more readiness to admit to drug use, and thus far less under-reporting than in countries where drug users fear that such information could be used against them. Against this background, significantly lower methamphetamine abuse rates reported from East and South-East Asia do not necessarily mean that abuse levels are substantially lower. Even such conservative estimates suggest that about half of all users of amphetamines worldwide are already found in Asia, mostly in East and South-East Asia. In a number of these countries, including Japan, the Republic of Korea, Taiwan, Province of China, the Philippines and Thailand, use of methamphetamine already exceeds that of the opiates, the traditional substance of abuse in the region. In addition to the instrumental use of

Table 7. Estimated number of ecstasy abusers (annual prevalence)

	Number of people (in million)	in % of population age 15 and above
Oceania	**0.4**	**1.6**
Western Europe	2.3	0.6
Eastern Europe	0.3	0.1
Europe	**2.6**	**0.4**
North America	1.2	0.4
South America	0.02	0.01
Americas	**1.2**	**0.2**
Africa	0.1	0.02
Asia	**0.2**	**0.01**
Global	**4.5**	**0.1**

above global average*
close to global average:
below global average**

* at least double the global prevalence rate.
** less than half the global prevalence rate.

Source: UNDCP, DELTA (including UNDCP estimates).

Table 8. Estimated number of cocaine abusers (annual prevalence)

	Number of people (in million)	in % of population age 15 and above
North America	7.0	2.2
South America	3.1	1.1
Americas	**10.1**	**1.7**
Oceania	**0.2**	**0.9**
Western Europe	2.2	0.7
Eastern Europe	0.1	0.04
Europe	**2.3**	**0.4**
Africa	**1.3**	**0.3**
Asia	**0.2**	**0.01**
Global	**14.0**	**0.3**

above global average*
close to global average:
below global average**

* at least double the global prevalence rate.
** less than half the global prevalence rate.

Source: UNDCP, DELTA (including UNDCP estimates).

Map 15. Abuse and trafficking of cocaine and other coca related products.

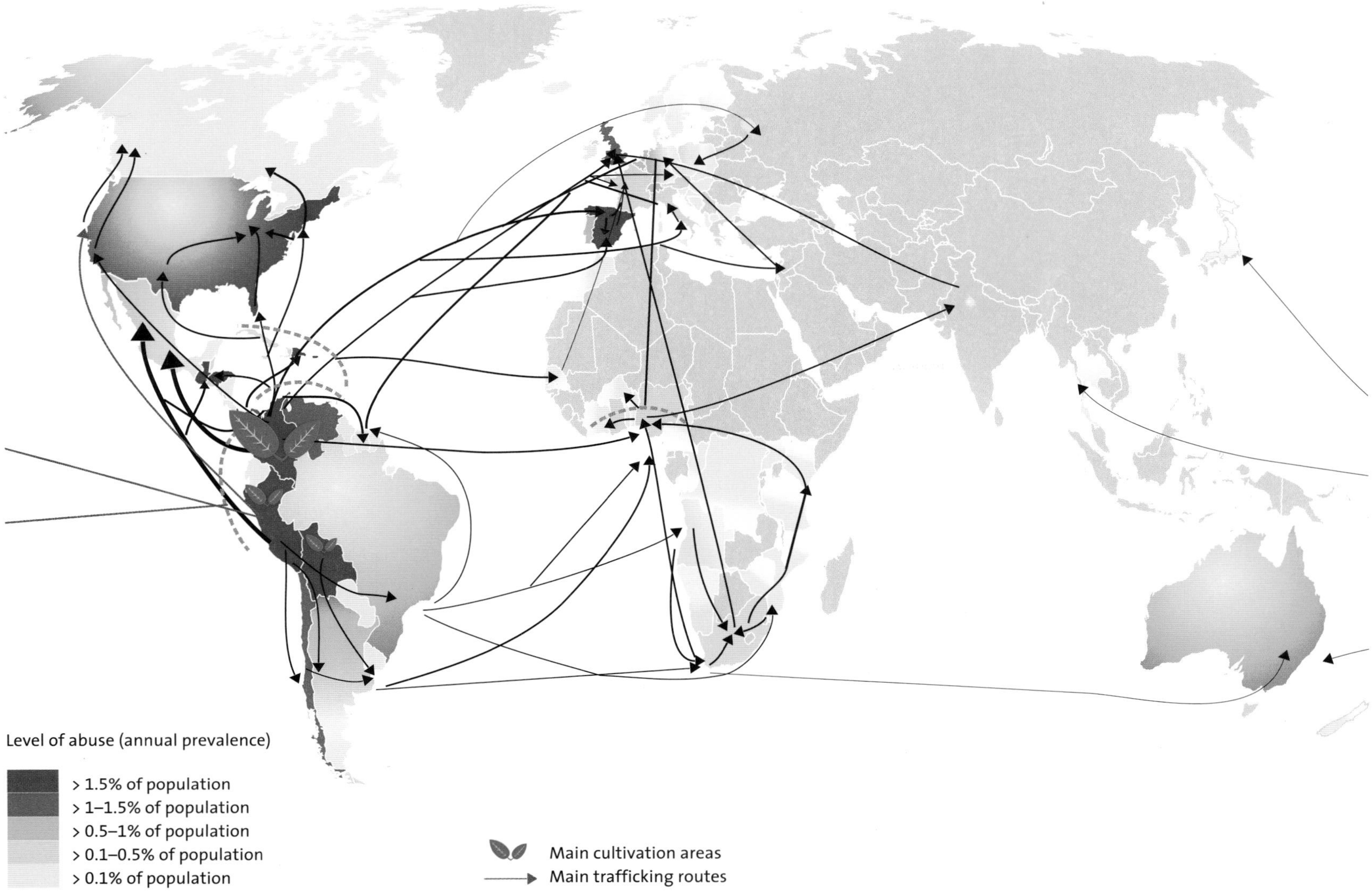

Level of abuse (annual prevalence)

> 1.5% of population
> 1–1.5% of population
> 0.5–1% of population
> 0.1–0.5% of population
> 0.1% of population

🌱 Main cultivation areas
→ Main trafficking routes

Note: The boundaries and names shown and the designations used on this map do not imply official endorsement or acceptance by the United Nations. Routes shown are not necessarily documented actual routes, but are rather general indications of the directions of illicit drug flows.

75

methamphetamine for truck drivers, fisher-men, students, sex-workers and other groups in the entertainment industry, which has been known in the region for decades, large-scale recreational use among high-school and uni-versity students has started spreading.

In Western Europe, abuse of amphetamines is 0.8% of the population aged 15 years and above, which is a little more than in the Americas (0.7%). The UK, Spain, and in relative terms (i.e. compared to overall level of drug abuse) the Scandinavian countries, are faced with high levels of consumption of amphetamines, mostly amphetamine.[111] In the USA, by contrast, life-time prevalence data show that about half of ATS abuse is related to the more potent metham-phetamine.[112] The high levels of ATS abuse reported from South Americas is linked to the use of licit ATS anorectics,[113] while ATS in North

America, Western Europe and increasingly in Asia, are mostly illicitly manufactured sub-stances. Use of ATS in Africa is found all across the continent though it is particularly concen-trated in Western Africa, where these substances are frequently sold in parallel markets.[114]

The strongest growth in recent years, however, was in abuse of the ecstasy drugs, notably MDMA (ecstasy) itself, even though in a number of locations less than half of the pills sold under the name of ecstasy actually contained MDMA. UNDCP estimates that some 4.5 million people – mostly teenagers and young adults – took ecstasy in the late 1990s (see Table 7). In contrast to the wide regional spread of amphetamines, *ecstasy* is still concentrated in a few regions: Europe (mainly Western Europe), North Amer-ica and Oceania (mainly Australia). Strong con-centrations of ecstasy use are found in Australia

Table 9. Estimated number of opiate abusers (annual prevalence)

	Number of people (in million)	in % of population age 15 and above
Oceania	0.13	0.58
Western Europe	1.22	0.34
Eastern Europe	1.46	0.54
Europe	**2.68**	**0.42**
Asia	**8.62**	**0.35**
North America	1.12	0.36
South America	0.32	0.12
Americas	**1.44**	**0.20**
Africa	**0.63**	**0.13**
Global	13.50	0.33

above global average*
close to global average:
below global average**

*   at least double the global prevalence rate.
** less than half the global prevalence rate.

Source: UNDCP, DELTA (including UNDCP estimates).

Table 10. Estimated number of heroin abusers (annual prevalence)

	Number of people (in million)	in % of population age 15 and above
Oceania	0.60	0.27
Europe	**1.51**	**0.24**
Asia	**5.74**	**0.24**
Americas	**1.31**	**0.22**
Africa	**0.57**	**0.12**
Global	9.18	0.22

above global average*
close to global average:
below global average**

*   at least double the global prevalence rate.
** less than half the global prevalence rate.

Source: UNDCP, DELTA (including UNDCP estimates).

Map 16. Abuse and trafficking of opiates (including heroin)

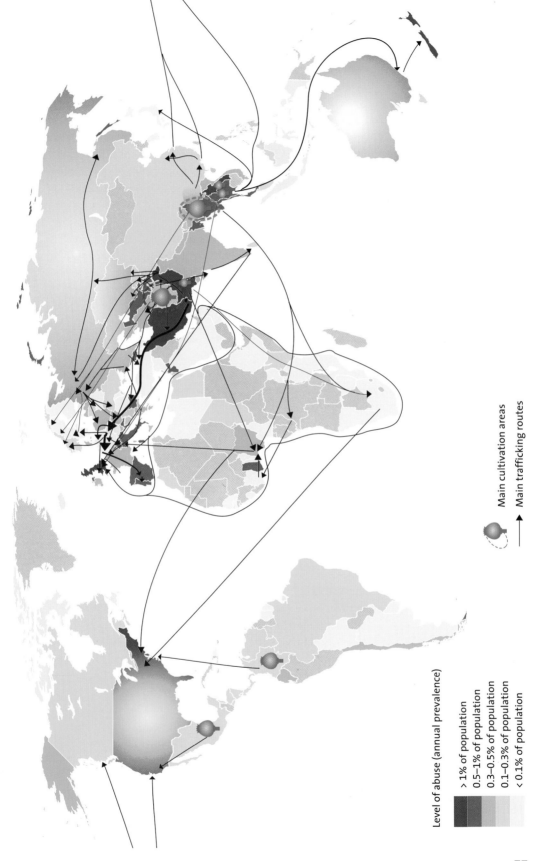

Level of abuse (annual prevalence)

> 1% of population
0.5–1% of population
0.3–0.5% of population
0.1–0.3% of population
< 0.1% of population

Main cultivation areas

Main trafficking routes

Note: The boundaries and names shown and the designations used on this map do not imply official endorsement or acceptance by the United Nations. Routes shown are not necessarily documented actual routes, but are rather general indications of the directions of illicit drug flows.

(annual prevalence of 2.4% in 1998, including other designer drugs, among the general population aged 14 years and above)[115], the UK (1%) and in Spain (0.9% in 1997)[116]. In a few European countries, including Germany, the Netherlands and Switzerland, ecstasy is already the second most widely abused substance after cannabis. In line with the globalization of popular youth culture, ecstasy now seems to be spreading rapidly across the globe.

Some 14 million people are estimated to take cocaine worldwide (see Map 15 and Table 8). In the USA, the world's largest cocaine market, abuse declined strongly over the last decade. Household survey data show a decline in the annual prevalence rate from 5.1% of the population aged 12 years and above in 1985 to 2.1% in 1992, and 1.7% in 1998.[117] Nonetheless, including marginalized groups not covered by a household survey, the prevalence rate is estimated by the authorities to be equivalent to 3% of the population age 15 and above, about ten times the global average. Even though prevalence rates are lower in Canada and Mexico, about half of the world's cocaine users are found in North America. The next largest markets are South America (1.1%), Oceania (0.9%; mainly Australia) and Western Europe (0.7%). Highest abuse levels within Europe are reported from Spain (1.6% in 1997),[118] at least partly a consequence of strong links between Spain and countries in Latin America. Abuse levels in Eastern Europe, though rising, are still significantly lower (far less than 0.1%). Cocaine abuse in Africa is estimated at close to the global average, with a concentration in Western Africa (notably Nigeria) and in the south of the continent (Republic of South Africa). Given the lack of comprehensive national surveys, estimates for countries in Africa are, however, subject to far higher levels of potential error than data from other regions. Cocaine consumption in Asia is clearly below global average, and almost negligible from an international perspective. This is partly explained by the large-scale availability of cheap methamphetamine and other amphetamine-type stimulants.

About 13.5 million people or 0.3% of the global population aged 15 years and above are estimated to consume opiates; most of this is heroin consumption which amounts to some 9 million people (see Map 16 and Tables 9 and 10). Almost two thirds of all users of opiates are found in Asia; Europe accounts for some 20%. Oceania, Europe and Asia also have the highest per capita consumption of opiates – ranging from 0.4%-0.6% of the population aged 15 years and above, while abuse of opiates in the Americas (0.2%) and Africa (0.1%) is below the global average. In South America abuse of opiates is still at very low levels, though this could change if the current expansion of production in Colombia were to continue.

The highest levels of abuse in Asia – clearly exceeding 1% of the population aged 15 years and above – have been reported from the Lao PDR, Iran and Pakistan,[119] i.e. either opium producing or transit countries for opiates. The largest number in absolute terms is found in India (though the prevalence of less than 0.5% of the population aged 15 years and above is smaller than in some of India's neighbouring countries). The mean estimates for India converge towards a figure of around 3 million people,[120] slightly more than the total estimate for Europe as a whole. Total estimates for Eastern Europe (close to 1.5 million) exceed those for Western Europe (1 to 1.5 million people; with an average of about 1.2 million) where abuse of opiates has stabilized or declined in recent years.

The highest levels of opiate abuse in Western Europe among the larger countries are still reported from Italy,[121] though these have been going down in the 1990s, and from the UK, one of a few countries in Western Europe where consumption, notably of smokeable heroin, is still on the rise. The largest market for opiates in Eastern Europe is the Russian Federation. Russian authorities estimate some 3 million drug abusers of which at least a third are addicted to opiates.[122] All available indicators clearly show that abuse is rising fast in Russia.

Even though available estimates are not very precise, there is little doubt that opiate abuse in a number of countries of Eastern Europe, particularly those along transit corridors, has reached problematic proportions in recent years. One half of 1% of the population aged 15 years and above, on average, are estimated to consume opiates, often in the form of 'kompot' (in Russia, the Ukraine and Poland), a brew made out poppy straw that is injected. Heroin abuse is still below levels found in Western Europe, but is increasing rapidly.

There was also a general increase in the number of opiate abusers in North America in the 1990s: most of this is heroin related. Estimates provided by the US authorities suggest that there may have been almost one million hard-core heroin abusers in the late 1990s.[123]

Another major market for opiates, which has been growing in recent years, is China. Estimates provided by the authorities in China are still rather small, given the size of the country's population (0.06% of the population aged 15 years and above). However, the reported rise of addiction to opiate addiction in the 1990s has been strong (from 250,000 registered users in 1993/94 to some 600,000 registered users in 1998/99), and it is possible that the actual number could well be larger. Some 80% of opiate abuse is already linked to heroin.

ENDNOTES

1. UNDCP, Afghanistan Opium Poppy Survey 1999, p. 1.

2. UNDCP, *Global Illicit Drug Trends, 2000* (ODCCP Studies on Drugs and Crime), Vienna 2000, p. 39.

3. A likely turnover of drug sales of US$ 360 billion for 1995 (range US$ 100-US$ 1,000 billion) had been calculated. UNDCP, *Economic and Social Consequences of Drug Abuse and Illicit Trafficking* (UNDCP Technical Series, Vienna 1997, p. 51.

4. Office of National Drug Control Policy, *National Drug Control Strategy, 2000 Annual Report,* p. 28, referring to National Institute on Drug Abuse, National Institute on Alcohol Abuse and Alcoholism, *The Economic Costs of Alcohol and Drug Abuse in the United States* (Rockville, MD: U.S. Department of Health and Human Services, 1998), http://www.nida.nih.gov/Economic-Costs/Chapter1.html #1.10, January 11, 2000. Both economic costs and US GDP data are for 1995. GDP data based on OECD, *National Accounts of OECD countries*, vol. 1, March, 2000.

5. Office of National Drug Control Policy, *National Drug Control Strategy, 2000 Annual Report,* p. 81.

6. International Narcotics Control Board, *Report 1999,* New York 2000, p. 34.

7. UNDCP, Annual Reports Questionnaire Data.

8. Office of National Drug Control Policy, *National Drug Control Strategy, 2000 Annual Report,* p. 81.

9. Institute for Defense Analyses, *An Empirical Examination of Counterdrug Interdiction Program Effectiveness,* January 1997, IV-6.

10. Bureau of International Narcotics and Law Enforcement Affairs, *1999 International Narcotics Control Strategy Report,* (Policy and Program Development), p. 27.

11. Alvaro Camacho Guizado, Andrés López Restrepo, "Perspectivas Criticas Sobre El Narcotráfico en Colombia: Analysis de Una Encuesta, in: Alvaro Camacho Guizado, Andrés López Restrepo, Francisco E. Thoumi, *Las Drogas: Una Guerra Fallida, Visiones Criticas,* pp. 1-91 (notably pp. 52-55).

12. Institute for Defense Analyses, An Empirical Examination of Counterdrug Interdiction Program Effectiveness, January 1997, IV-6.

13. UNDCP (Research Section), 'Cannabis as an illicit narcotic crop: a review of the global situation of cannabis consumption, trafficking and production', in UNDCP, *Bulletin on Narcotics,* 'Double issue on cannabis: recent developments', *Vol. XLIX (1997) and (1998), New York 1999,* pp. 45-85.

14. Interpol, *Cannabis World Report 1999,* Lyon, 1999, p. 6.

15. UNDCP, Annual Reports Questionnaire Data.

16. INCSR 1999. Bureau of International Narcotics and Law Enforcement Affairs, *1999 International Narcotics Control Strategy Report,* (Chapter on Colombia, p. 1), Washington, March 2000.

17. Interpol, *Cannabis World Report 1999,* Lyons, 1999, p. 11.

18. Van der Werf, R., 'Registration of illegal production in the national accounts of the Netherlands', joint OECD/ECE/Eurostat meeting on National Accounts, Paris, 3-6 June 1997 (Voorburg, Statistics Netherlands, 1997), quoted

in Trimbos Institute (Reitox Focal Point), National Report 1997, the Netherlands, draft version, p. 61.

19. UNDCP, *Global Illicit Drug Trends, 2000* (ODCCP Studies on Drugs and Crime), Vienna 2000, p. 198.

20. *Ibid*, p. 34.

21. *Ibid*, pp. 62 and 92.

22. Interpol, *1999 Trends and Patterns of Illicit Drug Traffic,* March 2000.

23. Interpol, Cannabis World Report 1999, Lyon 1999.

24. UNDCP, *Trends 2000, op.cit.,* pp. 10-21.

25. Interpol, *1999 Trends and Patterns of Illicit Drug Traffic,* March 2000, p. 4.

26. Ministry of Interior – Turkish National Police Department of Anti-Smuggling and Organized Crime, *Turkish Drug Report '99,* Ankara 2000, pp. 6-8.

27. Interpol, *1999 Trends and Patterns of Illicit Drug Traffic,* March 2000, p. 4.

28. Interpol, *Heroin World Report 1999,* Lyon, 1999, p. 30.

29. UNDCP, *Trends 2000, op.cit.,* p. 182.

30. UNDCP, *1999 Afghanistan Opium Poppy Survey 1999,* Islamabad 1999.

31. UNDCP, *Trends 2000, op.cit.,* pp. 85-88.

32. *Ibid.*

33. Interpol, *1999 Trends and Patterns of Illicit Drug Traffic, Lyon,* March 2000, p. 5.

34. Interpol, *Heroin World Report 1999,* Lyon, 1999, pp. 7-8.

35. Office of National Drug Control Policy, *The National Drug Control Strategy: 2000* (and previous years), Washington 2000 (and previous years).

36. Interpol, *1999 Trends, op.cit.,* p. 8.

37. *Ibid.*

38. Francisco Thoumi, 'Las Drogas Illegales y Relaciones Exteriores de Colombia: Una Vision desde el Exterior', in A. C. Guizado, A.L. Restrepo, F. Thoumi, *Las Drogas: Una Guerra Fallida – Visiones críticas,* (TM Editores, IEPRI (UN)) Santafé de Bogota, 1999, p. 124.

39. U.S. Drug Enforcement Agency, 'Russian Organized Crime and the Drug Trade: a domestic intelligence brief', January 1998.

40. Interpol, *1999 Trends and Patterns of Illicit Drug Traffic,* March 2000, p. 7.

41. UNDCP, *Trends 2000, op.cit.*

42. International Narcotics Control Board, *Report 1999,* New York 2000, p. 41.

43. Substance Abuse and Mental Health Services Administration (SAMHSA), *National Household Survey on Drug Abuse,* 1999, Washington 2000 and previous years.

44. Office of National Drug Control Policy (ONDCP), *The National Drug Control Strategy, 1996: Program, Resource, and Evaluation,* Washington 1996 and ONCDP, *The National Drug Control Strategy,* 2000, Washington 2000.

45. Australian Institute of Health and Welfare, *1998 National Drug Strategy Household Survey, First results,* Canberra, p. 5.

46. UNDCP, *Trends 2000, op.cit.*

47. SAMHSA, *National Household Survey on Drug Abuse, 1999 and previous years, op.cit.*

48. European Monitoring Centre for Drugs and Drug Addiction, *Annual Report on the state of the drugs problem in the European Union,* 1999, Lisbon 1999 (and previous years).

49. UNDCP, *Trends 2000, op.cit.*

50. Interpol, *1999 Trends, op.cit.,* p. 13.

51. International Narcotics Control Board, *Report 1999,* New York 2000, p. 37.

52. UNDCP, *Trends 2000, op.cit.*

53. *Ibid.*

54. UNDCP, ICPO, WCO, 'Significant Seizures Data Base', 2000 (based on information collected in UNDCP/ICPO/WCO seizure data sharing project).

55. Interpol, *1999 Trends, op.cit.,* p. 12.

56. UNDCP, ICPO, WCO, 'Significant Seizures Data Base', 2000.

57. Interpol, *Cannabis World Report 1999,* Lyon, 1999, p. 18.

58. *Ibid.*

59. UNDCP, *South Asia, Drug Demand Reduction Report,* New Dehli, 1998.

60. UNDCP, *Trends 2000, op.cit.*

61. *Ibid.*

62. Interpol, *Cannabis.., op.cit.,* p. 8.

63. UNDCP, *Trends 2000, op.cit.*

64. Interpol, *1999 Trends.., op.cit.,* p. 13.

65. Interpol, *Cannabis.., op.cit.,* p. 8.

66. United States Department of State, *International Narcotics Control Strategy Report,* March 1997, p. 464.

67. UNDCP, 'Cannabis as an illicit narcotic crop: a review of the global situation of cannabis consumption, trafficking and production', in UNDCP, Bulletin on Narcotics,

Double issue on cannabis: recent development, Volume XLIX and L, New York 1999, pp. 45-83.

68. Interpol, *1999 Trends..*, *op.cit.*, p. 12.

69. UNDCP, *Cannabis..*, *op.cit.*, p. 48.

70. UNDCP, *Amphetamine-type Stimulants: A Global Review*, Vienna 1996.

71. Hilary Klee, 'Patterns of Amphetamine-Misuse in Seven Nations: Factors Affecting Growth and Decline', in Hilary Klee, *Amphetamine Misuse, International Perspectives on Current Trends*, 1997, pp. 291-319.

72. UNDCP, *Trends 2000, op.cit.*, pp. 10-21.

73. UNDCP, ICPO, WCO, 'Significant Seizures Data Base', 2000.

74. UNDCP, *Trends 2000, op.cit.*, pp. 10-21.

75. *Ibid*, pp. 132-139.

76. *Ibid*, pp. 10-21.

77. International Narcotics Control Board, *Report 1999*, New York 2000, p. 42.

78. *Ibid*, p. 44.

79. Ministry of Interior/Turkish National Police, *Turkish Drug Report '99*, Ankara 2000, pp. 21-22.

80. UNDCP, *Amphetamine-type Stimulants ...*, *op.cit.*, p. 73.

81. UNDCP, *Trends 2000, op.cit.*, pp.10-21.

82. UNDCP, *Amphetamine-type Stimulants ...*, *op.cit.*, p. 48.

83. Interpol, *1999 Trends..*, *op.cit.*, p. 17.

84. *Ibid*, p. 16.

85. UNDCP, *Trends 2000, op.cit.*, pp. 178-209.

86. Council of Europe, Cooperation Group to Combat Drug Abuse and Illicit Trafficking in Drugs (Pompidou Group), *Treated Drug Users in 23 European Cities – Data 1997, Trends 1996-97, Pompidou Group Project on Treatment Demand: Final Report* (Council of Europe Publishing), Strasbourg, October 1999 and European Monitoring Centre for Drugs and Drug Addiction (EMCDDA), *Extended annual report on the state of the drugs problem in the European Union, 1999, Lisbon 1999*.

87. Centre for Drug Research (WHO Research and Training Centre: Universiti Sains Malaysia), *Report of the Asian Multicity Epidemiology Work Group, 1997*, Penang (Malaysia) and UNDCP, Annual Reports Questionnaire Data.

88. UNDCP, *Trends 2000, op.cit.*, pp. 210-213.

89. Office of the Narcotics Control Board, *Thailand Narcotics Annual Report 1998-1999*, Bangkok 1999, pp. 51-56 (and previous years).

90. Council of Europe, *Treated Drug Users ...*, *op.cit.*, pp.55-56.

91. EMCDDA, *Extended annual report 1999...*, *op.cit.*, p. 54.

92. UNDCP, *Trends 2000, op.cit.*, pp. 210-213.

93. *Ibid.*

94. Council of Europe, *Treated Drug Users ...*, *op.cit.*, p. 104.

95. UNDCP, *Trends 2000, op.cit.*, p. 213.

96. Comision Interamericana para el Control del Abuso de Drogas (CICAD), *Resumen Estadístico sobre Drogas*, 1999, Washington D.C., Sept. 1999, pp. 64-65, *and CICAD/OAS, SIDUC 1998 Preliminary Report*, Washington 1998, p. 27.

97. UNDCP, *Trends 2000, op.cit.*, p. 213.

98. Substance Abuse and Mental Health Services Administration (SAMHSA), Treatment Episode Data Set (TEDS), 1992-1997.

99. *Ibid.*

100. *Ibid.*

101. CICAD, *Resumen ..*, *op.cit.*, pp. 64-65; Canadian Centre on Substance Abuse (CCSA) and Addiction Research, *Canadian Drug Profile*, 1999, and SAMHSA, *Treatment ...*, *op.cit.*

102. UNDCP, UNICRI, Behman Hospital, 'UNDCP Global Study on Illicit Drug Markets – Study in Greater Cairo', (Draft), Cairo, 2000, p. 19.

103. Unweighted average of treatment in Johannesburg/Pretoria, Cape Town, Durban, Port Elizabeth, in Medical Research Council, *South African Community Epidemiology Network on Drug Use (SACENDU), Monitoring Alcohol and Drug Abuse Trends, Proceedings of Report Back Meetings, March 2000, July-December 1999*, May 2000.

104. UNDCP, *The Drug Nexus in Africa* (ODCCP Studies on Drugs and Crime), Vienna, March 1999, p. 25.

105. *Ibid*, p. 26.

106. Home Office, *Drug Misuse Declared in 1998: Results form the British Crime Survey* (Research Study 197), London 1999.

107. Substance Abuse and Mental Health Services Administration (SAMHSA), *National Household Survey on Drug Abuse*, 1998, Rockville, MD, 1999.

108. Australian Institute of Health and Welfare (AIHW), *1998 National Drug Strategy Household Survey*, Canberra, August 1999.

109. Home Office, *British Crime Survey, op.cit.*

110. EMCDDA, *1999 Annual Report, op.cit.*, p. 52.

111. *Ibid.*

112. SAMHSA, *National Household Survey 1998, op.cit.*

113. INCB, *Report 1999, op.cit.*, p. 42.

114. UNDCP, *Drug Nexus, op.cit.,* pp. 20-21.

115. SAMHSA, *National Household Survey 1998, op.cit.*

116. EMCDDA, *1999 Annual Report, op.cit.,* p. 52.

117. SAMHSA, *National Household Survey 1998, op.cit.*

118. EMCDDA, *1999 Annual Report, op.cit.,* p. 52.

119. UNDCP, *Trends 2000, op.cit.,* p. 182-185.

120. UNDCP, *South Asia Drug Demand Reduction Report,* New Delhi, p. 260.

121. EMCDDA, *1999 Annual Report, op.cit.,* p. 52.

122. UNDCP, *Trends 2000, op.cit.,* p. 182-185.

123. Office of National Drug Control Policy, *National Drug Control Strategy: 2000 Annual Report,* Washington 2000, p. 116.

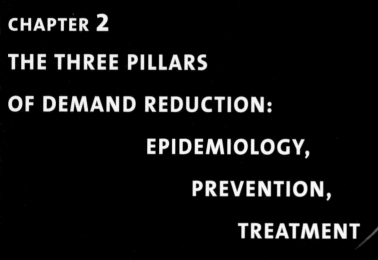

CHAPTER **2**
THE THREE PILLARS
OF DEMAND REDUCTION:

EPIDEMIOLOGY,

PREVENTION,

TREATMENT

EMIOLOGY | DEFINITIONAL ASPECTS | PREVAILING METHODS | THE DIFFICUL-
OF MONITORING DRUG ABUSE AND THE WAY AHEAD | PREVENTION | FROM
LY SUBSTANCE ABUSE PREVENTION TO MODERN APPROACHES | BASES FOR
ECTIVE PREVENTION | DRUG VULNERABILITY – RISK AND PROTECTIVE
TORS | TARGETS AND TYPES OF PREVENTION | SOCIAL ENVIRONMENT/
1AINS FOR PREVENTION | KNOWLEDGE DEVELOPMENT AND TRANSFER

INTRODUCTION

The aim of this chapter is to analyze the three 'pillars' of demand reduction – epidemiology (and related research), prevention and treatment.

Much of the research has so far been conducted in the industrialized countries, notably Northern America, Western Europe and Australia, as they – until recently – had a greater share of drug addiction and drug-related disease problems (as well as more resources to devote to drug research) than developing countries. The largest funds for systematic research into understanding the problem of drug abuse and for implementing prevention and treatment programmes, have been made available over the last decade in the USA. Spending on demand reduction (research, prevention and treatment) increased at the federal level from US$ 0.9 billion in 1985 to US$ 5.6[a] billion in 1999, equivalent to US$ 20 per inhabitant (a very high figure by international standards[b]), or a third of all drug control spending in the country. Even if inflation is taken into account, there was a more than fourfold increase in annual spending for demand reduction over the 1985-1999 period.[c] Parallel to increased spending, drug abuse (annual prevalence as well as current use of all drugs as revealed in the annual household surveys) fell by some 40% and cocaine abuse fell by as much as 70% over the 1985-1998/99 period.[d] Though changes in human

---

a) In 1986 US federal expenditure on drug abuse prevention amounted to US$ 146 million, on treatment to US$ 625 million and on research to US$ 94 million, of which US$ 88 million was allocated for various demand-related research activities. By 1999, expenditure on drug abuse prevention had increased to US$ 1,954 million (a thirteen fold increase), on treatment to US$ 2,949 million (a five-fold increase), and on research to US$ 781 million of which US$ 668 million was allocated for various demand-related research activities (a more than seven fold increase). (Office of National Drug Control Policy (ONCDP), *The National Drug Control Strategy, 1996: Programme, Resources, and Evaluation, and ONDCP, National Drug Control Strategy Budget Summary*, February 2000)

b) This is a large amount compared to other countries. In France, for instance, overall demand reduction related expenditure in 1995 amounted to ECU 124 million, equivalent to US$ 160 million or US$ 2.8 per inhabitant. In the same year, US demand reduction expenditure was US$ 4,692 million or US$ 17.5 per inhabitant. (European Monitoring Centre for Drugs and Drug Addiction, Annual Report on the State of the Drugs Problem in the European Union 1997, Lisbon 1997 and Office of National Drug Control Policy (ONCDP), *The National Drug Control Strategy, 1996: Programme, Resources, and Evaluation*, Washington 1996.)

c) Demand related expenditure for 1985, expressed in constant 1999 dollars, would have amounted to US$ 1,331 million, less than a fourth of actual demand related expenditure in 1999 (US$ 5,571 million). (Office of National Drug Control Policy (ONCDP), *The National Drug Control Strategy, 1996: Programme, Resources, and Evaluation*, and ONDCP, *National Drug Control Strategy Budget Summary*, February 2000)

d) The number of current users of illicit drugs (at least once in the month prior to the survey) fell from 23.3 million in 1985 to 13.6 million in 1998. The number of current cocaine abusers fell from 5.7 million in 1985 to 1.8 million in 1998. The national household survey conducted in 1999 showed past month use affecting 7% of the population aged 12 and older, down from 12.1% in 1985. The proportion of the population taking cocaine in the past month prior to the survey fell from 3% in 1985 to 0.8% in 1999. (Substance Abuse and Mental Health Services Administration, *US National Household Survey, 1999* (and previous years)).

behavior are usually the result of a multitude of factors, the above example indicates, nonetheless, that a massive increase in demand reduction efforts, based on in-depth research of the problem, seems to play an important role in curbing drug abuse.

As the drug abuse problem differs from country to country (and often within countries), a simple replication of prevention and treatment programmes does not work. This is even more true if programmes from industrialized countries are implemented in developing countries. Programmes, even if successful in one country, have to be carefully adapted to the specific social and cultural conditions in each individual country. Given the growing drug abuse problem in many developing countries, there is still a need for more research to take account of the specific factors affecting drug demand. Against this background, UNDCP, in co-operation with other partners, has been engaged in developing a number of model programmes on prevention

and treatment, which are designed in the light of differing local resources and conditions.

2.1. EPIDEMIOLOGY

Epidemiological research forms a key element for understanding the drug problem, developing responses and measuring their appropriateness so that the interventions can be modified and adapted to changing conditions. Systematic epidemiological analysis can be compared to the functions of an accounting system in an enterprise. Managers operating without a functioning accounting system could steer enterprises into a wrong direction, and are likely to take remedial action only when it is too late. The same is true for policy makers who have to deal with problems of drug abuse, unless such information systems are built. Epidemiological research provides policy makers with an information tool to target interventions, and acts as a necessary feedback mecha-

Fig. 1: Demand reduction expenditure (in million US$) and development of annual prevalence of drug abuse (age 12 and above) in the USA

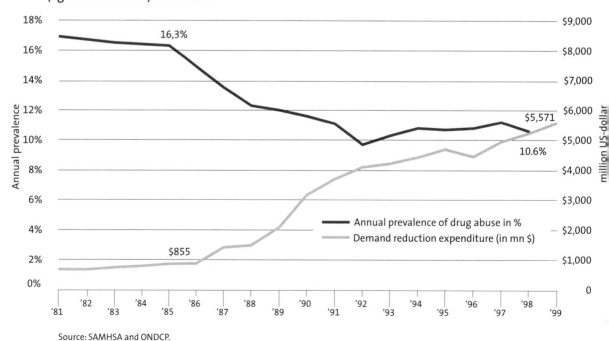

Source: SAMHSA and ONDCP.

Box 2A: The Declaration on the Guiding Principles of Drug Demand Reduction

In the *Political Declaration* adopted by the General Assembly at its twentieth Special Session on the World Drug Problem, Member States recognized that demand reduction was indispensable to solving the drug problem. Member States committed themselves to:

(i)   establishing the year 2003 as a target date for having in place new or enhanced demand reduction strategies and programmes in close collaboration with public health, social welfare and law enforcement authorities;

(ii) achieving significant and measurable results in the field of demand reduction by the year 2008; and

(iii) introducing in their national programmes and strategies the provisions set out in the *Declaration on the Guiding Principles of Drug Demand Reduction,* also adopted by the General Assembly at its twentieth special session;

The General Assembly has also adopted an *Action Plan for the Implementation of the Declaration on the Guiding Principles of Drug Demand Reduction.* The Action Plan is offered as guidance to Member States in implementing the Demand Reduction Declaration and in meeting the commitments of the twentieth Special Session of the General Assembly. It foresees two principal ways for UNDCP and other relevant international and regional organizations to assist Member States in their efforts.

First, it requires UNDCP to provide guidance and assistance to those requesting it for the development of demand reduction strategies and programmes, incorporating the principles of the Demand Reduction Declaration. Secondly, it envisages UNDCP and other relevant international and regional organizations facilitating the sharing of information of 'best practices' in all areas of demand reduction.

The Demand Reduction Declaration advocates that responses to drug abuse be based on regular assessments of the drug problem. They should also build on knowledge acquired from research as well as lessons derived from past programmes ('best practices'). Policy makers and practitioners should be trained on the design, execution and evaluation of demand reduction strategies, and the strategies and activities should be thoroughly evaluated.

Demand reduction programmes should cover all areas of prevention, from discouraging initial use to reducing the negative health and social consequences of drug abuse. They should be integrated into broader social welfare and health promotion policies and should encourage a community-wide participatory and partnership approach.

They should be designed to address the needs of the population in general, as well as those of specific population groups, particularly youth. Where appropriate, governments should consider providing treatment and rehabilitation to drug abusing offenders, either as an alternative or in addition to conviction or punishment.

The Demand Reduction Declaration also stresses the importance of sending the right message. States should seek to raise public consciousness about the hazards of drug abuse, and counter the promotion of drug use in popular culture. Every attempt should be made to ensure credibility, avoid sensationalism, promote trust and enhance effectiveness of the messages.

nism to see whether measures taken are appropriate and cost effective. Drug epidemiological monitoring is thus – and should be – an essential component any national drug strategy.

2.1.1. DEFINITIONAL ASPECTS

Websters Dictionary defines epidemiology as '1: a science that deals with the incidence, distribution, and control of disease in a population 2: the sum of the factors controlling the presence or absence of a disease or pathogen'.[1]

The requirements of epidemiological monitoring include the identification and measurement of three constellations of variables. These are a) patterns of drug abuse, b) the consequences of drug abuse, and c) correlates, or factors, which link drug abuse to contingent circumstances.

The analysis of drug abuse patterns looks at the 'prevalence' or magnitude of the problem with respect to the overall population, its 'incidence' (the number of new users), the frequency or intensity with which the behaviour occurs, the routes of administration (e.g. nasal inhalation, injecting or oral use), and the settings in which consumption takes place. The consequences of drug abuse involve both acute and chronic health effects as well as possible social effects. Thus, in addition to measuring drug abuse, information is required on the socio-demographic correlates of drug abuse – e.g., age, gender, income, education, occupation, ethnicity, community size, region – as well as other factors such as attitudes towards drugs, involvement in activities or exposure to specific factors which are associated with an increased vulnerability to drug abuse problems.

2.1.2. PREVAILING METHODS

The study of a largely hidden and stigmatized behaviour presents serious methodological challenges. The difficulties are amplified because of the diverse nature of drug consumption patterns and because of the complex interactions between drug abuse and other health and social problems. Often, the most serious consequences of drug consumption are found among those most socially marginalized. Such groups are difficult to research and poorly represented in households and ongoing registers. Because of the problems inherent in collecting information in this area, multi-method and multi-source approaches are considered the most appropriate for developing a comprehensive understanding of patterns of drug abuse. The strengths and weaknesses of the various methods are discussed below.

Surveys and other methods to measure prevalence and incidence
Understanding the extent and frequency of illicit drug consumption in any population is the starting point for policy discussions. Generating general population prevalence and incidence estimates is a key task of a drug information system. One common method used for measuring the prevalence and incidence of drug abuse is the *general population survey*. Such surveys, if systematically repeated (and without changes in methodology), are good instru-

ments to identify abuse trends over time. Even though they have deficiencies (as discussed below), the shortcomings tend to remain rather stable and usually do not affect, at least not to any large degree, the results from trend analyses which are needed in a rational policy making process.

Surveys can also provide basic information on the socio-demographic and other risk factors associated with drug consumption, and may thus fulfil some early warning functions. In all countries – for which information is available – drug abuse, for instance, was found to be significantly higher among

- the young adult population than the general population;
- males (though rates among females are rising in several countries);
- the unemployed;
- other marginalized and stigmatized groups of society, such as street children and
- special professional categories, such as people working in the entertainment industry (notably sex-workers), long-distance truck drivers, etc.

Moreover, in most countries, drug abuse is higher in urban than in rural areas though these differences are becoming less pronounced. A number of studies have been indicating that drug use among youth correlates positively with the frequency of going out at night and participating at rave events. Religious beliefs usually correlate negatively with drug abuse (though there are a few exceptions). In a number of countries drug use was found to correlate negatively with the perceived harmfulness of drugs. The relationships are less universally clear with regard to levels of income and education. In a number of countries a U-function seems to exist, which means that drug use is relatively high among the poorer sections of society, declines among the middle class, and increases again in the upper classes. These results vary, however, depending on the specific substances concerned, and are not the same for all countries. Nonetheless, in-depth analysis of such kinds of socio-demographic information and their relationships with drug using behaviour can be of assistance in filling data gaps, developing forecasting models, and improving the targeting of interventions.

The main pieces of information collected in household surveys are information on drug use *per se*, i.e. a measure of life-time prevalence or 'ever use' of a particular drug; a measure of current prevalence levels, such as use in the past year ('annual prevalence') or past 30 days ('monthly prevalence'). In some countries, additional information is collected in order to establish estimates of the incidence levels, usually the number of people who have started use of a particular drug over the past year. Some intensity measure may be included as well to allow regular consumers to be distinguished from those who have only experimented with a drug on a few occasions.

While short-term (year on year) changes in household surveys have to be treated with a degree of caution, as they can be the result of some differences in the selected samples or are simply not statistically significant, the analysis of changes over longer periods of time provides in general a fair reflection of underlying trends in drug using behaviours, at least as long as the methodological approaches to arrive at the results are not frequently changed.

Data for the USA, for instance, show a clear decline in the drug using behaviour in the general population over the 1985-1999 period cutting across all drug categories. Overall drug use fell by some 40%; use of drugs other than cannabis declined by about 50% and cocaine use fell by some 70% over the 1985-1999 period (see Figure 2).

Similar successes are not apparent in other countries. Nevertheless, most surveys conducted

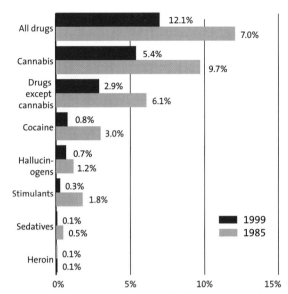

Fig. 2: Drug abuse in the USA, 1985-1999: monthly prevalence (age 12 and above)

Source: SAMHSA, *National Household Surveys 1998 and 1999*.

in Western Europe in the late 1990s indicated at least some stabilization of drug use.

• This has even been true for the UK, one of Europe's most rapidly growing drug markets in the 1980s and early 1990s (see Figure 3). The 1998 British Crime Survey, compared to the previous one conducted in 1996, showed a marginal increase in overall illicit drug use, but found no further increases for cannabis, amphetamine, LSD, ecstasy, cocaine or heroin among the general population.[e] Current use of drugs (past month prevalence) remained stable at 6% of the population age 16-59 over the 1996-98 period, slightly below the corresponding rate in the USA (7% in 1999).

• In Germany, which – among the larger EU countries – has one of the lowest rates of drug abuse, the upward trend of the early 1990s did not continue either; some declines were reported (see Figure 4).

e) The annual prevalence rates for cannabis among the general population (age 16-59) remained unchanged at 9%, for amphetamine at 3%, for LSD, ecstasy and cocaine at 1% each. Prevalence of heroin abuse remained at less than 0.5% (range: 0.2%-0.4% in 1998) (Home Office, *Drug Misuse Declared in 1998: results from the British Crime Survey*, London 1999, pp. 24-26).

Fig. 3: Drug abuse in the UK, annual prevelence among 16-59 year-olds

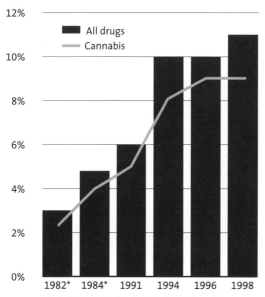

* Data for 'all drugs' for 1982 and 1984 have been extrapolated from cannabis use data.

Sources: Home Office, *Self-reported Drug Misuse in England and Wales – findings from the 1992 British Crime Survey*, London 1995; and Home Office, *Drug Misuse Declared in 1998: results from the British Crime Survey*, London 1999.

Fig. 4: Drug abuse in Germany in the late 1990s annual prevalence, 18-59 year olds

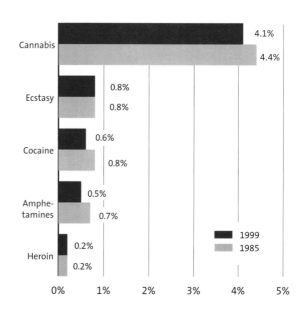

Sources: Ministry of Health, *Repräsentativerhebung 1995 and 1997*, Bonn 1995 and 1997.

Fig. 5: Drug abuse in Spain in the late 1990s annual prevalence

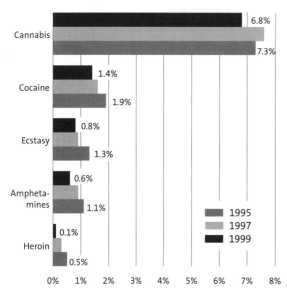

Source: EMCDDA, *Extended annual report on the state of the drugs problem in the European Union*, Lisbon 1999. Ministry of Interior, *Plan Nacional sobre Drogas*, 1996 and 2000, Madrid, 2000.

- National surveys conducted in Spain – which has invested heavily in a comprehensive national anti-drug strategy, including a strong focus on demand reduction[f] – showed a marked decrease in the overall levels of drug abuse over the 1995-99 period, notably for heroin (see Figure 5).

In general, prevention activities were apparently successful in keeping illicit drug use in the European Union more than a third below the levels reported from the USA, even though in a few countries (notably the UK) prevalence rates of drug use are approaching the US levels. Prevalence of cocaine use – as reflected in household

---

f) A systematic approach to drug control, encompassing both demand and supply elements, has been followed in Spain since the approval of the first *"Plan Nacional sobre Drogas"* in 1985. In 1997 a *"Plan de medidas para luchar contra las drogas"* was set up, and in December 1999 the Council of Ministers passed the *"Estrategia Nacional sobre Drogas"*. (Ministry of Interior, *Plan Nacional sobre Drogas – Estrategia Nacional sobre Drogas, 2000-2008*, Madrid 2000.)

surveys – is about 60% lower in the European Union than in the USA (annual prevalence of 0.7% of the population age 15 and above in the EU versus 1.7% in the USA in 1998).

As illicit drug use is often a low frequency event, large sample sizes are, however, necessary to generate sufficient cases for analysis. In the USA, for instance, the 1998 annual household survey on drug abuse was based on a sample of 25,500 people who were interviewed. In European countries, samples range from 1,500 people (Sweden) to some 10,000 people for countries such as the UK or Spain; in the Netherlands as many as 22,000 people were interviewed. Large samples are particularly needed to arrive at reasonable estimates for less prevalent drugs, such as heroin, and for monthly prevalence rates as opposed to annual or life-time use.[g]

Methodological and practical problems associated with conducting survey work in the drug area mean, however, that the information obtained through national household surveys cannot be assumed to provide a fully comprehensive picture of the drug-using population in a country. Household surveys show rather good results with regard to the overall level of drug use and the use of widely consumed substances, such as cannabis, but less so for typical problem drugs which are usually concentrated among marginalized sections of society. Drug using behaviour that is strongly stigmatized, such as heroin abuse, injecting drug use in general, or use of crack-cocaine, is usually only partially covered by household surveys. For problem drugs, household surveys may represent only between 30% (opiates) and 60% (cocaine) of the likely total size of the respective drug using population. Table 1 shows this for the USA, where national household survey data, reflecting drug use among the residential non-institutionalized population, have been compared

with the more comprehensive estimates provided by the Office of National Drug Control Policy (ONDCP). The latter explicitly take into account drug consumption patterns among marginalized groups such as homeless, people in jail, people in treatment, etc. Though the coverage levels differ from country to country, most countries – for which estimates are available – confirm the US patterns of far lower levels of problem drug use reflected in household surveys than in more comprehensive estimates which explicitly target the population at risk.

Problems of under-reporting are exacerbated in countries where drug consumers fear that the information they provide could be used against them. This means that the application of the very same methods can lead to different results in countries of different cultural backgrounds. This may explain why in a number of Asian countries, for instance, surveys on drug abuse have shown very low prevalence rates. Given other available drug indicators, such rates are unlikely to reflect reality but have to be seen in the cultural context in which such surveys have taken place. By contrast, surveys undertaken in Latin American countries do not appear to suffer from this problem. Nonetheless, many of these surveys, even if conducted within short periods of time, have been characterized by strongly diverging results which, of course, raises questions as to their reliability.

For all of these reasons, information gained from general population surveys has to be supplemented by special studies utilizing, for example, ethnographic methods (methods of describing social behavior based on direct observation) to describe the behaviour of 'hard-to-reach' groups, if a more complete picture on the overall extent of drug abuse is to be obtained. In addition, various indirect estimation techniques have been developed, either to complement data derived from survey methods

---

g) The lack of large enough samples (for cost reasons) is one of the reasons why information on life-time use – the least interesting element of drug information – is collected and analyzed. Another reason is that drug users may admit to have taken drugs at some stage in the past, but are not likely to admit that they took them over the last year or the last month, fearing that this could entail legal consequences.

Table 1: Estimated number of users of cocaine and heroin in the USA (in thousands) and as a percentage of the population age 12 and above

Drug	Year	ONDCP Estimates				National household survey (annual prevalence)		Coverage of drug users in national household survey
		Occasional users*	Hardcore users**	All users		Absolute	in %	
				Absolute	in %			
Cocaine	1996	3,425	3,410	6,835	3.2%	4,033	1.9%	59%
	1997	3,487	3,503	6,990	3.2%	4,169	1.9%	60%
	1998	3,216	3,343	6,559	3.0%	3,811	1.7%	58%
	avg 96-98	3,376	3,419	6,795	3.2%	4,004	1.9%	59%
Heroin	1996	455	917	1,372	0.6%	455	0.2%	33%
	1997	597	935	1,532	0.7%	597	0.3%	39%
	1998	253	980	1,233	0.6%	253	0.1%	21%
	avg 96-98	435	944	1,379	0.6%	435	0.2%	32%

* people using drugs less than once a week.
** people using drugs at least once a week.

Sources: SAMHSA, *1998 National Household Survey* and Office of National Drug Control Policy (ONDCP), *What America's Users Spend on Illegal Drugs, 1998-1998,* Washington 1999.

or to provide a better picture of the scale of the drug abuse problem. The methods[2], usually based on some further in-depth studies, include (i) the identification of appropriate multipliers to extrapolate from existing registers (such as arrests, treatment, mortality, etc.) the total number of 'problem users'[h], (ii) the use of 'capture-recapture' methods [i], (iii) back-calculations, e.g. based on HIV/AIDS statistics, and (iv) multivariate methods.[j]

One problem is that these alternative methods do not provide precise results, but only broad ranges that are usually not adequate for trend analysis. Nonetheless, such estimates on the likely orders of magnitude of the 'core drug problem' in a country yield important information. This is crucial as 'problem drug users' are usually responsible not only for the bulk of overall consumption of drugs such as opiates and cocaine, but also for the main drug related social problems, including crime, violence, drug related morbidity and death.

h) If, for instance, 2000 people are treated in a country and an in-depth study among drug users reveals that 20% of them had been to treatment in the previous year, it can be estimated that the total number of drug users could be around 10,000 people.

i) Such methods have been initially developed for estimates of the size of animal populations. If, for instance, 200 fish are caught ("captured"), marked, and released back into a lake, and the next day 100 fish are fished, of which 10 were already marked ("re-captured"), probability considerations suggest that the number of fish captured the first day were 10% of the total size of the population. Thus, the total population of the lake can be estimated at around 2,000 fish. Though the actual models are far more sophisticated, the same principle is applied to the estimation of the numbers of drug users based on their identification in various registers (arrests, ambulance services, treatment etc.). One problem, however, is that the "capture" and "re-capture"of drug users in these registers is frequently not independent from one another (e.g. people arrested may be sent to treatment), which violates some of the preconditions for the application of such probability considerations.

j) Based on the identification of the size of the drug abusing population in some local areas (e.g. based on a case-finding study, or based on capture/recapture methods) and the identification of some key variables which are likely to be good predictors for the level of drug abuse (e.g. drug-related arrests, drug-related treatment, drug-related mortality etc.), multivariate methods assist in the extrapolation of the local results to the national level.

Table 2: Estimates for 'problem drug users' per 1000 inhabitants, age 15-64, in the late 1990s in countries of Western Europe and North America

	Nordic countries				Selected other West European countries									USA[f]
	Finland	Sweden	Denmark	Norway	Germany	Austria	Ireland	France	Spain	Benelux[d]	UK	Switzer-land[i]	Italy	
Range of estimates	0.5-4.2	2.5-3.5	2.9-4.0	3.2-4.6	1.4-3.0	2.9-3.4	1.9-5.7	3.2-4.6	3.1-6.6	2.3-7.7	2.3-8.9	6.0-6.2	4.4-8.3	18.6-24.0
Mid-range estimate	2.4	3.0	3.4	3.9	2.2 (2.7)[c]	3.2	3.8	3.9	4.9	5.0	5.6	6.1	6.4	21.3 (5.4)[g]
Mean estimate[b]	1.9	3.0	3.6	3.9	2.2 (2.7)[c]	3.2	3.4	4.1	4.9	2.8	6.2	6.1	6.6	21.3 (5.4)[g]

a) 'Problem drug use' as defined by EMCDDA: drug addiction, notably to opiates and stimulants, injecting drug use, or drug use associated with criminal behaviour.

b) Average of all available estimates; estimation methods include extrapolations from treatment and police data, capture-recapture methods, mortality multipliers, back-calculations from HIV)AIDS figures and multivariate indicators.

c) Estimate for West Germany only.

d) Belgium, Luxembourg, Netherlands.

e) Based on an estimate of around 30,000 regular users of opiates and cocaine, provided by the Swiss authorities to UNDCP.

f) 'Problem drug use' data for the USA refer to 'hard-core' (= at least weekly) use of 'cocaine' (low estimate), respectively to 'cocaine & heroin' use (high estimate); whereas the low end of the range assumes that all hard-core heroin users are included in the group of hard-core cocaine users, the high-end of the range assumes that hard-core heroin and hard-core cocaine users are two distinct groups of people; the mean estimate assumes that half of the heroin users also use cocaine. There were 3.3 million hard-core cocaine and 0.98 million hard-core heroin users in the USA in 1998 according to ONDCP.

g) Estimate for heroin only.

Sources: EMCDDA, *2000 Annual Report on the State of the Drugs Problem in the European Union, Lisbon 2000*; ONDCP, *The National Drug Control Strategy: 2000, Annual Report*, Washington 2000; UNDCP, Annual Reports Questionnaire Data.

It goes without saying that such estimates, particularly if used for cross-country comparisons, have to be treated with caution. Nonetheless, they do provide results which can help to put problems into perspective and assist in the overall evaluation of the effectiveness of demand reduction efforts. Calculations for countries in Western Europe on the levels of 'problem drug use', provided by the European Monitoring Centre for Drugs and Drug Addiction (EMCDDA), and for the United States, provided by ONDCP ('hard-core use' of cocaine and heroin) show, for instance, that despite a strong fall in drug use in the USA over the past 15 years, 'problem drug use' is still a more serious phenomenon in the USA than in Western Europe. There were some 21 'hard-core' users per 1000 inhabitants age 15-64 of cocaine and heroin in the USA in 1998 (range 18-24). Estimates for hard-core heroin abuse alone were equivalent to 5 1/2 users per 1000 inhabitants, and thus similar to overall problem drug use reported from Europe. Esti-mates for Western Europe indicate that 'problem drug use' affects on average 4 1/2 persons per 1000 inhabitants age 15-64 (mean estimate of 15 countries). Estimates range from an average 2-3 in Finland and Sweden and some other countries of continental Europe, including Germany and Austria, to levels of around 4 in France, 5 in Spain and 6-7 in the UK, Switzerland, Italy and Luxembourg (see Table 2).

Even though definitions and methodological approaches for calculating 'problem drug use' differ, they are unlikely to explain all of the differences between the USA and Western Europe. 'Hard-core' users, according to the US definition, are people who use cocaine or heroin at least once a week.[3] 'Problem drug use', according to the definition applied by EMCDDA, is "intravenous drug use (IDU) or long-duration/regular use of opiates, cocaine or amphetamines". The definition of 'problem drug use' applied by EMCDDA excludes cannabis and ecstasy users and those who do not use, or at least not regularly, opiates, cocaine and amphetamines[4]; it is thus not too different from the US concept of 'hard-core' drug use. The lowest estimate for the USA (18 hard-core cocaine users per 1000 people age 15-64) is still twice as high as the upper range of estimates for European countries (8-9 in Italy or the UK).

The most in-depth data set (covering the last twenty-five years) for high-school students is the 'Monitoring the Future Project', which surveys 8th, 10th and 12th graders across the United States. One of the best data sets for cross-country analysis in Europe is the European ESPAD (European School Survey Project on Alcohol and Other Drugs) survey which, first in 1995 (26 countries)[5], and again a few years later asked cohorts of school children (in some 40 countries) questions about alcohol and drug use.[k] These studies, done according to the same methodological procedures, provide unique possibilities for comparison among European countries, including countries in Eastern Europe, and by focusing on the same age cohort over a number of years, also show a picture of trends in drug use among the youth population. The results apply, of course, only to youth regularly attending school. This caveat is important as youth who are frequently absent from school are less likely to be included in the survey sample though they are disproportionately more likely to use drugs.[6] The same is even more true for school dropouts.

Though school surveys cannot substitute for national household surveys, some of the main trends, nonetheless, are reflected in such surveys as well. Both types of surveys, for instance, showed strong increases of drug consumption in the USA in the 1970s and a decline in the 1980s. By the late 1990s both types of surveys showed signs of stabilization at levels that were below those reported in the mid 1980s. In the UK both household surveys and school surveys found increases in drug consumption up to the mid 1990s, but no continuation of this upward trend thereafter. Current use of drugs in the general population remained stable while national school surveys even showed a decline in the late 1990s.[l]

The relative position of countries with respect to the levels of drug abuse is also rather well reflected in school surveys. Countries reporting high levels of substance abuse among youth tend to also have rather high levels of drug use among the general population, and *vice versa*. Figure 6 shows such correlation of drug use between the group of 15-16 year-old pupils and the use of cannabis among the general population in 10 industrialized countries (R=0.87). As cannabis accounts for about 90% of total illegal drug use among 15-16 year-olds in both Western Europe and the USA, the extent of cannabis use is at the same time a good proxy for overall levels of drug use, including for drugs other than cannabis. The analysis of the drug using behavior of 15-16 year-olds in 21 countries, for which detailed data have been made available in the ESPAD study, suggests that there is a positive correlation between the level of cannabis use among 15-16 year-olds in a country and the use of other illegal drugs in this age group (R=0.80).

Morbidity and mortality information sources
Although some information on the problems associated with drug abuse may be obtained from surveys, other sources are more commonly used to obtain basic data on adverse health and social consequences. These include targeted research and monitoring activities designed specifically to collect information on drug abuse, and the extraction of drug-related data from other more general information sources. Chronic and acute health consequences can sometimes be monitored through the national health care reporting systems. For example, diagnostic data on deaths and hospitalizations may be recorded and reported annually using

---

k) At the time of writing this Report, not all ESPAD survey results of the second phase among high-school students have been published.
l) Life-time prevalence of drug use among the 14-15 year olds, for instance, fell from 31% in 1995/96 to 27% in 1998. DrugScope, *Drug Situation in the UK: Trends & Updates*, London 2000.

Fig. 6 : Cannabis use reflected in school surveys (15-16 years olds) and among the general population in industrialized countries in the late 1990s

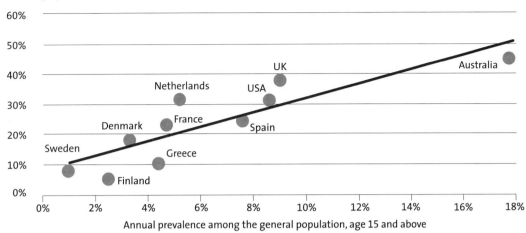

Annual prevalence among the general population, age 15 and above

Source: EMCDDA, *Extended annual report on the state of the drugs problem in the European Union*, Lisbon 1999; NIDA, *Monitoring the Future*, 1975-1999, Centre for Behavioural Research in Cancer, *Australia secondary student's use of over-the counter and illict substances in 1996*, in Nov. 1998; Australian Institute of Health and Welfare, *1998 National Drug Strategy Household Survey*, Canberra, August 1999.

the International Classification of Diseases (ICD). Where this is done comprehensively and with attention to detail, useful information can be extracted.

In other countries, separate drug-specific reporting systems have been developed. Some countries have established specialist *treatment registers* for those seeking help with a drug problem, for those in treatment, or for those leaving treatment. Such registers reflect the demand for treatment as well as its availability and attractiveness. As drug abusers typically consume drugs for some considerable time before seeking help, treatment attendance must be viewed as a delayed or 'lagged' indicator of prevalence. Studies suggest that West European heroin abusers will typically have used the drug for between three and six years before first entering treatment, which means that increases in treatment demand may continue even though the levels of drug abuse are already declining. A related problem is the relapsing of drug addicts which impacts on treatment demand. This can lead to potentially erroneous conclusions that prevention is not working, even though *de facto* it may be highly successful. The example of Spain can be used

to demonstrate this point. While there was an increase in treatment demand for heroin abuse up until 1996, a breakdown shows that the number of people that entered the treatment system for the first time, has actually been falling since 1992, by some 40% up until 1998 (see Figure 7). Such simple breakdowns – though highly policy relevant – are unfortunately not available from many other countries.

In countries, where such data are not published regularly, treatment data can still be used for the identification of underlying abuse trends. In Italy, for example, the total number of people in treatment was growing up until 1997. The actual stabilization of abuse trends, however, started a couple of years earlier. This is indirectly reflected in the changes of the growth rates of treatment demand. While the number of people in treatment had increased by more than a third in 1991, a consequence of the heroin epidemic of the late 1980s, the growth rate declined to 12% in 1992 and 6% in 1997 before turning negative in 1998 (-0.4%) and 1999 (-2%) (see Figure 8). The general stabilization/decline was even more pronounced with regard to heroin. Treatment demand for heroin fell between 1997 and 1999 by 7%,

Fig. 7: Drug addicts treated for heroin abuse in Spain

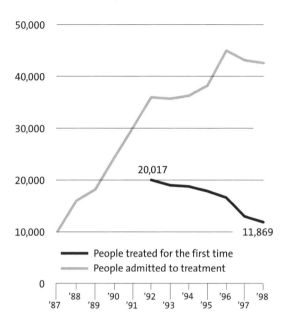

Fig. 8: Drug treatment in Italy

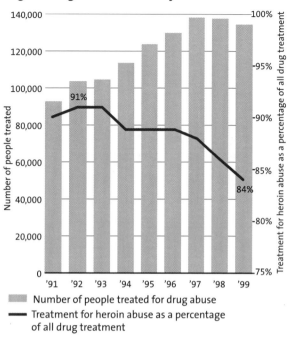

Source: Observatorio Espanol sobre Drogas, Informe No. 3, March 2000 and Plan Nacional Sobre Drogas, State Information System on Drug Abuse, 1995 Report, Madrid 1995.

Source: Ministry of the Interior, *Annual Report on the State of the Drugs Problem in Italy for the European Monitoring Centre on Drugs and Drug Addiction*, Rome 1996 and Presidenza del Consiglio dei Ministri Dipartimento per gli Affari Sociali, *Tossicodipendenze, Relazione Annuala al Parlamenta sullo Statu delle Tossicodipedenze in Italia*, 1999, Rome 2000.

more than twice as much as treatment demand in general, reflecting the long-term downward trend of the proportion of heroin in Italy's overall drug treatment demand (92% in 1990; 84% in 1999). In parallel, the average age of people in treatment was rising.

In recent years, Italian researchers, under the auspices of EMCDDA, have developed more sophisticated models which, based on treatment data and the history of clients in treatment centres, have been able to create a fairly good picture on the development of drug incidence over time. All of these models indicated that Italy's heroin epidemic of the 1980s peaked around 1991, fell strongly thereafter and more or less stabilized at lower levels after 1993. The models proved to be valuable tools to forecast treatment demand a couple of years in advance. Attempts are currently under way to adapt such models to the institutional context of other European countries as well.

A simple treatment-related indicator is the *mean age of people in treatment*. Available data for 12 EU countries showed, for instance, that – with only two exceptions – the mean age of people in treatment was growing in the 1990s, reflecting the ageing of the drug using population, notably of heroin addicts (see Figure 9). The average growth of the mean age in treatment was about one year over the 1994-98 period. Even stronger increases in the mean age were reported from Greece, Spain, Italy, Portugal, France, Belgium and Denmark. These are usually positive signs. They indicate a flattening or even a possible downward trend as less new (i.e. younger) users are entering the treatment system. Of course, an increase in the mean age also raises some questions about the adequacy of the treatment available. In the past, the treatment systems in Europe were largely geared towards caring for heroin addicts, whose numbers are apparently declining. But it may still

Fig. 9: Changes in mean age treatment for drug problems in the late 1990s in EU countries

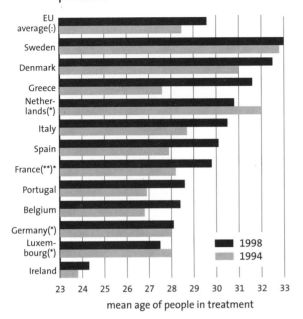

mean age of people in treatment

1998
1994

(:) Unweighted average of 12 EU countries;
(*) 1995 starting year;
(**) 1993 starting year;
*   1997 latest year available

Source: EMCDDA, *2000 Annual Report on the State of the Drugs Problem in the European Union*, Lisbon 2000 and previous years.

take some time until the systems are adequately reoriented to fulfill the needs and requirements of users of other drugs as well.

Drug treatment reporting registers are used most commonly in countries that have developed specialist drug treatment services. As help for drug problems can be provided by a diverse range of institutions and individuals which include self-help groups, general practitioners, non-governmental organizations and various elements of the mainstream health and social services, the development of specialist drug treatment registers needs to be carefully tailored to match the patterns of service provision and help-seeking behaviour found within the country in question.

The systematic collection of treatment data, however, has also been shown to provide relatively good and reliable information on the drug problem in a number of developing countries. With regard to cross-country efforts among developing countries, the Asian Multicity Epidemiology Work Group and CICAD with its SIDUC system (Inter-American Uniform Drug Use Data System) have done pioneering work in this area in the 1990s, largely improving the understanding and the transparency of existing trends across countries in the two regions. These systems are partly based on the model of the Community Epidemiology Work Group (CEWG), set up a couple of years ago with the assistance of NIDA in the USA. CEWG has proven to be successful in the early identification of trends at the local level and the sharing of such information with representatives from other parts of the country in order to be able to respond to problems even before they occur. A similar system at the national level was also introduced in the Republic of South Africa ('South African Community Epidemiology Network') which may be expanded to neighbouring countries as well.

In addition to registers on drug abusers who seek treatment, other epidemiological data on the health consequences of drug consumption have been collected by monitoring *emergency room visits*. An example of this kind of information system is the DAWN (Drug Abuse Warning Network) in the United States, which over the years developed into a key up-to date information system on trends in problem drug use in the USA.

One particularly worrying consequence of drug abuse is that of viral infection in general and *HIV infection* in particular. Drug injection is a major risk factor for HIV infection in many parts of the world. Non-injecting drug users may also be at elevated risk because of an association with specific patterns of drug abuse and/or sexually risky behaviour. Drug epidemiological systems have been developed to record HIV infection rates among drug injectors and to measure the extent of HIV risk behaviour among drug-using populations. Drug injection can spread rapidly in areas

Fig. 10: Incidence of AIDS cases related to injecting drug use in the EU per milion population

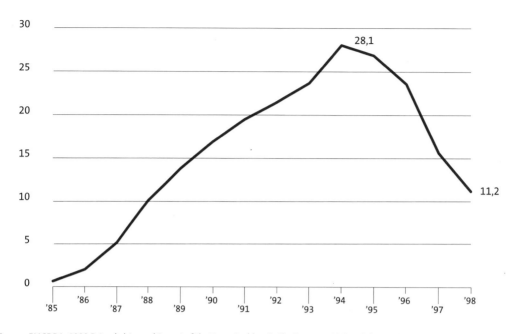

Source: EMCDDA, *1999 Extended Annual Report of the Drugs Problem in the European Union,* Lisbon 1999.

where it has been previously unknown and information systems are needed to identify the emergence and spread of injecting practices. This work is both methodologically and practically challenging because many drug injectors are not in contact with services and therefore research activities have to take place in community settings. However, such information is vital to the targeting and evaluation of interventions. Its systematic collection in a number of countries has definitely increased awareness of the problem which is a first step towards finding solutions. In the countries of Western Europe, for instance, this has led to significantly improved services and prevention work and enabled a great reduction in the incidence of AIDS cases related to injecting drug use from 28 per million inhabitants in 1994 to 11 in 1998, about the same level as a decade earlier (see Figure 10). All EU countries reported reductions. The strongest declines over the 1994-98 period were reported from Spain, Italy and France. Over the 1985-98 period some 23% of AIDS cases in the countries of the European Union

were related to injecting drug use (unweighted average of the 15 countries). This compares with a rate of 36% for the USA over the same period. The share reported from the USA is, however, within the range of results reported from individual European countries which goes from 3.8% in Finland to 65% in Spain. While HIV has been one of the main concerns of policy makers, progress with regard to hepatitis B, C and tubercular infections, all of which also cause major health problems among drug injectors, was less pronounced.

The development of *drug-related mortality* is sometimes seen as the ultimate success or failure of countries' drug policies. The effectiveness of both drug prevention and treatment is eventually reflected in drug-related mortality data. A more immediate impact in reducing drug related deaths can be usually achieved by improving availability and effectiveness of treatment services. Even though they cannot prevent all drug-related deaths as not all drug addicts are willing to undergo treatment and relapse rates tend to be high, they usually help, at least, to elevate the average age of drug-related deaths. This is more than a simple postponement of drug-related death. It means that drug users are offered extended opportunities to get rid of their addiction.

In the long run, falling numbers of deaths, however, will be only possible if prevention works, i.e. if the number of new drug addicts can be lowered. But, even if this is achieved, it can take several years until this is reflected in the death statistics. Drug epidemics are dynamic processes which, once started, tend to expand exponentially. They may come to an end by themselves, but this could well take fifteen years or longer and cost the lives of many more young men and women. Against such a background, any stabilization following years of a major upward trend, may be regarded as a success.

Data provided by the European Monitoring Centre for Drugs and Drug Addiction suggest that a stabilization – following a strong intensification of demand reduction efforts – was actually achieved in the countries of the European Union in the 1990s. Following strong increases in the 1980s, the number of acute drug deaths stagnated in the European Union in the 1990s. If the trends of the 1980s had continued – which might have been the case without appropriate interventions – the number of acute drug-related death cases, less than 7,000 a year in the late 1990s, could well have been three times higher in the late 1990s (See Figure 11). The number of acute drug-related deaths in the European Union was less than half the number in the United States (about 16,000 in 1997, according to ICD-9 classification[m]) and less than a third in per capita terms (less than 20 drug-related deaths per million inhabitants in the EU as compared to 59 in the USA). A majority of West European countries located on the continent already reported declines in drug-related death cases over the 1992-1998, including France, Spain, Germany, Italy, and if the 1994-98 period is looked at, Austria, Luxembourg and Switzerland.

How reliable are such mortality data and how good are they to identify drug trends and make cross-country comparisons? The answer to the first question depends largely on the countries collecting such data. In developing countries and countries in transition, but also in some developed countries, the accuracy and comprehensiveness of mortality registers may be questionable. Detail necessary to compile reliable drug mortality statistics is often absent. In other cases, various kinds of social pressures inhibit the recording of drug abuse as cause of death which may lead to under reporting.

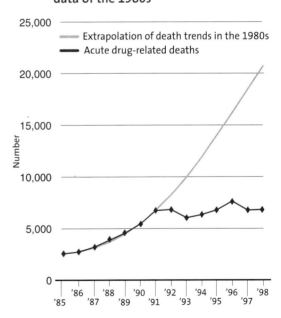

Fig. 11: Drug deaths in the EU: actual death cases compared to extrapolated trend data of the 1980s

Source: EMCDDA, *2000 Annual Report on the State of the Drugs Problem in the European Union*, Lisbon 2000.

---

m) ICD 9 includes deaths attributable to drug psychoses; drug dependence; non-dependent use of drugs (excluding alcohol and tobacco); accidental poisoning by drugs and medicaments; suicide by drugs and medicaments; assault from poisoning by drugs and medicaments; poisoning by drugs and medicaments undetermined whether accidentally or purposely inflicted. Drug induced cases exclude, however, accidents, homicides and other causes indirectly related to drug use. Also excluded are newborn deaths associated with a mother's drug use.

Not all patterns of drug abuse result in significant levels of mortality, and for those that do, the relative number of individuals dying in any particular time period may be relatively small. Mortality data are usually closely linked to the use of a few problem drugs, such as heroin and other opiates (Europe), cocaine and heroin (USA) or methamphetamine and heroin (East Asia). The consequence is that trends derived from mortality data at the national level reflect abuse patterns of specific drugs, rather than of all drugs. As such trends may be based on small numbers of observations, they may not be very meaningful for smaller countries; this does not mean, however, that reasonable conclusions cannot be drawn once data are analyzed within a broader subregional or regional context.

Definitional problems also exist which are more significant than for other drug indicators. In fact, even in countries where considerable efforts have been made to develop comprehensive drug-related mortality registers, problems remain, particularly if data are to be used for cross-country comparisons. The link between drug use and death is seen differently from country to country. In some classification systems, for instance, drug-related suicide is exempted even though distinguishing between an accidental and a deliberate overdose is often difficult. In some countries, AIDS developed through needle sharing is seen as a drug-related death, in others not. In some countries, a traffic accident which involves a person with traces of cannabis in the blood, is registered as a drug death, while in others a person, under the influence of heroin, falling under a train, is recorded as a traffic accident, not a drug death. Indeed, in most countries, the role of drug abuse in accidental deaths such as those caused by traffic accidents, goes largely unreported. The more general problem is that drug abuse may be just one of several possible causal factors, or even one among a range of factors con-

tributing to death. Drug abusers may be using a range of substances, including high levels of alcohol, which complicates the attribution of a causal link between death and any particular substance. This again is handled differently among countries.[n]

For years, attempts have been made to standardize the drug-related death indicator. In practice, however, this has remained a highly complicated endeavor, even within groups of countries, such as the EU Member States, which otherwise work closely together. The most widely used indicators for inter-country comparison, at the moment, are those where the nature of the causal link between drug consumption and the recorded event (death) is as far as possible unambiguous, such as drug overdose leading to death.

Adverse social consequences of drug abuse
Other methods and data sources are required to estimate adverse social consequences, particularly drug-related crime and lost productivity due to drug abuse.

There is little doubt that drug abuse is related to crime: in many countries illicit drug use is a criminal offence, and it is a contributory cause in some property crimes and crimes of violence. The nature of the relationship, however, is not so simple. While many criminals take drugs and many drug addicts commit crimes, it is likely that both drug abuse and crime are related to a similar set of socio-demographic and personality variables such as poverty, poor future career or income prospects, low self esteem and poor social integration. These factors may be underlying causes of both criminality and illicit drug use. But, even if this were the case, illicit drug use and crime can be still seen as mutually reinforcing forms of behavior. This has important policy implications. A fall in the levels of drug abuse is likely to contribute to an overall reduc-

---

n) In response to this, indirect methods have been developed to determine the attributable portion of mortality and morbidity that is due to illicit drug abuse. These combine prevalence data with the relative risk of particular disorders for drug abusers versus non-abusers to estimate the proportion of cases that can be attributed to the abuse of drugs. At present the necessary data to develop robust estimates in this area is however largely lacking.

tion in the levels of crime. US data point in this direction. While drug abuse rates – notably of cocaine abuse – were clearly lower by the end of the 1990s than a decade earlier, both the total crime rate and the property crime rate fell by 20%, the violent crime rate by 23%, murders by 28% and murders related to the narcotics drug laws by 50% over the 1990-98 period.[o] Once the crime costs and other related costs to drug abuse are quantified on a regular basis, they could provide a powerful instrument to measure the cost effectiveness of various kinds of drug-related interventions.

Law enforcement data on the number of drug crimes, property crimes and violent crimes are thus increasingly seen as important areas for developing monitoring capacity. Data on violations of drug law are included in most drug information systems and in some countries may be the only routinely collected indicator of drug abuse. They are, of course, not without problems. In countries where drugs are produced or which lie along trafficking routes, a distinction is useful to make between drug law violations and seizures relating to drugs for domestic use, and those relating to drugs intended for export. It should also be remembered that such data reflect changes in consumption patterns as well as the priorities and efficiency of law enforcement agencies. The possibility of a phenomenon known as 'deviancy amplification' has been noted, whereby an increase in interdiction activities resulting from political or public concern leads to increased arrests which in turn generate even more public concern and further calls for increased activities by law enforcement bodies. This usually does not affect long-term trends, but it may have a significant impact on short-term trends.

The analysis of drug supply and drug markets is, of course, not restricted to statistics on arrests for drug violations or on the numbers of seizures made. Other relevant information sources include: survey data on the relative ease with which respondents are able to obtain illicit drugs; police reports or at least anecdotal data on the price of drugs at the street level; information from or studies of drug abusers; and laboratory analyses of the composition and potency of street drugs.

Another input to epidemiological study is the loss of worker productivity due to problems of acute or chronic drug abuse. This may show up in statistics on workplace accidents; absenteeism or disciplinary problems. Sources of information on drug abuse in the workplace stem mainly from specific studies which analyze the relationship between employee drug test results and accidents, absenteeism and turnover. Lower status workers, young persons, males and workers in particular industries are particularly prone to drug abuse. Aspects of the work environment such as stress, organizational and co-worker norms, and ready availability will influence levels of alcohol and drug use on the job. A relationship has been found between drug abuse and unemployment, turnover and absenteeism; but the evidence regarding the relationship of drug abuse to workplace accidents is less compelling. In the absence of more specific data on the adverse consequences of drug abuse in the workplace, economic cost studies rely on indirect methods to estimate productivity losses. Most cost-of-illness studies estimate productivity losses by comparing the wages of drug-dependent persons to other workers, using this as a crude measure of lower productivity attributable to drugs. It goes without saying that this approach remains problematic. It suggests that productivity losses are exclusively borne by the drug-taking person who accepts lower wages while enterprises would bear no costs. This is not the case. But even with these caveats in mind, the calculated magnitudes of productivity costs arising from drug

---

o) The total crime rate in the USA per 100,000 inhabitants showed a fall from 5,820 in 1990 to 4,615 in 1998; the property crime rate fell from 5,088 to 4,049 and the violent crime rate from 731 to 566. The total number of murders fell from 23,438 to 16,914; the murders related to the drug laws fell from 1,367 to 679. (U.S. Department of Justice (Federal Bureau of Investigation), *Crime in the United States: Uniform Crime Reports (1990-99)*, Washington 2000.)

abuse are significant. One NIDA study calculated the productivity losses due to drug abuse (lost earnings of drug-related crime victims and lost earnings of drug users due to illness and premature death) at US$ 78 billion[7] in 1995, equivalent to 1.1% of GDP.

2.1.3. THE DIFFICULTIES OF MONITORING DRUG ABUSE AND THE WAY AHEAD

Each of the primary sources of information required for epidemiological monitoring has particular constraints and limitations, as already noted.

Yet epidemiological monitoring systems are essential to achieve sustainable progress in the field of demand reduction. Improving the epidemiological framework of drug demand requires basically multiple indicators and multiple methods. No one method is entirely adequate. Surveys provide reasonably reliable and generalizable data on drug use, but fail to capture important high-risk groups and behaviours such as drug injecting. Law enforcement data provide important insights into the drug situation in a country, but are influenced by other factors as well. Health care data are sometimes limited to the most severe health consequences of drug abuse, which only represent the tip of the iceberg. In order to obtain a fair understanding of underlying trends, all of the above mentioned sources have to be pooled and compared with the aim of using *multiple indicators,* methods and sources of data on drug abuse, its adverse consequences and associated risk factors to overcome the problems associated with individual indices. In this context, for countries seeking to establish or develop drug information systems, it is definitely an advantage to be able to build on the experiences of countries where considerable investment in such fields has already been made.

Everywhere, information deficits are apparent and systems are slow to respond to new trends. Nonetheless, there is now know-how available of how to use a few key indicators of drug demand to construct a reliable knowledge base. This development is acknowledged to be of critical importance for the formulation and evaluation of effective polices and interventions. UNDCP is working with other international organizations and regional drug epidemiology groups to reach consensus on the key indicators that are appropriate for standardization, and this in turn will lead to improved comparability of epidemiological monitoring over time and between countries.

Yet it is not sufficient to have agreement on sound measurement systems if countries lack the capacity to collect data in the first place. Improvements in epidemiological methods and systems are most apparent in the industrialized countries where drug abuse has been a major concern for a considerable time, and where resources have been available for the development and support of monitoring systems. But drug abuse has now become a major issue for governments in both the developed and the developing world. Many countries are currently experiencing serious drug problems, yet lack the basic information necessary to develop appropriate responses. Today's challenge is not only to improve existing information systems and to develop a more sophisticated understanding of the costs associated with drug-related behaviour, but also to build the capacity to collect information in parts of the world where it is currently lacking. With this objective, UNDCP is helping countries to develop their own epidemiological information systems. The Global Assessment Programme on Drug Abuse (GAP) will support the establishment of national drug information systems and regional epidemiology networks (see Box number 2B).

Box 2B: UNDCP Supporting Drug Epidemiology

National governments, as well as regional and global bodies have all made a commitment to improving the quality and comparability of the information collected on illicit drug consumption. This consensus is enshrined in the *Political Declaration on the Guiding Principles of Demand Reduction* where countries commit themselves to base their demand reduction response on regular assessments, to be undertaken in a comprehensive and systematic manner. Interest in the epidemiologial situation, however, goes much further. Understanding the development of drug abuse is not only a matter of local or national interest but increasingly a topic of interest for the international community as a whole. In today's ever more integrated world, drug epidemics of drug abuse do not respect national borders.

Against this background, UNDCP sees one of its key roles in the developing a better understanding of global trends in drug abuse, as well as in supporting countries to improve their information resources – a precondition for successful demand reduction interventions and for informing member states about emerging trends.

The formal mechanism by which Member States report on the drug abuse situation is the Annual Reports Questionnaire (ARQ). The completed questionnaires, together with other information, are synthesised in UNDCP's annual reports to the Commission on Narcotic Drugs (CND), the main policy making body of the United Nations on issues related to illegal drugs. ARQ data also form the basis of much of the information contained in this and the previous *World Drug Report,* and for the production of a statistical review, *Global Illicit Drug Trends* which is published annually. Following a decision of the CND, the ARQ is currently being revised in order to simplify it, sharpen its focus and reduce duplication. The revised ARQ will include a set of core indicators – similar to those already in use, or in the process of being developed by regional organisations – that should allow for better and more comparable reporting as well as assist Member States in the establishment of efficient drug monitoring systems.

One of the preconditions for the system to work is, of course, that countries are able to collect epidemiological information. While even more sophisticated methods of collecting such information are now available and investments made by countries into drug epidemiology over the last decade are starting to show dividends, the majority of developing countries has not benefitted from these advances. In many parts of the world very little information is available and correspondingly the understanding of the dynamics and patterns of illicit drug consumption remains poor. This can create a vicious circle. Anecdotal information on the drug abuse situation is not a sufficient basis for development assistance to build demand reduction programmes. At the same time, the lack of economic resources and the existence of more pressing needs may prevent countries from investing in the establishment of drug monitoring systems.

UNDCP's Global Assessment Programme (GAP) aims to break this vicious circle by actively assisting countries to develop data collection systems and improve the quality and comparability of the information collected. GAP regional epidemiological advisors are currently helping to coordinate improvements in data collection in Central and Southern Africa and in Central and South-West Asia. The programme also encourages the development of sustainable data collection activities that reflect the core information topics found in the ARQ. These *include measuring the extent of drug abuse and its adverse consequences,* such as drug-related deaths, treatment and HIV infections. A GAP 'methodological toolkit' will be shortly available, providing a practical planning guide for countries wishing to adapt state-of-the-art data collection methods to their own national circumstances. In parallel, UNDCP has been assisting various Latin American countries, including countries that have already an advanced research capacity, in conducting *epidemiological surveys* in a way that results become directly comparable across countries. Moreover, UNDCP has been conducting a number of *rapid assessment studies,* notably in a number of countries in Africa, to obtain basic information on patterns of drug abuse and thus have a basis for targeting interventions.

Despite of all of these efforts, the challenge of developing a timely and comprehensive understanding of the dynamics of global drug abuse is considerable, and much remains to be done. The demands of globalization and the need for evidence based responses mean that such an understanding of the drug abuse situation and its development are critical. This is increasingly being recognised. Progress can and is being made and UNDCP remains an active and committed partner to this endeavour.

2.2. PREVENTION

2.2.1. FROM EARLY SUBSTANCE ABUSE PREVENTION TO MODERN APPROACHES

In general terms, drug prevention aims at preventing the occurrence of substance abuse in society, as it is clearly better, and more cost effective, to prevent problems in the first place rather than to have to deal with them later. As a majority of people first use drugs during school age, prevention work has to set in earlier.

One slightly more operational goal is to reduce or delay the onset of substance abuse in society, reflecting the fact that the vulnerability to substance abuse generally reduces with age. The longer the onset can be delayed, the less likely it becomes that a person will eventually turn to drugs. Other goals, pursued in some countries, include the prevention of the progression to full-scale drug addiction. The chances of success are greatest if intervention starts at the earliest possible moment. There is also a possibility of 'maturing out' of drug use as circumstances change. This process, again, can be facilitated and shortened through prevention activities.

By targeting various risk groups – similar to the market segmentation approach by commercial companies – attempts are made to tailor the messages and interventions to specific needs and thus to increase the overall chances for success. While this is necessary, care has to be taken that the messages and intervention in this process remain consistent with one another which, in today's ever more integrated world, is a difficult exercise. Even if potential risk groups are successfully targeted, there are limitations to what prevention can do. The best marketing efforts will not convince all potential buyers of the advantages of a specific product, and similarly, the best identification of risk groups, and tailoring of messages and interventions, will not make all potential drug takers refrain. In the end, each individual is different, and what might be a valid argument for one person may still fail to convince another one. There are also limitations to prevention work once drug use has set in. An effective demand reduction strategy therefore requires a balance, an integration of both prevention and treatment: the latter has to be available if the first has failed.

It is clear that without a successful prevention strategy, all drug policies are likely to fail eventually. While laws that forbid trafficking and possession of drugs are important elements in a national drug strategy as they document, in general terms, the norms of behaviour in society, they are not sufficient unless potential users themselves come to the conclusion that the use of drugs is against their own interests. It is this internalization of social norms which is one of the core functions of prevention. Though usually much less tangible than other elements in the drug field, prevention remains the key to long-term success.

Substance abuse prevention in its earliest form was essentially based on opinion rather than science. The dominant approach was *information dissemination*, based on the assumption that once people knew the negative consequences of drug use, they would choose not to use drugs.

Evaluations have shown that *pure information dissemination* approaches increase knowledge of the adverse consequences of using drugs. They may also increase anti-drug attitudes, but there are also some examples showing an opposite outcome, of people being better informed – and taking more drugs. Results also seem to be location dependent. While in several developing countries there is still a need for basic information on drugs, this is already widely available in developed countries. The additional value added of more detailed drug information may thus be limited. There is a lack of serious long-term studies to investigate whether prevention approaches which are exclusively based on information dissemination have an impact on future behavior. A consensus, however, seems to emerge that information dissemination is a necessary, though not a sufficient condition for successful prevention.

Far more controversial has been the additional use of *scare tactics*, which have been repeatedly applied in prevention activities across the world since the beginning of the 20th century. Research in western countries suggested that prevention initiatives which overemphasized or exaggerated the negative consequences of drug consumption, made the information less trustworthy to the target population. The wisdom of prevention campaigns which concentrated more on scaring individuals than on providing sound facts, were therefore questioned. While a majority of people may have even reacted as expected, for certain groups at risk, the propagated dangers of drugs made them even more attractive for experimentation. The loss of credibility proved to be an additional hurdle at a later stage for these groups to make use of counselling services. Some countries outside North America and Europe, by contrast, appear to have had some success with deterrence models. This may change, however, as communication flows across countries increases.

A different though related issue is media response to specific events, and the use of scare tactics to transport the message. In the UK, for instance, a major, unofficial, nationwide media campaign, lasting for several months, followed the death of a young woman from ecstasy use in December 1995. This death received much coverage as the parents had allowed photographs to be taken in the intensive care unit before their daughter died. The unofficial media campaign appears to have been successful in the short term. A nationwide school survey among 15-16 year-old students in 1997 showed lifetime prevalence of ecstasy use at 3% and use of amphetamines at 7.3%, while a nationwide school survey among the same age group two years earlier had shown prevalence rates of 8% and 13%, respectively.[p] Differences

in methodologial approaches may explain some, but are unlikely to explain all of the change. However, the momentum created by the event could not be maintained. In 1998, the British Crime Survey, showed that the effects had largely waned. Substance abuse, including use of ecstasy, returned to previous levels.

The example shows that the whole issue remains complicated and still requires further investigation. A tentative conclusion, however, suggests that even though some short-term gains could be obtained, scare tactics may be counterproductive in the long-run. The international experts designing the Declaration on the Guiding Principles of Drug Demand Reduction, passed by the June 1998 Special Session of the General Assembly, came to the same conclusion: "Information utilized in ... prevention programmes should be clear, scientifically accurate and reliable, culturally valid, timely and, where possible, tested with a target population. Every attempt should be made to ensure credibility, avoid sensationalism, promote trust and enhance effectiveness...."[q]

Another frequent weakness of many prevention efforts in the past was the tendency for the *prevention agency to play a central role* in defining problems and organizing solutions for the target group. More recently, and based on the results of evaluations, the active role of the community and the 'target group' in defining the problem and finding the solution to it has been emphasized.

To date, most of the research into the effectiveness of drug prevention has been carried out in the industrialized world, notably in the United States, and the '*scientific approach*' to prevention has been showing success. Prevalence rates fell significantly in the USA. In many other western countries, the upward trend in

---

p) Lifetime prevalence of ecstasy use among 15-16 year-olds fell from 8% in 1995 to 3% in 1997, use of amphetamines from 13% to 7,3%, and use of cannabis from 41% to 37.5%.(EMCDDA, *Extended Annual Report on the State of the Drugs Problem in the European Union*, 1999, p. 53 and EMCDDA, 1998 Annual Report, Lisbon 1998, p. 47.)

q) United Nations, *Special Session of the General Assembly Devoted to Countering the World Drug Problem Together – Political Declaration, Guiding Principles of Drug Demand Reduction and Measures to Enhance International Cooperation to Counter the World Drug Problem*, New York, 8-10 June 1998, Declaration on the Guiding Principles of Drug Demand Reduction: IV. E. 15.

drug abuse was stopped, and in some countries it was even lowered. By contrast, many developing countries have been faced with ongoing increases in substance abuse. The extent to which lessons learned in developed countries can be applied to developing ones still needs to be assessed. It is clear, however, that the evidence based approach to prevention – research and identification of baseline data → design of prevention strategies → constant monitoring and evaluation → adaptation of interventions – has universal applicability. UNDCP is thus actively involved in assisting developing countries to formulate and implement comprehensive prevention packages.

2.2.2. BASES FOR EFFECTIVE PREVENTION

The provision of *accurate information* on the nature and extent of substance abuse is a critically important input to prevention. Such information is *inter-alia* generated through prevalence and longitudinal studies. *Prevalence studies,* conducted at regular intervals in a given country, are not only useful in estimating the size, nature and trends in substance abuse, but they may also serve to raise public awareness of the problem, both in the process and once the results are communicated to the general public. *Longitudinal studies* – which analyse the behaviour of a single group over an extended period of time – contribute to a better understanding of the impact of risk factors and interventions over a number of years.

Accurate information on the nature of substance abuse problems in a community is fundamental to the development of clear and realistic goals. Those who plan prevention efforts need to *engage the targeted community* or group and help *them to assume primary responsibility* for finding solutions. This means working cooperatively with, and supporting credible representatives of the targeted group as they clarify the problem, determine appropriate goals, design, possibly deliver, and help to eval-

uate the prevention activity. Imposing solutions on an unwilling or uninvolved group is rarely effective and may lead to negative consequences that were not intended.[8]

Substance abuse is intertwined with a number of other *social problems* and behaviours and may be influenced by the same underlying factors or determinants. The feeling of being excluded socially is a contributing factor in substance abuse as well as in other health and social problems. Similarly, in some communities, poverty has been shown to be a risk factor not only for unwanted pregnancy, violence among young people but also substance abuse. Substance abuse prevention efforts that address these kinds of *broad risk factors* can be integrated with other strategies that aim to improve the lives of people and communities.[9] On this basis, a substance abuse prevention plan or strategy may be embedded within a larger crime prevention, safety or health promotion initiative. To introduce comprehensive action on substance abuse is to acknowledge that the social and economic costs arising from the abuse of legally available substances such as alcohol, various medications and tobacco are also significant, and need to be addressed alongside the illicit substances.[10]

The active *contribution of a broad range of scientific disciplines* – psychology, sociology, education, medicine, public health, economics, communications and criminal justice – is required within a comprehensive prevention policy.[11] It may also mean drawing in individuals who have not traditionally played a role in substance abuse prevention, such as urban planners, housing authorities and employment policy makers[12], or experts in social marketing.

Similarly, at the *local level*, many sectors, including schools, enforcement services, neighbourhoods, community agencies, and the business, religious, arts and sports communities need to be made aware of their special role in prevention and have to be brought together to cooperate. It is generally acknowledged that approaches which bring together these various sectors of a community to address individual and environmental factors in a *coordinated and sustained fashion*, have the best chances to be effective. Indeed, the best results – irrespective of the concrete drug policies pursued – have been achieved in communities where such coordination between various social services, enforcement services and representatives of civil society, could be created and maintained.

Moreover, UNDCP's experience has shown that prevention programmes are more likely to be successful if they *combine the results of scientific research with the practical experience* of practitioners doing real prevention work. Practitioners involved in field-testing programme models can offer important practical advice on implementing and sustaining programmes, as can representatives of the target group while researchers can point to general principles and considerations for programme design.

Politicians and governments must provide *leadership and commitment* for prevention to be effective. Leadership in this sense means establishing a policy (which should be based – as far as possible – on empirical evidence), making resources available and setting standards of acceptable practice. It also means maintaining a long term commitment, even when resources are scarce or when crises divert attention. Governments can also exercise leadership by bringing together representatives of business, the media and non-government organisations to seek solutions.

2.2.3. DRUG VULNERABILITY – RISK AND PROTECTIVE FACTORS

As with most health and social problems, substance abuse rarely has a single cause. Research has identified a set of factors which increase the individual's risk of using drugs ('risk factors') and a set of factors which protect the individual from using drugs ('protective or resiliency factors'), i.e. those which serve to strengthen or protect individuals, families, com-

munities and societies.[13] The factors are complex and constantly changing at the individual, community and societal levels. While some of them are universal, such as curiosity, boredom, and loneliness, others are more specific, and the mix and weight of factors will vary from person to person and from community to community. The reasons behind an individual's use of drugs have been recognized to be the result of a complex interaction with individual, family social and environmental factors as well as factors relating to genetics, biology and personality.

The strongest influences on initial drug use are often interpersonal relationships – the *family* and *peer groups*. The following key risk factors have been identified:

- In terms of *family risk factors*, there is a large body of research on the influence of family structure, parenting style, quality of parent – child relationship, parental monitoring, and the strength of the extended family network on the development of drug use. Family disruption, weak family relationships, criminality and drug abuse of parents and siblings, as well as inconsistent enforcement of rules and norms and ineffective supervision, have been identified as critical predisposing factors for later problems.[14]

- Epidemiological research points to the importance of *peer networks* on both the initiation and escalation of drug use. The transition to adolescence is characterized by a shift in values from those of the parents to those of the peer group, implying that friends and peers are important in providing opportunities for drug use and supporting this behaviour.[15]

- Further links have been found between drug use and other *social factors*, such as poor school attendance, poor school performance, and early drop out from school.[16]

- *Environmental influence* is also important, including the availability of psychoactive substances, the social rules, values and norms with regard to the use of tobacco, alcohol and illicit drugs (lack of community wide anti-drug use messages and norms), as well as lack of recreational programmes for children and adolescents after school and during weekend hours (which is the case in many countries).

- A consistent finding of many longitudinal studies of young people has been *that early onset of tobacco smoking and alcohol drinking* is associated with experimentation with cannabis and other drugs.[17] This does not imply that someone who drinks alcohol at an early age will automatically use cannabis or other drugs. Rather, it shows that among tobacco smokers and alcohol users, the risk of progression to cannabis and other drugs is much higher than if an individual has never smoked or consumed alcohol.[18] For this reason, some prevention activity has attempted to delay onset of smoking and alcohol use as a key objective. This assumption rests on the notion that early onset is a causal factor for drug consumption rather than an associated one.

- A number of risk factors associated with the *individual* himself or herself, have also been identified through research. These include low self-esteem ('shy'), poor self-control ('aggressive', 'impulsive personality traits'), inadequate social coping skills, sensation seeking, depression, anxiety and stressful life events.[19]

While much of the research in earlier years concentrated on the identification of risk factors, research in recent years started focussing more on the identification of *protective factors*. This shift was the result of apparent limitations in prevention programmes, concentrating too much on the reduction of risk factors which was not always possible. The strengthening of protective factors is nowadays seen to be at least as important (if not more important) than the reduction of risk factors. Some of the key findings have been:

- The *family* still plays a key role. Bonding and positive relationships with at least one caregiver or another significant adult outside the immediate family have shown to have a protective effect, as has high and consistent parental supervision. Children have to learn that their are limits of what they can do and what they are not allowed to do.

- Research also showed that *association with peers* who hold conventional attitudes, acts as a protective factor. Notably at a younger age, parents can still influence the selection of peers for their children.

- *Educational factors* such as high education aspirations and good teacher-student relations have shown to be protective factors.

- *Individual characteristics* such as a high self-esteem, low impulsivity, i.e. a stable temperament, as well as a high degree of motivation, were found to be protective factors.[20]

- General personal and *social competence* is important as well, and is reflected in 'feeling in control of one's life', feeling optimistic about the future, being able to detach from conflict in the home or neighbourhood, and being willing to seek support. Bonding to pro-social institutions, another expression of social competence, was also found to be a protective factor.

The risk and protective factors that are a part of a person's life may be seen as a *balance*. An accumulation of protective factors may counteract the negative influences of risk factors. The more risk factors a person is subjected to, the more likely substance abuse and related problems will occur.

Studies have shown that some individuals may experience several risk factors (e.g., poverty, chaotic neighbourhood and poor home life) and still avoid significant problems.[21] These individuals have been termed 'resilient'. They have been able to offset stress and adversity through their ability to cope and find support. However, when risks outweigh protective factors, even individuals who have been resilient in the past may develop problems. The balance is not simply determined by the number of risk and protective factors, but by their respective frequency, duration and severity, as well as the developmental stage at which they occur. Families, schools and community agencies can promote resiliency in young people by providing care and support, by presenting the child with positive expectations and by offering opportunities for participation.[22] Promoting resiliency or strengthening protective factors in a person is increasingly seen as preferable to focussing on weaknesses and problems.

A clear advantage of the risk/protective factor approach in modern prevention work is the awareness that many social and health problems are linked by the same *root causes*. This can lead to better integration of strategies and an economizing of resources. Although there is still something to be learned about risk and protective factors and how they interact, notably in developing countries, prevention programmes which pay attention to these factors are more likely to reach the roots of the problem and facilitate its solution than other, more superficial approaches which simply target some of the symptoms of drug abuse.

2.2.4. TARGETS AND TYPES OF PREVENTION

The complexity of the paths that lead to drug use have led to the development of several broad *prevention strategies*. All of these intend to provide tailor-made solutions to the specific problems of the groups at risk and associated groups.

Children and youth are common targets for prevention, as are parents and families. Other groups, which have particular risks associated with them, are often also considered priorities for prevention efforts. As a rule, the higher the risk for a group, the greater the needed inten-

Awareness raising, Viet Nam
© T. Haley/UNDCP

sity in prevention efforts.[23] Broad, lower-intensity efforts are usually aimed at the population in general. They aim at preventing people from engaging in risk behavior, and, if already involved, in leading individuals to contemplate changing their risk behaviours, or to recognize that they have a problem and request participation in a more personalized or intensive form of programme.[24]

As prevention budgets in many countries are limited, there is a need to search for the most cost-effective strategies. UNDCP, as well as many other agencies working in this field, have had considerable success in targeting potential '*multipliers*', such as teachers and social workers, or even one stage earlier, targeting institutions which educate teachers and social workers, to become familiar with drug prevention work and incorporate it into curricula and training seminars.

Prevention activities are sometimes divided into *primary* (preventing people from using drugs), *secondary* (convincing drug users, at the earliest possible point in time, to give up use and/or undergo treatment) and *tertiary prevention* (reducing some of the risks related to drug use, such as preventing needle sharing among injecting drug users in order to reduce the HIV

109

infection risk).[r] While all of these 'prevention goals' have their justification, care, however, must be taken that messages and interventions at one level do not endanger success of interventions at another level. Policy dilemmas in this field are, nonetheless, unavoidable. These dilemmas are resolved differently across the globe. While in the USA and in several Asian countries, for instance, 'primary prevention' is given clear supremacy, in several West European countries as well as in Canada and Australia, more emphasis – in cases of conflicting priorities – is given to secondary and tertiary prevention efforts.

Another categorization of prevention is: 'universal', 'selective' and 'indicated', according to the target group that is to be reached:[s]

- A broad or *'universal' prevention* programme aims to reach the general population or some broad sections of society to promote health and prevent the onset of substance use. Children and youth are usually the focus of universal prevention efforts. Measures associated with universal prevention include campaigns to raise awareness of the hazards of substance abuse, school drug education programmes, multi-component community initiatives, and, in the case of licit substances, warning labels.

- *'Selective' prevention* programmes target groups at risk such as children of drug users, students with poor school achievement, persons facing difficulties with relationships, or difficulties due to disability, problems of poverty, financial hardship etc. Selective prevention programmes aim generally to reduce the influence of these risk factors and to prevent or reduce substance abuse by building on

strengths such as coping strategies and other life skills. Notably children from difficult environments are often targeted to benefit from such 'selective prevention interventions', including at the pre- and early school ages.

- *'Indicated prevention* programmes' are designed for people who are already experimenting with drugs or who exhibit other risk-related behaviours that make them prone to hard-core drug abuse.

The various types of prevention approaches may include structural approaches, which aim at influencing the environment to make it less conducive to drug use, and communicative approaches[25], which are person oriented.

- Examples of *structural approaches* are programmes to reduce social problems related to substance abuse, like income support, employment and housing programmes. Perhaps even more important are initiatives that offer drug-free alternatives, like youth centres, sporting facilities and cultural events. Many of UNDCP's current programmes in developing countries contain a structural component. Law enforcement efforts to reduce the availability of drugs can also be considered structural approaches.

- *Communicative approaches* include (i) providing factual information and (ii) promoting psychosocial competence, so called 'life skills' training. Young people are informed about substances through many different sources like mass media, the Internet, peers, teachers, etc. The information, if not accurate, may work in two directions: to exaggerate the positive aspects as well as the risks. Even though *information dissemination* alone does not

---

r) According to WHO the definitions of primary, secondary and tertiary prevention are as follows: *"The aim of primary prevention is to ensure that a disorder, a process or a problem does not develop. The aim of secondary prevention is to recognise, determine or change a disorder, a process or a problem at the earliest possible point in time. The aim of tertiary prevention is to stop or delay the progress of a disorder, a process or a problem and the consequences thereof, even if the underlying condition continues to exist."*

s) The terms Universal, Selected and Indicative Prevention were described by R. Gordon in 1987, to replace the terms, primary, secondary and tertiary prevention. The model was adapted by the US Institute of Medicine Committee on prevention of mental disorders in 1994, and applied to substance abuse by the National Institute on Drug Abuse in a 1997 publication, *Preventing drug use among children and adolescents: a research-based guide.*

seem to have a measurable immediate impact on substance use in the target population, it is critical as part of other prevention activities. It can be argued that experience has shown the usefulness of factual information, the example of information on the harmful effects of tobacco smoking perhaps being the most striking. The key element of modern prevention work, however, centres on so-called *life skills development*. This includes teaching techniques and personal and social skills to deal effectively with demands and challenges of everyday life. Typical examples of such skills are:

- decision making,
- problem solving,
- effective communication,
- social skills,
- coping with stress,
- critical thinking,
- improving self-control,
- resistance to social pressure.

Research clearly shows that interaction is a key element in life skills training and that traditional, didactic teaching methods alone do not deliver an appropriate life skills education. A number of innovative approaches are frequently used to acquire such skills. Role plays to develop the skills to resist social pressure, for instance, have been shown to be effective in coping with peer pressure.

In a number of countries such kinds of prevention programmes are already being integrated into normal school curricula – and are showing promising results. In the Netherlands, for instance, a programme ('Healthy School and Stimulants') has been introduced in secondary schools which teaches facts relating to the risks of substance abuse and how to resist peer pressure. A subsequent evaluation showed that pupils participating in the programme had a

prevalence rate of drug use that was a third lower than those of the control group which had not participated in the programme.[t] A UNDCP prevention programme in Bogota, Colombia also shows evidence of success in its use of communicative approaches.

2.2.5. SOCIAL ENVIRONMENT/ DOMAINS FOR PREVENTION

Another frequently used categorization of prevention efforts is according to the 'key domains'. This categorization is useful because it highlights strengths and weaknesses of current prevention work.

Parents and families
Parenting is a particularly challenging role; yet in most countries, young parents receive little, if any, formal parenting preparation. This is particularly problematic as family and parental influence has repeatedly been found to be a significant factor affecting substance abuse and other risk behaviours by youth, particularly during early childhood when parental influence is greater than that of peers. Ideally, substance abuse prevention programming for parents should be provided during each phase of the child's growth:

- Early childhood education programmes that involve and support parents in nurturing their children may be effective in preventing substance abuse and a range of other later problems.[26] Interventions that aim to improve parenting practices have been found to reduce the onset of drug use, even when these interventions target adolescents.[27]

- Throughout later childhood and adolescence, prevention programmes can enhance parents' communication and discipline skills, while providing drug information and

---

t) Use of cannabis in the experimental group was 9.1%; in the control group it was 13.5%. Progress was also achieved with regard to licit substances: alcohol: 58.3% versus 66.7% and tobacco: 25.4% versus 29.3%. Weerdt I de, Jonkers R., Nierkens V., Jonkind S., "Begeleidend onderzoek De Gezonde School en Genotmiddelen: Stand van zaaken van het effect- en implementatieonderzoek per november 1997", Haarlem, 1997, quoted in EMCDDA, *1998 Annual Report on the State of the Drugs Problem in the European Union*, Lisbon 1998, p. 45.

access to counselling. The intensity of effort depends on the general level of risk associated with a target group and ranges from awareness-raising to multi-session programmes focusing on skills development and counselling.

Programmes should be based in the local community, and be made available over the course of a number of years so that they become integrated into the life of the community, as opposed to simply offering 'one-off' sessions. Parents are more likely to be committed to a prevention programme if they perceive it as being established and as having a good track record. Given the interconnectedness of drug problems with other social problems, integrating drug prevention activity into programmes designed to address other social problems would be appropriate.[28]

Schools

For a majority of drug users, substance use is initiated during the school years. In the USA, for example, two thirds of all initiation to drug use in 1998 took place among those 12 to 17 years-old.[29] Consequently, substance use prevention education programmes have been developed that – with variations – are intended for use at all educational levels. Such programmes may stand alone or, even better, be incorporated into a broader health or social skills module. A *typical programme* may include

- *for the early school years*, discussion of hazardous products, including solvents;

- through *the middle years* of schooling, prevention elements that aim at delaying initial use of alcohol and tobacco, and at deterring use of illicit drugs;

- by the *end of the school years*, components that caution against dangerous practices, including binge drinking, driving while under the influence of alcohol, mixing drugs, and engaging in unsafe sex.

School-based prevention is the most researched prevention area worldwide. Evidence supports an approach that lasts throughout the school career and which involves both students and parents. It also indicates that substance abuse prevention in the school setting is most successfully delivered as part of a comprehensive, community-wide approach, which integrates evidence-based health and drug education with school policies that promote general health. Active student participation, from the earliest years onwards, stimulates a positive, supportive climate.[30]

Research in the field of school-based prevention has furthermore come to the conclusion that prevention programmes for children and adolescents[31] should:

- be designed to enhance protective factors and attempt to reverse or reduce known risk factors;
- target all forms of drug abuse, including tobacco, alcohol, cannabis and solvents;
- include skills to resist drugs when offered; strengthen personal commitments not to use drugs; increase social competency (in communication, peer relationships, self-efficacy and assertiveness);
- when targeted at adolescents, include interactive methods, such as peer discussion groups rather than didactic teaching techniques alone;
- include a component for parents or caregivers that reinforces what the children are learning, and that provides opportunities for family discussion;
- be long term, taking place throughout the school career with repeat interventions to reinforce the original prevention goals;
- strengthen norms against drug use in all drug-abuse prevention settings (family, school, community);
- be adapted to address the specific nature of the drug-abuse problem in the local community;
- be more intensive and begin earlier the higher the level of risk experienced by the target population; and
- be age-specific, developmentally appropriate, and sensitive to culture and gender.

Out-of-school youth programmes

Out-of-school youth programmes provide an important setting for peer experiences. They can help to reduce a number of the 'precursors' to drug use, such as aggression, conduct disorders, lack of self-discipline, shyness, lack of school and family attachment, etc. The programmes vary widely, and range from theatre and dance groups to sport teams, business ventures and community service groups. Common to all is their offer of 'something to do' to fill leisure time and a sense of belonging to a group. Programmes that offer alternatives to drug use – providing opportunities for recognition and personal achievement through involvement in 'self-help' activities – have been found to be most effective for those most vulnerable to drug abuse.[32] Research indicates that the preventive value can be enhanced by encouraging participants to be involved in the management of the activities and by creating an environment of care, support and clear expectations. If basic drug education messages are incorporated into the regular activity of a sports team or arts group, this may greatly enhance the degree of credibility for those involved and reinforce messages received in other domains. Key elements are: establishing

Sports against drugs
UNDCP awareness raising programme   © UNDCP

prevention as a high-priority issue; choosing the 'right' leaders and providing them with support; creating a special group identity, and gaining the support of the local community.

Alternative programmes, including those involving some measure of risk (e.g., rock climbing, motocross racing), have been shown to be of value with high-risk youth.[33] These programmes are characterized by concerted, creative outreach and non-traditional prevention agents such as reformed gang leaders. Trained peers supported by professionals can be an effective method of reaching out to these people. Opportunities for leadership and skill-building are important, as is case management of the various problems facing the target group. In addition, close coordination of various services – health, social, housing and employment – is crucial in supporting high-risk youth.

Religious groups/communities

Different religious faiths reflect a wide range of attitudes regarding alcohol and other drug use; however, active affiliation is generally considered to be a protective factor in relation to substance abuse. Faith can be helpful in addressing some of the risk factors associated with substance abuse, such as feelings of isolation and lack of attachment. Because they are one of the few domains that attract both the elderly and the young, religious groups have the opportunity to foster contact and volunteer service between them. Many have been historically active in reaching out to marginalized people. A challenge and opportunity for such groups is to expand their outreach, focusing particularly on marginalized youth and young adults.

Workplace

Enterprises, however large or small, play a crucial role for prevention through their corporate policies and practices. Much of this lies in the simple assertion that work is central to people's lives. Business is most effective in contributing to substance abuse prevention when it promotes an approach that values *workplace well-being and safety*. When employees are healthy, it pays off for the company. Drug abuse can cause absenteeism, accidents, tardiness, and poor quality work. Clear and consistent messages against the use of drugs are crucial. At the same time, programmes should send a clear signal to the employees that they are valued and that the company recognizes the connection between their health and that of the company. A balanced approach recognizes that the company and its workers share the responsibilities and the benefits associated with effective action on substance abuse.[34] It also recognizes that the workplace can contribute to an environment that is less prone to substance abuse through certain working conditions or practices.[35] A policy which deals with a company's particular concerns, conforms with its corporate culture and includes a coordinated mix of several measures has proven to be most effective. This type of comprehensive action usually involves careful recruiting, employee education, supervisor training, providing means for identifying problems, and access to assistance for those requiring it. It is beneficial both for the company and the employee that offers of assistance are preferred to disciplinary measures.[36] Programme elements should be framed within a policy that draws broadly on employee input and is well communicated within the organization. The example of the USA has shown that the adoption of anti-drug programmes in the private sector contributed to a two-thirds reduction in the rate of positive drug test results over the 1988 to 1999 period.[u]

A positive outcome of such programmes is also achieveable in developing countries and countries in transition. A collaborative UNDCP/ILO/WHO model programme on drug and alcohol abuse prevention among workers and their families was implemented in a total of 38 workplace sites located in Egypt, Mexico, Namibia, Poland and Sri Lanka. At the end of 1997, when the model programme was independently evaluated, it was reported that following the introduction of the programme, the rate of absenteeism among workers had decreased in 66% of the workplace sites. In 59% of the sites there had been fewer disciplinary problems. In 47% of the sites there had been less on-the-job accidents and injuries and in 50% of the sites a substantial reduction in substance abuse-related problems (mainly alcohol-related) had occurred".[37]

Mass Media

Mass media campaigns are commonly used in the prevention of substance abuse. They help to increase awareness, though – unless carefully planned and tested – may be less effective in changing attitudes and behaviour. Media campaigns, however, have proven to be powerful instruments for primary prevention purposes. They have a strong potential to affirm existing anti-drug attitudes of youth who are not involved in drugs. Messages in the past, which were intended to simply arouse fear, by contrast, did not prove to be effective. Modern media campaigns, such as ONDCP's current five-year National Youth Anti-Drug Campaign (US$ 200 million), which started in 1997, use more sophisticated and targeted approaches, developed in close consultation with experts from various behavioural sciences, drug prevention, medicine as well as experts from teen marketing and advertising, and representatives from various professional, civic and community based organisations.[38] The approach has been, *inter alia*, based on evidence that social marketing, which involves all parties concerned, segments the audience and tailors messages, usually obtains better results. Prior to starting the campaign at the national level, messages were carefully elaborated and tested among representatives of the various target groups, and the campaign was well integrated into broader ongoing prevention activities. The results achieved thus far are impressive. The strong upward trend in drug use among youths (in contrast to the US population as a whole), observed over the 1991-1996 period, was reversed, notably among the younger age groups. The Monitoring the Future studies, which indepen-

---

u) Positive drug tests fell from 13.6% in 1988 to 4.7% in 1999 in the USA. ONDCP, *2000 National Drug Control Strategy*, Washington 2000, p. 48.

dently collect data on substance abuse among US high school students, showed that annual prevalence of drug use among 8th graders (14 year-olds) in the USA fell between 1996 and 1999 by 12%, and was in 1999 a third lower than could have been expected if the prior upward trend had continued (see Figure 12).

It is generally agreed that one of the greatest values of the mass media is in setting the agenda for broad community-wide prevention initiatives, that is to raise awareness of programmes, to promote participation in them, and to reinforce programme messages.[39] In other words, media campaigns have the strongest impact if they are integrated into broader anti-drug programmes and other outreach initiatives.

Experience has also shown that media campaigns aimed at young people are more likely to be effective if they take account of popular cultures that embody contemporary beliefs, tastes in music and fashion, and interest in new technologies. Youth cultures transcend borders, trends evolve rapidly and it is important to have representatives of the particular group concerned involved in designing and delivering prevention messages.

In addition to the classical media – magazines, radio and television – the *Internet* has proven in recent years to have a considerable potential for raising awareness of contemporary issues. As more people gain access to the Internet and use it to obtain information, web sites devoted to substance abuse reach ever-larger audiences.[40] The Internet, however, is also a medium for the diffusion of pro-drug messages, as well as for the exchange of information on illicit drug availability and production. As a consequence, contradictory messages about drug use and its desirability are readily available on the Internet. Against this background, every effort should be made to facilitate the setting up of sites which combine the provision of accurate, relevant information with attractive presentation for the respective target group. One of the key challenges for prevention programmers,

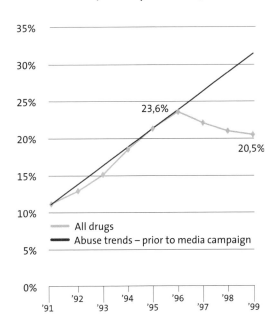

Fig. 12: Substance abuse among 8th graders in the USA (annual prevalence)

Legend:
- All drugs
- Abuse trends – prior to media campaign

Source: NIDA, *Monitoring the Future*, 1975-1999.

using Internet as a vehicle, is to segment the audience accordingly, and to provide targeted and developmentally appropriate substance abuse messages. Preliminary research indicates that Internet substance abuse prevention or health promotion sites are most useful when linked to other local prevention activities.[41]

Law Enforcement

Police officers are frequent participants in school and civic *educational efforts* in many societies. *Community policing*, an approach to enforcement that places emphasis on crime prevention through collaboration between police and the residents and community leaders in a neighbourhood, has the potential for reducing substance abuse in a community.

Law enforcement officers may be able to use the point of contact or arrest to provide information or referral. Typically, the percentage of those who take up services on this basis is low, but when this approach is well resourced, with project workers operating closely with police and making contact with those arrested at the police station or in court, it can be effective.[42]

Another approach – which has proven effective with regard to *secondary prevention* – has been the development of specialized *Drug Courts*. They attempt to prevent future drug use and other drug-related criminal behaviour through comprehensive court-directed treatment and rehabilitation programmes, usually integrating multidisciplinary teams of professionals committed to these goals. The system is based on swift, certain and consistent sanctions and rewards for non-compliance and compliance.[43]

2.2.6. KNOWLEDGE DEVELOPMENT AND TRANSFER – THE ROLE OF EVALUATION

A key element for successful knowledge transfer in the prevention field, of 'best practice' (i.e. of what works and what does not work), are project and programme *evaluations*. Evaluation is a specialized task requiring knowledge of experimental designs and statistics – expertise that many prevention practitioners lack. A successful prevention policy in the long run cannot exist without systematic evaluation of existing programmes and projects. UNDCP thus promotes the systematic evaluation of programmes and projects which are being implemented under its auspices. The only drawback is that evaluations tend to be rather expensive. Many prevention organizations are thus unwilling, and sometimes unable, to afford the associated costs. Yet, without proper evaluations, efforts and resources may be wasted. Some interventions may make things even worse. Effective programmes cannot be differentiated from poor ones, unless independent outcome evaluations take place.

Evaluations are also one of the main bases for research in the prevention field, which helps to generalize findings and provides input for improved prevention strategies in the future. As evaluation has become more common, research

is now beginning to demonstrate the effectiveness of some of the school prevention programmes.[44] This analysis needs to be extended to prevention activities in other domains and other target groups. There is also a vital need for the worlds of the 'practitioner' and the 'researcher' to be bridged and for more exchange and feedback between the two. These barriers can be overcome if funding bodies give evaluation greater priority by highlighting the benefits of continuously improving a programme, and, most importantly, by offering the financial and technical means to do so.[45] As practitioner competence and research rigour increase, and as theoretical foundations, core knowledge and training standards develop, prevention will be increasingly seen as a specialized field of study and practice – and evaluations will for obvious reasons form an integral part in this process.

In spite of the challenges and limitations, knowledge about prevention is now being generated at an unprecedented rate – and evaluations – in many countries – already play a key part in this process. Against this background, advocates of substance abuse prevention, however, should not only bemoan the low priority and the lack of funds made available for this key task in many countries, but must build on the progress made to date to demonstrate what many people innately believe – that prevention represents a sound social investment.

2.3. TREATMENT

2.3.1. TREATMENT AS A DEMAND REDUCTION STRATEGY

The term 'treatment' refers to a variety of activities and processes that focus on helping individuals with drug-related problems. Treatment has been defined by the experts of the World Health Organization[46] as the process that begins when psychoactive substance users come into contact with a health provider or other community service, and may continue through a succession of specific interventions until the highest attainable level of health and well-being is reached'. 'Treatment and rehabilitation' are seen as a 'comprehensive approach to identification, assistance, health care, and social integration of persons presenting problems caused by any psychoactive substance use'. The Expert Committee suggests that treatment should have three broad objectives:

- to reduce dependence on psychoactive substances;
- to reduce the morbidity and mortality caused by, or associated with, the use of psychoactive substances; and
- to ensure that users are able to maximize their physical, mental and social abilities and their access to services and opportunities, and to achieve full social integration.

Treatment is generally recognized as an essential component of a comprehensive demand reduction strategy, including in the Declaration on the Guiding Principles of Drug Demand Reduction.[47] In addition to helping individuals to reduce drug consumption, improve health status, reduce criminality and improve social functioning[48], treatment reduces drug abuse in an important segment of the population which, in most countries, is responsible for the bulk of the consumption of drugs such as heroin or cocaine. Estimates for the USA, for instance, suggest that a quarter of the cocaine using population accounts for two thirds of the consumption of this substance[49], and an even stronger concentration seems to apply for heroin. If treatment is readily available and a high percentage of drug abusers receive it, it can have a measurable effect on the overall demand for illicit drugs. With fewer untreated abusers involved in the recruitment of new users, prevalence of drug abuse is likely to decline as well.

For treatment to be an effective strategy which has an overall impact on drug demand, two conditions have to be fulfilled: (i) treatment has to be effective in reducing drug consumption, and (ii) a large enough number of drug dependent persons must have access to treatment so that the effectiveness is translated into an overall reduction with a measurable impact on the drug market.

Effectiveness of treatment

While it is well known that treatment is a long-term process in which 'relapses' are common, there is an increasing body of evidence which shows that despite this, treatment is an effective strategy in reducing drug consumption and related health and social problems. This also reflects the fact that drug treatment has made significant progress over the last two decades. Expertise in a number of treatment related fields has grown and ever more specific programmes are now available, at least in developed countries, to accommodate the specific needs and requirements of drug dependent persons.

A national treatment outcome study in the UK conducted in the late 1990s among 1,075 patients, for instance, showed that regular heroin use of people in residential treatment was 43% lower two years after the end of treatment. Regular use of cocaine and amphetamines fell by more than 60%, of benzodiazepines by 70%. In parallel, the rates of complete abstinence doubled for the use of opiates (from 24% to 51%) and for cocaine and amphetamines (from 30% to 65%) (see Figure 13). The total volume of acquisitive crime committed by people treated fell by more than three quarters, drug trafficking activities by more than 80%. These declines were even more important than the drop in the number of people who gave up trafficking and other illegal activities. Given the strong reductions in crime, calculations of economic costs suggested that every extra GBP 1 spent on treatment interventions, actually yielded GBP 3 in terms of immediate cost savings associated with lower levels of victim costs of crime and reduced demands upon the criminal justice system.[50]

Methadone maintenance and reduction programmes were also found to be effective. They showed even better results for curbing heroin abuse. They were, however, less successful than residential treatment programmes in reducing

Fig. 13: Residential treatment in the UK
2 year follow-up study on 'regular use'

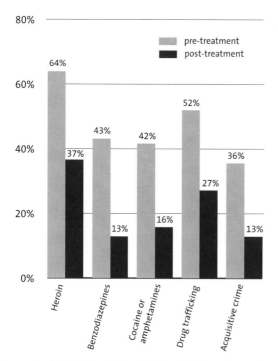

Source: Dept. of Health, *National Treatment Outcome Research Study*, London 1999.

Fig. 14: Treatment in the USA
1 year follow-up study on people treated in publicly-funded substance abuse programs in the 1990s

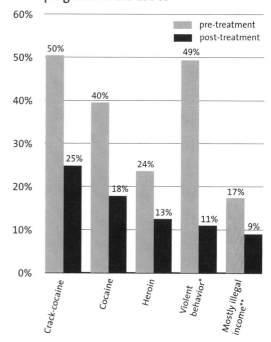

* 'beating up people'
** most support arises from illegal activities.

Source: SAMHSA, *National Treatment Improvement Study(NITIS)*, Sept. 1996.

regular use of cocaine and amphetamines, and in reducing the volume of acquisitive crime (see Table 3).

Similarly positive results for treatment outcome were also found in the USA. *The National Treatment Improvement Evaluation Study* (n = 5,388), which investigated the effectiveness of publicly funded treatment programmes, found a 47% decline in heroin use (annual prevalence) one year after treatment (see Figure 14). In the case of crack-cocaine and cocaine the improvements were even better: annual prevalence fell by more than half. Reports of the participants in the study were validated by urine tests in order to avoid under-reporting.[v] In parallel, violent behaviour declined by three quarters, which was also indirectly confirmed by a reduction in the

number of arrests by two thirds. Reliance on income from illegal activities dropped by almost half while income from regular employment rose by almost 20%. Homelessness fell by more than 40%. General risk behaviours also reduced significantly: unprotected sex fell by a third among heterosexuals and by about 60% among homosexuals and prostitutes.

The positive results of treatment were also confirmed in the *Drug Abuse Treatment Outcome Studies (DATOS)* – one of the largest such research efforts on the effectiveness of treatment worldwide – which were conducted in the 1990s under the auspices of the US National Institute on

---

v) The validation process revealed a tendency to under-report recent use (use during the last 30 days), but not the use over the past year. In self reports participants admitted – one year after treatment – recent use of cocaine/crack of 20.4% while urine tests (undertaken in half of the sample) found 28.7%; recent heroin use was admitted by 11.3% while urine tests found use by 16.2%. These deviations, however, do not affect the overall positive evaluation of treatment activities. (SAMHSA, *National Treatment Improvement Evaluation Study* (NTIES), Sept. 1996.)

Table 3: UK: National Treatment Outcome Study* follow-up 2 years later

	Residential treatment (data in % of people)			Methadone treatment		
	pre-treatment	post-treatment	change	pre-treatment	post-treatment	change
Regular heroin use	63.9%	36.6%	-43%	78.9%	40.0%	-49%
Regular benzodiazepine use	43.1%	12.9%	-70%	35.1%	14.9%	-58%
Regular use of cocaine and amphetamines	41.6%	15.8%	-62%	20.8%	10.8%	-48%
Injecting drugs	63.9%	36.6%	-43%	60.3%	42.2%	-30%
Injectors sharing needles	32.6%	13.5%	-59%	21.5%	11.5%	-47%
Abstinence from heroin	24.3%	51.0%	110%	10.0%	37.0%	270%
Abstinence from benzodiazepines	40.1%	76.7%	91%	48.9%	72.2%	48%
Abstinence from cocaine and amphetamines	29.7%	65.3%	120%	47.6%	66.8%	40%
Acquisitive crime (% of clients)	52%	27.2%	-48%	45.4%	21.4%	-53%
Average number of acquisitive crimes per client	22.5	5.1	-77%	23.4	8.7	-63%
Drug trafficking (% of clients)	35.6%	12.9%	-64%	24.3%	9.5%	-61%
Average number of drug selling crimes per client	48.1	8.3	-83%	25.3	5.2	-79%

* based on 1075 people entering treatment in 1995.

Source: Gossop, M., Marsden, J., Stewart, D., & Rolfe, A, "The National Treatment Outcome Research Study: Changes in substance use, health and crime: Fourth Bulletin"; Department of Health, London, 1999.

Drug Abuse (NIDA). The studies analyzed the treatment results of 96 programmes, and the situation of 10,010 patients in substance abuse treatment across the USA. The main success indicator used in these studies was reduction in 'hard-core use', i.e. use of drugs at least weekly. Applying this indicator, the results of treatment become particularly impressive. The studies – conducted one year after the end of treatment – found declines in the consumption levels of both cocaine and heroin by about two thirds, and a reduction in the involvement in illegal activities by more than half. The time span between initiation of drug use and treatment was 7 years.

As compared to the *National Multi-Modality Treatment Outcome Evaluation – part of the Drug Abuse Reporting Programme* (DARP) that studied the development of 44,000 clients admitted to 139 programmes between 1969-1972, the DATOS

results of the 1990s indicated improvements, notably with regard to heroin. The decline in heroin use in long-term residential treatment programmes, measured one year after the end of treatment, improved from 61% to 65%; in outpatient methadone treatment programmes from 64% to 69%.[51] Outcomes – in both the DARP and the DATOS studies tended to be better the longer clients stayed in treatment. For most programmes, three months were found to be a critical minimum level. Clients staying less than three months in treatment, in general, did worse than those remaining longer in treatment. Dropouts fared worse than people who remained in treatment.[52] Early engagement in treatment was associated with higher levels of post-treatment abstinence. *'Long-term residential treatment'* programmes (i.e. programmes which usually last from 4 months to 2 years) seem to achieve the best results overall but, they are also the most expensive. According to the

DATOS study of the 1990s, both weekly cocaine use and weekly heroin use were two thirds lower one year after having successfully completed treatment. Such results were even better than the success for the treatment of heavy alcohol consumption (see Figure 15).

The main difference – compared to other programmes – was the fall in illegal activities. Such activities dropped in long-term residential treatment programmes by some 60%, more than in other programmes. Based on in-depth interviews with a nationwide sample of cocaine-dependent clients, the average crime costs per client in 'long-term residential treatment' programmes were calculated to amount to US$ 20,700 p.a. prior to treatment. In the year following the end of treatment, such costs were shown to have fallen to, on average, US$ 4,600 p.a., equivalent to a reduction of drug abuse related crime costs by 78% (similar results as in the UK). Given average treatment cost in long-term residential treatment programmes of US$ 72 per day, a cost benefit ratio of 1.94 was calculated. This means that for each US$ 1 spent on treatment, one might expect savings on crime-costs of about US$ 2.[53]

Other programmes were found to be significantly cheaper (e.g. US$ 9 per day per client for drug-free outpatient programmes). As clients participating in these programmes were, in general, less involved in criminal activities prior to entering the treatment system, the cost-benefit ratios turned out to be slightly lower, though they remained clearly positive (savings of US$ 1.6 of reduced crime costs for each US$ 1 spent in drug-free outpatient programmes).

Drug-free outpatient programmes' (where clients are usually expected to stay from 3 to 6 months) were, nonetheless, found to be highly effective. Despite far lower costs per client treated (daily costs were just ⅛th of those in long-term residential treatment programmes), weekly cocaine use was still almost 60% lower one year after the end of treatment. It should be noted, however, that since the target populations of the

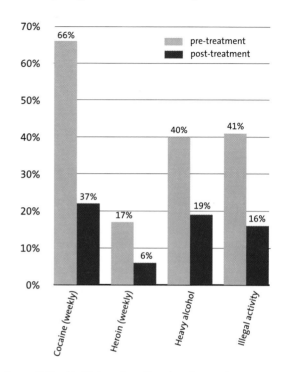

Fig. 15: Long-term Residential Treatment in US (one year after treatment)

Source: National Institute on Drug Abuse (NIDA), Drug Abuse Treatment Outcome Studies (DATOS), 1999.

different types of programmes are different, direct comparisons of cost effectiveness are difficult (see Table 4).

Good results were also achieved in the case of *'short-term inpatient treatment'* programmes, which usually last only up to 30 days. Weekly cocaine use was found to be two thirds lower in the follow-up study a year after the end of treatment. However, people admitted to these programmes usually have far less severe problems in the first place.

Similar to the UK example, outpatient methadone treatment programmes showed a substantial fall in weekly heroin use that was above average. The reduction use of cocaine, which is usually the secondary drug in these programmes was below average though still significant (almost half). However, no positive effects on heavy alcohol use could be identified. Engagement in illegal activities fell by half, but

Table 4: US Drug Abuse Treatment Outcome Studies – one year follow-up*

	Long-term residential treatment (21 programmes) in %; N = 2774			Short-term inpatient treatment (14 programmes) in %; N = 3,122			Outpatient drug-free treatment (32 programmes) in %; N = 2,574			20 Outpatient methadone treatment (29 programmes) in %; N = 1,540			Change (un-weighted average)
	pre	post	change	pre	post	change	pre	post	change	pre	post	change	
Cocaine weekly	66	22	-67%	67	21	-69%	42%	18%	-57%	42	22	-48%	-64%**
Heroin weekly	17	6	-65%	n/a	n/a	n/a	n/a	n/a	n/a	89	28	-69%	-67%
Cannabis weekly	n/a	n/a	n/a	30	11	-63%	25%	9%	-64%	n/a	n/a	n/a	-64%**
Heavy alcohol	40	19	-53%	48	20	-58%	31%	15%	-52%	15	16	7%	-54%**
Illegal Activity	41	16	-61%	26	11	-58%	22%	14%	-36%	29	14	-52%	-52%

* The studies are based on information obtained from 10,010 treatment admission over the 1991-93 period.
** Unweighted average, excluding outpatient methadone treatment programmes.
Source: National Institute on Drug Abuse (NIDA), *Drug Abuse Treatment Outcome Studies (DATOS)*, Washington 1999.

this decline (like in the UK) was below the reductions achieved through long-term residential treatment programmes.

Whatever methodological problems exist for comparing different treatment programmes, the key point to emphasize is that drug treatment in all its complex manifestations remains a highly effective strategy in reducing substance abuse (For more details, see Box 2D).

Impact of treatment on overall drug demand

Despite a number of studies which have demonstrated the effectiveness of treatment, the effects of treatment on the overall demand for drugs have not, for the most part, been assessed systematically yet. One analysis, of cocaine abuse in the United States in the early 1990s[54] suggested that by treating 6,500 heavy cocaine abusers a year, cocaine consumption could be reduced by one tonne a year. If this is the case, the admissions to treatment (230,000)[w] for cocaine abuse in both 1997 and 1998 could have contributed to a potential reduction of the US cocaine market by some 35 tonnes p.a., equivalent to a third of federal-wide cocaine seizures or about 10% of the total estimated size of the US cocaine market. Though the potential margin of error for such calculations is not negligible, the results do suggest that overall consumption can be significantly reduced through treatment.

This seems to be even more true for heroin where – compared to the overall heroin consuming population – a significantly higher proportion is in contact with the treatment system. While the number of admissions to treatment for cocaine abuse in the USA (233,000 in 1998) were equivalent to 7% of the estimated number

w) The number of treatment admissions is not identical with the number of people being treated. People can be treated for more than one year. Also, one and the same person can undergo several treatment episodes in a year. There is also some under-reporting as not all people admitted to treatment facilities are actually registered. In Sept. 1998 the overall number of people in treatment for substance abuse (incl. alcohol) was 1,138,002. The total number of admissions to treatment in 1998 (incl. alcohol) was 1,564,156, more than a third higher than the number of people in treatment in the census period; over the 1992-98 period, the number of admission were, on average, two thirds higher than the number of people in treatment. SAMHSA, TEDS, 1993-1998, *Treatment Episode Data Set (TEDS): 1993-1998, National Admissions to Substance Abuse Treatment Services*, Rockville, Maryland, Sept. 2000.

of hard-core users (3.3 million), the 216,900 admissions to treatment for heroin abuse in 1998, were equivalent to 22% of the estimated number of hard-core users (0.98 million).

Even higher proportions of the opiate consuming population seem to be in contact with the treatment system in a number of European countries – though comparisons – due to differences in definition – have to be treated with caution. In Italy, for example, 121,000 people were treated for heroin abuse in 1997, equivalent to 46% of the total number of problem drug users (263,000; range:172,000-326,000). In France, 49,300 people were treated in specialized treatment centres in 1997 for abuse of opiates, equivalent to a third of the total number of problem drug users (mainly opiates) of 155,000 (range:124,000-164,000). If substitution treatment is added, treatment involved 94,400 persons[x], equivalent to some 60% of the total number of dependent users of opiates. In Switzerland 19,000 people, and thus almost two thirds of the estimated problem users were in one or another form of treatment in 1998. Similarly, in the Netherlands, some 19,000 people were treated for heroin abuse in 1999, equivalent to about 70% of the estimated number of heroin problem users (25,000-28,000) in the country.

By contrast, in most developing countries and countries in transition the numbers of drug addicts being given access to treatment services are far smaller, clearly indicating the need to strengthen and expand the treatment infrastructure. While in the USA 837,000 admissions into the treatment system for drug abuse were reported in 1998, i.e. more than 3,000 per million inhabitants, and more than 530,000 people or more than 1,500 per million inhabitants, were in treatment in Western Europe, the corresponding rates were around 300 per million

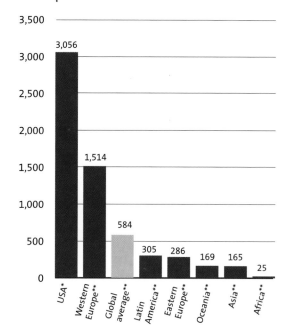

Fig. 16: Drug treatment per million inhabitants p.a. in the late 1990s

* Admittances to treatment (excluding alcohol) in 1998.
** 14 West European countries, 13 Latin American countries, 12 East European countries, 2 Oceanian countries, 25 Asian countries, 11 African countries; Global average based on information from 78 countries.

Source: UNDCP, DELTA.

inhabitants in Latin America, less than 300 in Eastern Europe, less than 200 in Asia and even less than 30 in Africa (see Figure 16).

Differences in the levels of addiction do not explain this huge gap between treatment in the developed and the developing countries. In most developing countries, the reported numbers of people treated range from a few dozen to a few thousand people compared to several thousand or more in a number of developed countries. Significant numbers of people being treated in developing countries were only reported from a handful of countries, including

x) The total number of people admitted to specialized treatment centres in France in 1997 was 60,170. 82% of treatment in specialized treatment was related to opiates (i.e. 49,340). Based on the sales of substitution substances – Subutex and methadone – the authorities estimated that 64,300 people in 1997 were under substitution treatment. In specialized treatment services, substitution treatment accounted for 32% of all treatment, i.e. 19,250. This means that 45,050 people were treated outside the specialized treatment sector. Together with overall treatment for opiates in the specialized sector, thus 94,390 people underwent treatment for opiates in France in 1997. (Observatoire Français des Drogues et des Toxicomanies, *Drogues et toxicomanies : Indicateurs et tendances – édition 1999, Paris 1999*, Chapter: 'Usagers de Drogues et Institutions'. http://www.drogues.gouv.fr/fr/index.html)

India (191,100 in 1999), the Islamic Republic of Iran (23,300 in 1997), Thailand (17,800 in 1998) and among former developing countries, Mexico (48,500 in 1999). Half of all treatment in Africa was reported from just one country, the Republic of South Africa. Significant treatment activities may take place in a few other developing countries, but they apparently do not have this information available. In most developing countries, there are, however, many forms of 'traditional healing'. Such kinds of treatment may be available to large sections of the drug abusing population, though this is not usually reflected in official treatment statistics.

There are, of course, limitations to treatment as a stand-alone demand reduction strategy. Not all drug abusers seek treatment, and those that do, tend to do so rather late in their drug abuse careers, which reduces the chances for success. Drug users also tend to relapse, and it may take several attempts until they can be considered cured.[y] Given the multiplicity of factors which affect both supply and demand, and the lack of

Celebration of the 26th of June the United Nations International Day Against Drugs, Peru © UNDCP

an appropriate treatment infrastructure in most countries, treatment, at the moment, is unlikely to play a significant role in reducing overall drug demand at the global level, even though it does this in a number of individual countries. This does not preclude treatment from playing such a role in the future. In any case, treatment in the context of a comprehensive drug strategy, can and should make an important contribution to demand reduction as a humane and cost-effective way of responding to those with drug problems. An increasing body of evidence from a number of countries supports the contention that treatment can represent a particularly cost-effective response to at least some patterns of drug abuse.

2.3.2. TREATMENT INTERVENTIONS

Treatment for drug abuse and dependence varies according to the activities and strategies used to relieve symptoms and induce change. The types of treatment offered are also distinguished by their underlying philosophies, goals, intended target groups and by the settings in which they are provided (outreach, outpatient or residential).

In general, five main modalities of treatment can be distinguished:
(1) biophysical
(2) pharmacological
(3) psychological
(4) therapeutic community, and
(5) traditional healing.

Mutual aid groups such as 'Narcotics Anonymous' are also an important resource for people seeking to overcome drug problems. As they, however, do not constitute a formal type of treatment, they are considered separately here. Programmes aimed at minimizing the adverse health and

---

y) The DARP studies in the USA mentioned earlier, which also investigated the outcome of treatment (which had taken place over the 1969-72 period) 12 years later, found that almost three quarters of the daily heroin users had relapsed one or more times to daily heroin use, and that they had, on average, 6 treatment admissions during their drug career. However, the study also found that 12 years after treatment, 75% had not used heroin on a daily basis during the past year, and 67% had not used it over the past three years, suggesting that two thirds of the people treated could be considered cured.

social consequences of drug abuse are not treatment programmes in a conventional sense, but they are often provided in tandem with treatment provision and may act as a conduit to treatment.

In practice, many agencies that provide treatment for substance abuse offer two or more modalities and also provide rehabilitation, relapse prevention and aftercare services. Programmes that provide pharmacological treatments usually offer some form of counselling or other psychological treatment as well. Various psychological approaches are used in therapeutic communities and in traditional healing. That said, differences between treatment regimens of the same type, even within countries, are often considerable. When one compares provision between countries, even more marked differences are found. It cannot be assumed that treatment provision of the same modality is uniformly delivered. Variations in therapeutic practice complicate the assessment of treatment effectiveness. Nevertheless, the list of modalities that follow, broadly characterizes the different therapeutic approaches found.

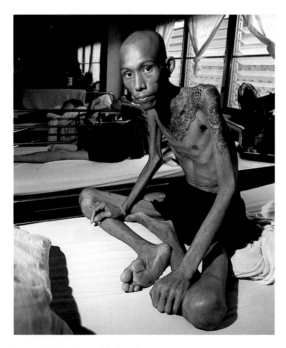

Treatment Centre, Thailand
© T. Haley/UNDCP

Detoxification

Although the term detoxification literally implies the elimination of toxic effects of drugs from the body, it is more widely used to refer to the management of the rebound symptoms of neuroadaption i.e. withdrawal and its associated physical and/or mental problems. In simple terms, the body having adapted in some way to the regular administration of a drug is actually thrown out of balance when the drug is no longer administered. This can produce a number of undesirable symptoms which the detoxification process is designed to manage. Detoxification is usually regarded as a distinct treatment modality. It can be also regarded as a 'precursor' for actual treatment. It deals with the withdrawal effects but does not address the psychological, social and behaviourial issues associated with drug abuse.

Complete detoxification is a requirement of most programmes with abstinence goals, and it may be a prerequisite for the successful treatment of some medical conditions. Detoxification is achieved either by the abrupt cessation of drug use or by a more gradual reduction. Support and monitoring need to be provided in accordance with the risks related to withdrawal from different substances since sudden withdrawal, notably from alcohol, barbiturates and benzodiazepines, can have life-threatening consequences. Support methods may include physiotherapy, acupuncture and herbal teas.

Acupuncture is used in detoxification programmes in several countries. There is some evidence for its effectiveness.[55] Though it is not entirely clear how it works from a medical perspective, practitioners claim that acupuncture stimulates the release of enkephalins and other endogenous opioids and thus reduces craving. Acupuncture may also have a strong placebo effect.

Pharmacotherapy may be used to support detoxification. It is most commonly used for detoxification from opioids, benzodiazepines and barbiturates. In the case of benzodiazepines and barbiturates, substances with similar pharmacological characteristics to the drug of dependence are used in decreasing doses over a short period of time.

Methadone, L-alpha-acetylmethadol (LAAM), buprenorphine, clonidine, and sedatives are among the substances most commonly used to facilitate the heroin detoxification process. Of these methadone (a synthetic opiate) and buprenorphine are the two most commonly used substances. A considerable research literature exists on the therapeutic use of these drugs in the heroin detoxification process.

Alternatively, accelerated or 'rapid' and 'ultra-rapid' detoxification methods have been used to a limited extent in some countries.[56] They involve the use of general anaesthesia which has raised concerns over the associated risks – and they tend to be costly. They thus remain controversial and are usually only appropriate in exceptional cases.[57] There is no strong evidence that accelerated detoxification increases the chances of long-term abstinence.[58]

Pharmacological Treatments

Pharmaceuticals are used in longer term therapies as well as in the management of acute drug withdrawal. In some cases, the aim is to treat depression or other mental health problems which coexist with substance abuse. However, there is an increasing interest in the use of pharmacotherapy to moderate processes in the brain that seem to contribute to persistent drug abuse.

Treatment for opioid dependence

Opioid[z] maintenance programmes aim at stabilizing addicts within the community and at helping them to move away from the use of illicit drugs to the point at which non-drug-use focused interventions can be introduced. Such programmes may maintain addicts on therapeutic doses of opioids for considerable peri-ods of time. Available evidence indicates that successful outcome is enhanced when a series of ancillary services are offered to the patients, such as counselling, interpersonal and social skills training, referral to medical and psychiatric services, HIV and other infectious diseases testing, education, vocational training and advice, and social support services such as housing. Opioid maintenance programmes tend to be strict with respect to enrolment and re-admission and require clients to submit to regular and supervised urine tests. The programmes are generally considered most suitable for older, long-term opiate abusers who have consistently failed to benefit from abstinence orientated programmes.

The use of rewards for abstinence from illicit drugs has been shown to reduce illicit drug use among clients.[59] These rewards may take the form of vouchers that can be exchanged for goods and services, and their value is increased with the number of consecutive drug-free urine samples provided.

The most commonly prescribed psychoactive drugs for the treatment of opiate dependence are shown in Box 2C. In adequate doses and with supportive therapy, opioid maintenance programmes were shown to reduce illicit opioid abuse and criminal activity, improve social functioning and productivity, reduce HIV transmission and improve pregnancy outcomes in addicted women.[60] Methadone, though not without problems, has been shown to be relatively safe for long-term use, and good outcomes are associated with retention in treatment.[61] Numerous studies have shown that LAAM can be as effective as methadone in reducing illicit drug abuse in opioid-dependent individuals.[62] Several clinical studies have shown that buprenorphine is effective in the treatment of opiate dependence as well.[63] Naltrexone has been

---

z) The term opioid is used as the generic term for any natural or synthetic drug that has morphine-like pharmacological actions although not necessarily sharing a similar chemical structure. It is also used to refer to the compounds occurring naturally in the brain which have opioid action such as the endorphins and enkephalins. The term 'opiate' is used for substances derived from the opium poppy and that are contained in opium, such as morphine and codeine; the term is also used for the semi-synthetic opioid diamorphine (heroin), which is manufactured from morphine. In practice, when the term opiate addiction is used it is usually referring to the abuse of heroin or opium.

investigated as a maintenance agent, but all the studies carried out reported high dropout rates early on in treatment. Naltrexone may be, nonetheless, useful in treating highly motivated individuals.[64] Clients starting on naltrexone must be free of opioids for at least seven to ten days prior to treatment, otherwise a withdrawal syndrome may be precipitated.

Substitution treatment is, of course, not without problems. Methadone, LAAM and buprenorphine are not effective in all cases. Some heroin addicts report that these drugs do not reduce their craving for heroin or that they have unpleasant side effects. This is frequently a question of dosage. While higher dosages can prevent heroin addicts from having feelings of craving, they strengthen the negative side-effects from the substitution substances, and *vice-versa*. The behavioral requirements of some substitution programmes have also limited their appeal for some addicts. A potentially more serious problem is that some of the substitution substances end up on the illicit markets as addicts manage to sell them in order to obtain the financial means for buying their

---

Box 2C: The main drugs used in the treatment of narcotic dependence

Name of drug: Methadone
Mode of action and main effects
Methadone is a synthetic opioid that binds to the same receptors as endogenous (opioids naturally produced in the body) and exogenous opioids (other opioids not produced in the body). Because of its similar pharmacological effects, methadone prevents withdrawal symptoms in opioid-dependent people. It is used in the management of opiate withdrawal and for the maintenance of addicts. The main advantages of methadone are that it can be taken orally and that its effects last for 24 hours

Name of drug: LAAM – L-alpha-acetylmethadol
Mode of action and main effects
LAAM is a synthetic opioid that can also be used as a maintenance drug. It is chemically related to methadone and like methadone is orally active, in other words produces its effect when taken by mouth. However, it has a longer duration of action (2-3 days). The onset of action is slower compared to methadone and the time to reach maintenance levels is also longer with LAAM (8-20 days) compared to methadone (5-8 days). LAAM should not be administered daily because of drug accumulation and the danger of overdose. LAAM has been available since 1993 in the USA for the treatment of opiate dependence, but it is not available in all countries.

Name of drug: Buprenorphine
Mode of action and main effects
Buprenorphine is a partial agonist (in simple terms an agonist is a drug that is capable of combining with a cell receptor and stimulating or initiates a biochemical response) which is dissolved under the tongue and used for opioid maintenance. It exhibits a ceiling effect (increasing the dose only increases the effect to a certain point). It is thus safer than full agonists such as morphine or heroin and less likely to produce respiratory distress. Buprenorphine withdrawal symptoms are milder than those for methadone. In order to reduce the abuse potential of buprenorphine, naloxone – a narcotic antagonist (in simple terms an antagonist is a substance that is capable of inhibiting the effect of a target substance by binding to a cell receptor and displacing the original drug and nullifying, counteting or reversing its effect) which reverses the respiratory, sedative and hypotensive effects of heroin overdose, has been added to some buprenorphine tablets. Buprenorphine is currently not available in all countries.

Name of drug Naltrexone
Mode of action and main effects
Naltrexone blocks the effects of opioid drugs, but it produces no pharmacological effects of its own. In a person who is opioid-free, naltrexone produces no discernible effects. However, if it is administered to someone who is physically dependent on opioids it will precipitate withdrawal. It will also cancel out the effects of other opioids taken concomitantly. It is orally active and long-acting (1-2 days). It has been indicated to help highly motivated drug addicts keep abstinent.

drugs of first choice as addicts are often reluctant to forgo the sense of euphoria (rush) that they experience when injecting heroin. Some death cases have already been associated with diverted substitution drugs. A related trend in a number of European cities in recent years, has been the increasing use of illegally acquired crack-cocaine by people in methadone maintenance programmes as these stimulants apparently provide them with the much desired sense of euphoria. The addiction problem is thus widened even further.

Some practitioners have advocated prescribing injectable preparations, such as injectable methadone. Far more rarely, and more controversially, some European countries have started to experiment with injectable diacetylmorphine (heroin). The medical prescription of heroin has long been a feature of treatment of heroin addiction in Britain. However, following some cases of diversion to clandestine markets and the dubious role played in this by at least one medical doctor in the 1960s, few British doctors are nowadays licensed to prescribe heroin for addiction and most of them rarely do so.[65] Injectable preparations of methadone are more commonly prescribed for intractable injectors – but again this remains a rare response. Oral preparations of methadone are most commonly used. In Switzerland, following a much publicized and still controversial evaluation[66], the medical prescription of heroin for the treatment of addiction has been approved. A major impetus for the Swiss heroin trials was the high incidence of HIV infection in the population of injecting drug users and the highly visible nature of the drug scene in Zurich and other cities. The External Evaluation Panel on the Evaluation of the Swiss Scientific Studies of Medically Prescribed Narcotics to Drug Addicts found improvements in the health status and social functioning in the individuals treated, but concluded that no causal link could be established between the prescription of heroin and these improvements[76]. A further evaluation of heroin prescription is proceeding in the Netherlands and additional trials have or are being developed or discussed in Australia, Belgium, Canada, Germany, and Spain. Alternative modes of delivery for heroin (including reefers for smoking, nasal sprays, and rectal suppositories) have been studied, but these have not generally been made available[68] to patients.

Problems associated with heroin prescription are – apart from serious ethical considerations – the high costs of such programmes – resulting from the need to take necessary precautions to prevent diversions. This makes such programmes, *de-facto*, not appropriate for implementation in developing countries, countries in transition and a number of developed countries with limited financial resources for treatment. The programmes also require trustworthy and dedicated staff who are not tempted by the opportunities to generate extra income. Societies which are so resilient to corruption are, however, not easy to find, in the developed or developing world. A more fundamental problem is whether the authorities should provide a dangerous and potentially lethal substance – which in a number of cases will lead to death – on the grounds that the overall likelihood of morbidity and mortality were higher if such a substance were to be bought through clandestine channels. This is a clear ethical dilemma (which to some extent also exists in the case of other substitution substances) that is not easy to solve. It should be clear, however, that heroin prescription, even in countries where it takes place, is not *the* solution to the drug problem. It can, at best, be the ultimate response for dealing with the small group of the most severe drug addicts who are heading towards almost certain death, and who would not be susceptible to any other form of treatment. An effective treatment infrastructure, however, should avoid such severe forms of addiction from developing in the first place.

Treatment for dependence on other drugs
There are no specific pharmacotherapies for the prevention of relapse among people dependent on sedatives or anxiolytics (central nervous system depressants with the capacity of

relieving anxiety and inducing calmness and sleep). Amphetamine has on occasion been prescribed for amphetamine dependence[69] but this remains a rare and largely experimental response. Further research on this treatment is currently being conducted in the United Kingdom. No strong evidence is available to allow the effectiveness of this response to be judged.

To date, no pharmacotherapeutic agents have been approved for the treatment of cocaine abuse and dependence. However recent research indicates the potential of two classes of drugs, *antidepressants* and *dopaminergic compounds*. The rationale for studying antidepressants is based on reports of depression following cessation of cocaine abuse. Several antidepressants have been tried, though with limited success.[70] The rationale for using dopaminergic agents was based on the finding that the reinforcing properties of cocaine are mediated through the neurotransmitter dopamine, and that chronic cocaine abuse over stimulates the dopaminergic reward system, resulting in dopamine depletion. Dopamine agonists have been used to counteract the effects of dopamine depletion. Although they have been shown to reduce cocaine abuse and cravings in some clinical trials[71], these effects have not been confirmed in others.[72] Many other pharmacological agents have been investigated with limited success.[73]

Recent animal studies have shown promising results with the use of vaccines against the behavioural effects of cocaine and nicotine.[74] These vaccines stimulate the immune system to create antibodies that bind to molecules of the active drug and form molecules that are too large to pass the blood/brain barrier. If the active drug cannot pass the blood/brain barrier it will not reach the brain and will not produce its psychotropic effects. Animal studies have shown a marked reduction in the reinforcing effects of drugs that stimulate drug-specific antibodies after vaccination. However, there are no studies of the effects of vaccines on drug use in humans and this remains a promising area for further research.

NON-PHARMACOLOGICAL INTERVENTIONS

Biophysical interventions
Acupuncture is used for treatment and in relapse prevention[75], especially in Eastern European countries and in the Middle and Far East. It is also increasingly used in some Western European countries as a complimentary therapy to other interventions. For example, to help relieve withdrawal distress during detoxification.

Psychological/counseling interventions
A wide range of activities and processes fall under this heading, although there is no clear consensus as to how they should be distinguished or classified. Two broad categories of psychological treatment are generally recognized – interventions based on *behavioural principles* and those based on *psychodynamic principles* – each of which reflects different assumptions about the nature of substance abuse and the recovery process. Behavioural treatments postulate that substance abuse is the result of maladaptive learning and that recovery involves relearning or unlearning patterns of behaviour that contribute to persistent substance abuse. In contrast, psychodynamic treatments are based on the assumption that substance abuse is a symptom of childhood conflicts and that recovery requires these conflicts to be resolved.

Further classification of treatments within these two categories is complicated by differences in the way they are described by different practitioners and researchers. Some 'named' treatment approaches involve several distinct components. For example, 'relapse prevention' can be described as a separate form of treatment or as a component of 'cognitive therapy'. Relapse prevention and other treatments outlined in a recent report from the US National Institute on Drug Abuse[76] encompass a variety of distinct treatment techniques. For example, some models consider relapse prevention, counselling and support, referral to self-help, education, urine testing and family and group therapy under the same heading.

A useful approach to understanding different forms of treatment is to focus on the key components of each one and to look at how these are utilized to achieve particular objectives at different stages in the rehabilitation and relapse prevention process.[77] A summary of treatment strategies and their effectiveness is provided in Box 2D. Most of these treatments are broadly based on behavioural principles. The exceptions are Ericsonian Psychotherapy, which has its roots in psychoanalysis, and a form of client-centred therapy influenced by the humanistic writings of Carl Rogers. Many other types of psychodynamic therapy have

been proposed, but few have been evaluated and their effectiveness is in doubt. Most are long term and only available to clients willing to pay the high fees charged by their practitioners. Brief descriptions and some indications of specific interventions are given below. Further evidence for the effectiveness of some other types of therapy is summarized in Box 2D on treatment effectiveness.

The technique of using *confrontation* to 'break through clients' denial' of drug problems is quite commonly used. Some approaches involve the forceful presentation of evidence of drug abuse

---

Box 2D: The effectiveness of services and treatments for substance abuse disorders

This box, based upon selected evaluations, summarizes the evidence on the impact of three major types of treatment: drug substitution, psychosocial counselling, and residential rehabilitation.

Background

The usual practice with treatment outcome evaluations is to first interview a representative sample of the people entering the particular treatment option. The extent of these clients' problems is then measured, typically across the core domains of substance use, health risk behaviour, physical and psychological health status and problems, and personal and social functioning (e.g. relationship difficulties, employment, housing, and criminal behaviour). Measures in these areas are then reassessed at one or more points during and after treatment. In addition to assessing change on these primary measures, research evaluators are increasingly interested in recording the costs of the treatments studied and evaluating their economic effectiveness. While clinical and economic measures can be relatively straightforward to gather, reporting outcome is more challenging. Nevertheless, there is a substantial literature which shows that well-structured treatment achieves positive gains, both during and after treatment.

Drug substitution

Opioid substitution prescribing is the most widely evaluated treatment for heroin and opioid dependence. Internationally, there is a well-established evidence base for substitution treatment with oral methadone (MMT) which is associated with lower rates of heroin consumption, reduced levels of crime, improved social functioning, lower mortality and reduced rates of HIV risk behaviours. In 1998, Marsch reported the results of a statistical meta-analysis of 11 MMT outcome studies and eight and 24 studies investigating the effect of MMT on HIV risk behaviours and criminal activities, respectively.[78] These analyses show a consistent, statistically significant relationship between treatment and the reduction of illicit opiate use, HIV risk behaviours and drug and property crimes.

Psychosocial counselling

Psychosocial counselling is an important treatment for people with drug problems and it is considered a valuable element of treatment programmes. It can be provided in residential or community/outpatient settings, but only some of the broad range of counselling modalities have been evaluated with drug abusing populations.

The overall goals of counselling relate to changes in substance use behaviours and improvements in several areas of personal and social functioning – including family and social relationships, employment, and crime. From the programmes studied, there is evidence of positive impact on these dimensions. For example, general outpatient abstinence-oriented counselling programmes in the USA have been evaluated as part of the national series of field evaluation studies and the results highlight reductions in drug use and crime involvement as well as improvements in health and well-being. Drug use outcomes for outpatient drug free programmes, which contain a counselling element reported by the Drug Abuse Treatment Outcome Study[79], show positive impact on the use of heroin, cocaine, cannabis and alcohol.

In terms of specific psychotherapy modalities, brief motivational therapy has been used successfully with opiate users in oral methadone maintenance treatment. Psychotherapies which are focused, time limited and incorporate behavioural elements, notably contingency reinforcement therapy, have also produced encouraging results. Relapse-prevention oriented, cognitive-behavioural therapies (CBT) have received the most frequent evaluation. Some 24 randomized controlled trials of CBT have been conducted among adult users of tobacco, alcohol, cocaine, marijuana and opiates. There is good evidence for the effectiveness of this approach, compared with no-treatment controls or in contrast with alternative therapies. In particular, positive results have been found in respect to treatment compliance and abstinence. Some studies have suggested that a CBT approach may be particularly appropriate for severely dependent or depressed users.

Residential rehabilitation programmes
There is good evidence from research conducted in several countries for the positive benefits of residential rehabilitation. The majority of studies have evaluated Therapeutic Community (TC) programmes and the evidence points to the considerable success of these services in achieving post-discharge reductions in illicit drug use. For example, in the Treatment Outcome Prospective Study (TOPS) regular use of illicit drugs (weekly or more frequent consumption) was reported by 31% of clients in the year prior to admission in residential programmes. For those clients who had received at least 23 months of treatment, this rate reduced to zero during the first 90 days of treatment, then stabilized across three further points: (i) three months after treatment (11%); (ii) one year after treatment (11%); and (ii) 3-5 years after treatment (12%). Drug use outcomes for long-term residential and short-term inpatient treatment programmes, as studied by the US – Drug Abuse Treatment Outcome Study (DATOS) also show positive outcomes for both types of treatment.

Similar data from the UK (National Treatment Outcome Research Study[80]) has reported outcomes after discharge from eight inpatient units and 16 residential rehabilitation programmes. One-year follow-up results show a decreases in the use of opiates stimulants, levels of injecting and HIV risk behaviour.

KEY ISSUES
Understanding treatment process: client, counsellor and environmental factors
In addition to gathering information on the outcomes of the treatments summarized above, important advances have been made in understanding what happens during treatment and how this has an impact on outcome. Various factors have been studied, including a client's readiness for change (motivation), initial engagement in the programme, and the establishment of a positive therapeutic working relationship with the counsellor. For example, treatment readiness has been found to be predictive of retention and early therapeutic engagement for clients entering long-term residential treatment, outpatient methadone and drug-free counselling programmes. Findings also suggest the importance of attributes of the counsellor. Effective counsellors have been found to possess good interpersonal skills, be organized in their work, see their clients more frequently, refer clients to ancillary services as needed and generally establish a practical and empathy "therapeutic alliance" with the client. Therefore it appears that both client and counsellor attributes are important in achieving positive treatment outcomes.

Outside of the therapeutic process, social supports and stressors (e.g. a substance dependent spouse) in the client's social environment can exert a powerful influence on outcome and treatment gains and may attenuate rapidly if his/her social resources are limited. This risk can be compounded by an imbalance found in many treatment programmes, which (due to understandable practical necessities) focus on initial behaviour change and substantially less on the maintenance of change in clients' social environment. Overall, those programmes which are able to help clients improve their community integration and stability, address life problems, family relationships and enhance personal resources, are more likely to be effective.

Expanding evaluation efforts
There are political imperatives to gather information on the routine performance of treatment services. Most evaluation studies have focused on the "main effects" of treatment for a sample of clients. Increasingly, treatment strategists and the research community are looking at the outcomes for priority groups, including young people; people with psychiatric and substance use co-morbidity, the homeless, and people from ethnic minority communities. Treatment process and outcome studies are now especially needed to inform the development of services in these areas. National drug control strategies are also using a performance measurement framework to assess the impact of treatment services, not just on one occasion, but regularly across time to assist in the evaluation of overall policy. For example, the US Drug Control Strategy has estab-

and related problems, while others involve less forceful presentation and information about the effects of drugs. Some limited evidence concerning the effectiveness of forceful confrontational methods with alcohol and drug abusers raise, however, some questions as to the appropriateness of this method.[81]

Many therapists use some type of *client-centred counselling* approach to increase client motivation. This was originally developed by Carl Rogers and is a type of therapy concerned with self-actualization and freedom of expression. It is often characterized as a holistic or *Gestalt* approach to treatment. The techniques of *motivational interviewing* or *motivational enhancement therapy*[82] are also grounded in Rogers' work. These involve an initial assessment and discussion about drug use to help clients identify personal reasons and objectives for change. Therapists then seek to strengthen motivation using interviewing techniques that focus on the issues felt by clients to be the most important. Where appropriate, therapists provide suggestions for dealing with high-risk situations. Over the course of treatment, therapists and clients review progress and continue to seek ways of achieving agreed-on objectives. Clients are sometimes encouraged to bring close friends or family members to treatment sessions.

Ericsonian psychotherapy is similar to hypnosis except that the therapists do not induce trance states, but use metaphors or storytelling to encourage clients to articulate problems and solutions. Storytelling helps clients to discuss issues that otherwise would raise too many anxieties. The goal of this approach is to help to reduce client resistance to change.

Cognitive therapies aim to identify and modify thoughts and beliefs that contribute to drug abuse. They are based on the assumption that drug abuse partly stems from negative emotional states that can be caused or aggravated by the ways in which the drug abuser thinks about him/herself and the world in general. These therapies require clients to monitor their thoughts to identify those that are irrational or maladaptive, and those associated with depression or craving for drugs. Therapists then help clients to develop different ways of thinking and new positive self-statements (e.g. I am trying hard to overcome my problems) that can be substituted for previous negative statements (e.g. I am a worthless person). Cognitive therapies that focus on relapse situations (see box on treatment effectiveness) have shown good results.

Thought stopping is another technique designed to alter cognitions. Clients are taught to say, 'Stop' either aloud or silently whenever they find themselves having intrusive, negative thoughts. They may also be advised then to think about something peaceful or relaxing.

Central to the principles of *behavioural therapy* is the view that all behaviour is determined by its expected or desired outcome. The underlying assumption is that learning processes play an important role in the development and continuation of abuse and dependence[83]. These therapies have specific objectives of altering the outcome and expectancies of drug-related behaviours through the development of coping strategies which will then allow positive reinforcement to arrive from non-drug-related activities. A very simple example would be for an individual whose reaction to stress was to use drugs, a behaviourial intervention that seeks to encourage an alternative rewarding behaviour. As indicated in Box 2D, several psychological treatments incorporating behavioural techniques have shown encouraging results in the

Community awareness raising
© UNDCP

treatment of dependence on different substances. Often in practice behaviourial therapy is combined with cognitive approaches. For example, typically relapse prevention interventions combine both behaviourial and cognitive elements. Some types of *marital/family therapy* also use behavioural principles and family members are taught how to reward appropriate forms of behaviour and to avoid others which reinforce or facilitate drug abuse and other inappropriate activities.

Alterations of environmental contingencies are central to *community reinforcement* treatment. This has proved successful in the treatment of alcoholism, and has shown promising results in several of the programmes for drug abusers described in recent reviews by NIDA.[84] In these programmes, therapists and clients seek to involve family members (sometimes employers and other agencies) in agreements to reward clients for abstinence or to withhold privileges should they use drugs. A contingency in this sense can be understood by the following example: when an individual demonstrates a positive behaviourial change, such as providing a drug clean urine sample at a drug treatment center, they are then rewarded for this in some way, for example with a food voucher – the reward is

therefore *contingent* upon the positive behavioural change. Employers may, for example, agree to provide random drug testing for clients who have had drug problems, and to sanction those who test positive. Families may also be asked not to contest criminal sanctions against members arrested for drug-related offences. Arrangements for the use of positive contingencies can also be made. For example, therapists may ask family members to support abstinent clients in their efforts to return to work and reintegrate into the community.[85]

Some interventions focus specifically on the circumstances of drug use. They may simply provide advice about ways of avoiding these situations or else focus on alternative uses of leisure time. Two 'named' interventions of this type are *self-control training* and *drug refusal training*. The first involves self-monitoring of urges to take drugs, setting goals for drug use (abstinence or limited use), developing self-initiated rewards for meeting these goals (e.g., using money saved to purchase goods) and the analysis of high risk situations. *Drug refusal training* involves teaching clients how to say 'no' to drugs. Often role playing is used, whereby clients practice establishing eye contact and using appropriate body language and words to indicate that they do not wish to take drugs, and which help them to avoid being pressured to do so.

Cue exposure is a form of counter-conditioning. Clients are helped to identify the internal and external cues that trigger the desire for drugs – for example, certain thoughts and feelings, sights, sounds or smells. Clients develop a hierarchy of cues ranging from the lowest to highest capacity to excite cravings. They are then taught how to achieve a state of deep relaxation, and are exposed to the cues in ascending order of powerfulness. Once clients are able to remain calm in the presence of a cue that previously induced anxiety, the therapist introduces a cue further up the hierarchy. Gradually clients learn to remain calm in the presence of all cues, and can transfer this ability to real-life situations.

Many treatment programmes include some kind of educational component. There is, however, little evidence that education *per se* reduces drug abuse among experienced drug users. A form of education known as *bibliotherapy* has been used with some success with early-stage problem drinkers. It involves the use of written self-help materials that give concrete advice about changing substance use and related habits.[86] Sometimes this is supplementary to therapist-led treatment.

Therapeutic communities

Therapeutic communities are nowadays found in a number of countries. Local traditions and cultures have influenced their development. Therapeutic communities aim to change the negative patterns of behaviour and feelings that are assumed to underlie drug abuse. In order to achieve this, they encourage socialization within a highly structured environment which rewards honesty, trust and self-help and discourages negative thoughts and behaviours. Components common to most therapeutic communities are (1) consistently reinforced expectations of certain types of behaviour (2) increased responsibilities and privileges contingent on appropriate behaviours (3) social learning and role-modelling processes, including peer pressure to participate in behaviour that expresses positive values such as acceptance of a non-violent, drug-free life and the healing power of the community. Increasingly, therapeutic communities also help clients to improve their educational and employment skills, and some have onsite programmes where these can be acquired.

Originally, therapeutic communities required residents to stay for lengthy periods, and in some cases, long-stay residents were recruited as staff members or encouraged to help found new communities. Currently, therapeutic communities differ widely with respect to their required length of stay. Some only require a short period of residence followed by a lengthy period of day or outpatient treatment. Research though suggests that longer stays are associated with better outcomes.[87]

Therapeutic communities sometimes include family programmes and programmes for women, adolescents, people with HIV and other special populations. Some mainly serve people from the correctional system. Many programmes in prisons are based on therapeutic community principles.

Traditional healing

Traditional healing involves the use of 'non-orthodox practices based on indigenous cultural treatment which operate outside official healthcare systems'.[88] These are often based on Islamic, Buddhist, Hindu and other religious beliefs and healing traditions, and are particularly widespread in Africa and Asia. However, programmes that incorporate beliefs and practices of indigenous peoples have also been developed in North and South America, Australia and New Zealand, which clearly shows that there is not only a North-South know-how transfer but also a South-North and a South-South transfer of knowledge of how to deal with problems of drug addiction. Common elements in these programmes are:

- Ritual and other ceremonies conducted by traditional healers who perform incantations and invocations, and make use of sacred objects and images;
- Cleansing rituals;
- Confessions, pledges and sacrifices, and various forms of catharsis, or purging.

Drug abusers, their families and other members of the community are frequently invited to participate in healing ceremonies, which is to strengthen the will of the drug dependent person to overcome his or her addiction and to facilitate social reintegration thereafter. In many developing countries, traditional healing is the only source of help available for drug abuse. Elsewhere, traditional and modern health services coexist and cooperate to a greater or lesser extent. In North America, for example, traditional native healing practices such as sweat lodges and sweet-grass ceremonies are sometimes used in programmes that also provide professional counselling.

Most traditional healing programmes have not been rigorously evaluated but there is much anecdotal evidence that they are helpful in many cases. Buddhist treatment centres in Thailand have been shown to have post-discharge abstinence rates comparable to those for modern medical institutions.[89] Experimental studies have shown that the herbal medicines used to treat addicts in Malaysia effectively reduce the craving for opiates.[90]

The major advantages of traditional healing methods are their low cost and high levels of acceptability. From the perspective of health care service planning and development, however, they are often secretive and difficult to regulate. Some procedures and remedies used in traditional healing practices may even have potentially harmful effects. However, experience shows that traditional healers and professionals can work together. Traditional healers are willing to share information with and take advice from professionals who show due respect for their beliefs. Descriptions of a number of traditional treatment methods were provided in UNDCP's *1997 World Drug Report*.

2.3.3. SOCIAL REINTEGRATION AND AFTERCARE

One of the most critical phases for ultimate success of treatment is the phase of social re-integration. Former addicts often face severe problems of adaption when moving from the protected and well-structured environment of a therapeutic community, back to 'normal life'. There is a considerable risk that, facing a number of frustrations in the reintegration process, they will eventually search for their old friends and acquaintances in the drug scene. Drug abusers engaged in a treatment process usually need help, not only to acquire social and vocational skills to be better prepared for the life outside, but to establish or re-establish links with the community and to find accommodation and employment. Case managers can play an important role in this process and, where

appropriate, they can assist clients in gaining access to appropriate services and programmes such as welfare, housing allowances and job training. Some programmes have alumni associations that assist discharged clients to establish themselves in the community, and these will draw on family members and friends to help in the process where possible.

Aftercare is usually understood as a phase of treatment that follows completion of a time-limited programme. The objective is to prevent relapse and to improve social and psychological functioning. In practice, aftercare ranges from the occasional telephone contact with a therapist or case manager to regular individual or group meetings. Many programmes refer clients to mutual aid groups for aftercare. A number of early studies have shown positive relationships between involvement in continuing care and improved post-treatment functioning of people treated for drug and alcohol problems.[91]

Mutual aid

Two types of mutual aid groups have been developed by people with drug problems. The best known and most common is Narcotics Anonymous, (NA) whose members seek to overcome their addiction through self-change. The other consists of networks or associations of active drug users which assist drug consumers to reduce high-risk behaviours (e.g., through information, education and the distribution of clean needles). Some of these networks are involved in programme and policy development, and seek to reduce the stigma of drug dependence. These groups have been most active in the Netherlands, but are now increasingly found in other countries.

Cocaine Anonymous is similar to Narcotics Anonymous. It operates mainly in the United States and aims to support people in the attempt to give up cocaine abuse. Both Cocaine Anonymous and Narcotics Anonymous have support groups for family members. NA has a core set of beliefs about the nature of addiction and the process of recovery which holds that addiction is an incurable disease, but one which can be kept at bay if individuals accept their inability to control their drug use and if they believe in a 'higher power'. NA members are encouraged to create a 'moral inventory', and to admit their faults to their higher power or to another human being. They are also expected to make honest attempts to overcome their faults and to make amends for the harm they have done to other people. There are over 25,000 NA groups worldwide which meet in over 50 countries. In addition, many NA meetings are held in correctional and treatment facilities.

Relationships between mutual aid groups and professionals vary. Some professionals actively encourage their clients to attend NA meetings, while others take little interest in it and make few referrals. Major advantages of mutual aid groups are their low cost and ready accessibility. They offer life long support to their members and thus may help to reduce the risk of relapse for those individuals who remain committed members. NA groups are quite diverse and many professionals emphasize the need to encourage drug-dependent people to attend a variety of different groups in order to find one in which they feel comfortable.

2.3.4. REDUCTION OF THE NEGATIVE HEALTH AND SOCIAL CONSEQUENCES OF DRUG ABUSE

In some countries (notably Australia, Canada and Western Europe) a number of flexible programmes have been developed to attract and retain a greater proportion of clients. *Low-threshold programmes* are by definition designed to be accessible and make it easy for new and former patients to gain admission or readmission. These programmes typically aim at reducing the adverse health and social consequences of drug abuse; they may also sometimes provide drug prescribing services, offer problem-based counselling, primary health care and referral to other specialist services.

A variety of non-pharmacological programmes or initiatives to reduce the health and social consequences of drug abuse have been proposed or developed.[92] These usually aim to improve the well-being of drug abusers, their families and their communities by discouraging high-risk behaviours, and by providing support and resources to promote self-care. They do not require those targeted to necessarily stop using drugs, but encourage practices such as the use of clean needles for self-injection and the use of less hazardous routes of administration such as inhalation rather than injection. Comprehensive programmes include outreach activities, peer information and education, access to social and health services, referral to treatment, provision of clean injecting equipment and cleansing means, condom distribution and information about safer sex and other lifestyle issues.

A major impetus for these efforts was the appearance of HIV infection and the risks associated with needle-sharing. The scope has since broadened to include additional risks associated with drug abuse. At present, initiatives such as needle exchanges and education on cleaning injecting equipment are well established in some countries, but remain controversial in others as the authorities in the latter fear that the existence of such programmes could be misinterpreted by potential users that drug consumption is a relatively harmless leisure time activity as long as some simple rules are respected. The art, of course, is to prevent both the most harmful consequences of drug abuse and such potential misinterpretation.

2.3.5. THE FUTURE OF TREATMENT

The evidence before us today indicates that drug abuse and dependence are treatable conditions if treatment is available, accessible and attractive to drug abusers.[93] Clearly, much remains to be done to reach these goals. Treatment systems need to be planned and developed in many parts of the world to take account of assessed local needs, the appropriate social context and current scientific knowledge. Treatment services need to be broader in scope and available for all groups in need, such as women, the very young, those with coexisting mental disorders, offenders and prisoners. Treatment options should be diversified and coordinated with other services in order to respond to the different needs and characteristics of drug abusers. Clients' own perspectives and experiences of treatment need to be better understood and taken into account in the design of treatment systems.[94] More research is needed to expand knowledge on appropriate and effective approaches for different types of problems and patients, and to understand which components of treatment work for them.

Research shows that the associated economic benefits of treatment exceed its costs.[95] Thus on cost grounds alone the provision of well-designed and effective treatment services should be viewed as an economic imperative and not only as an unaffordable luxury. When one adds the promotion of health and humanitarian concerns to economic practicalities, the arguments in favour of treatment provision are overwhelming. The establishment of substance abuse treatment services commensurate with the needs of the population should be pursued as a necessary and achievable objective by developed and developing countries alike.

REFERENCES:

1. *Webster's Third New International Dictionary*, Merriam-Webster Inc. Springfield, Massachusetts, 2000

2. A good review of the application of such models in practice can be found in EMCDDA, *Estimating Prevalence of Problem Drug Use in Europe*, ISBN 92-9168-006-0, Lisbon 1997.

3. Office of National Drug Control Policy, *National Drug Control Strategy 2000*, Washington, 2000.

4. European Monitoring Centre on Drugs and Drug Addiction (EMCDDA), *1999 Extended Annual Report in the State of the Drugs Problem in the European Union*, Lisbon, 1999 .

5. Council of Europe (Pompidou Group), *The 1995 ESPAD report – The European School Survey Project on Alcohol and Other Drugs, Alcohol and Other Drug Use Among Students in 26 European countries*, Stockholm 1997.

6. NIDA, *Monitoring the Future*, and SAMHSA, *National Household Surveys*.

7. National Institute on Drug Abuse and National Institute on Alcohol Abuse and Alcoholism, *The Economic Costs of Alcohol and Drug Abuse in the United State*, 1998.

8. Skirrow, J., Sawka, E., *The Dark Side of the Moon: The Unintended Prevention*, Alberta Alcohol and Drug Abuse Commission (1986).

9. Seivewright N., 'Combined risk factor for drug misuse must be recognized'. Comments on drug misuse and the enviornment: a recent British report, *Addiction 94 (9)*, p. 1301 (1999).

10. Single, E, Robson, L., Xie, X. & Rehm, J., *The Economic Costs of Substance Abuse in Canada*, Ottawa: Canadian Centre on Substance Abuse (1996).

11. Durlack, J.A., 'Primary Prevention in Schools', in Ollendick, T.H., Prinz, R.J. (Eds), *Advances in Clinical Child Psychology*, New York: Plenum Press (1997).

12. Advisory Council on the Misuse of Drugs, *Drugs Misuse and the Environment*, London: HMSO (1998).

13. Hawkins, D.J., Catalano, R.F., and Miller, J.Y., *Risk and Protective Factors*.

14. Sloboda, Z., 'State of the Art of Prevention Research in the United States', *Evaluating Drug Prevention in the European Union* (1998).

15. Boys, A., et al. (1999) 'What Influences Young People's Use of Drugs? A qualitative study of decision making', *Drugs: Education, Prevention and Policy*,Vol.6. No.3, 373-387.

16. Sloboda, Z., *op.cit.*

17. Kandel, D. et al, (1992) 'Stages of Progression in Drug Involvement from Adolescence to Adulthood: further Evidence for the Gateway Theory', *Journal of Studies on Alcohol*, 53(5), 447-457.

18. Sloboda, *op. cit.*

19. Sloboda, Z., *op.cit.*

20. ONDCP, *National Drug Control Strategy – 2000 Annual Report*, Washington 2000, pp. 39-40.

21. Werner, E.E., Smith, R.S., *Overcoming the Odds: High-risk Children from Birth to Adulthood*, Ithica, NY: Cornell University Press (1992)

22. Benard, B., *Fostering Resiliency in Kids: Protective Factors in the Family, School, and Community*. Portland, OR: Northwest Regional Educational Laboratory (1991).

23. National Institute on Drug Abuse, *Drug Abuse Prevention for At-risk Individuals.* Rockville MD: US National Institutes of Health (1997).

24. Abrams, D.B., Orleans, C.T., Niaura, R.S., Goldstein, M.G., Prochaska,J., Velicer,W., 'Integrating Individual and Public Health Perspectives for Treatment of Tobacco Dependence Under Managed Health Care: A Combined Stepped Care and Matching Model', *Tobacco Control 2* (suppl), S17-S37 (1993).

25. Uhl, A., 'Evaluation of Primary Prevention in the Field of Illicit Drugs, Definitions Concepts – Problems', *Cost A6 Evaluation Research in regard to Primary Prevention of Drug Abuse* (1998), 135-220.

26. Schweinhart, L.J., Barnes, H.V., Weikart, D.P., *Significant Benefits: the High Scope Perry Preschool Study Through Age 27*, Ypsilanti, MI: High Scope Press(1993)

27. Bry, B., and Canby, C. (1986), 'Decreasing adolescent drug use and school failure: long-term effects of targeted family problem-solving training', *Child and Family Behaviour Therapy*, 8(1), 43-59; Friedman, A. (1989); 'Family therapy versus parents groups: effects on adolescent drug abusers', *American Journal of Family Therapy*, 17(4), 335-347; and Lewis, R., et al.(1990), "Family-based intervention for helping drug-using adolescents", *Journal of Adolescent Research*, 6, 82-95.

28. Home Office Drug Prevention Initiative, *Guidance on good practice*, The Stationery Office, London, 1998

29. SAMHSA, *1999 National Household Survey.*

30. Allensworth D., Lawson, E., Nicholson, L., Wyche, J. *Schools and Health – Our Nation's Investment.* Institute of Medicine Washington, D.C. National Academy Press (1997)

31. Based on Nancy Tobler,1992, 'Drug prevention programs can work: research findings', *Journal of Addicitive Diseases*, 11 (13), 1-28.

32. Sloboda, *op.cit.*

33. Carmona, M., Stewart, K., A review of alternative activities and alternatives: programs in youth-oriented prevention. CSAP Technical Report 13. Rockville MD: *Substance Abuse and Mental Health Services Administration (1996).*

34. Butler, B., *Alcohol and Drugs in the Workplace.* Toronto: Butterworths (1993)

35. International Labour Office, *Workplace Initiatives to Prevent and Reduce Drug and Alcohol Problems.* Geneva: ILO (1998).

36. International Labour Office, *Management of Alcohol- and Drug-Related Issues in the Workplace.* Geneva: ILO 1996

37. Jean Paul Smith, *Model Programmes of Drug and Alcohol Abuse Prevention among Workers and their Families – Evaluation Report*, December 1997.

38. ONDCP, *National Drug Control Stratey, 2000 Annual Report*, Washington 2000, pp. 42-44.

39. Room, R., Paglia, A., Preventing substance use – problems among youth: a literature review and recommendations. Research document series #142; Toronto: Addiction Research Foundation (1998).

40. European monitoring centre for drugs and drug addiction. News Release: EU steps up use of the Internet to spread drugs awareness, 8 November, 1999 (http://www.emcdda.org)

41. Skinner, H.A., TeenNet: using the Internet to engage teens in health promotion. University of Toronto: http://www.cyberisle.org/teennet (1998)

42. Hough, M., *Drugs Misuse and the Criminal Justice System: A Review of the Literature.* London: Home Office: (1996)

43. UNODCCP, '*Expert Working Group – Improving Inter-Sectorial Impact in Drug Abuse Offender Casework*', (Draft), Vienna 2000.

44. Caulkins, J.P., et al. *An Ounce of Prevention – a Pound of Uncertainty: the Cost-Effectiveness of School-Based Drug Prevention programs.* Santa Monica: RAND (1999).

45. Carmona, MG, Stewart, Kgottreddson, DC, Gottfredson, GD, A guide for evaluating prevention effectiveness, CSAP Technical report. Rockville MD: *Substance Abuse and Mental Health Services Administration (1998).*

46. World Health Organization (WHO), Committee on Drug Dependence, 30th Report, WHO, Geneva, 1996

47. United Nations General Assembly Resolution S-20/3, 'Declaration on the Guiding Principles of Drug Demand Reduction', United Nations, New York, 1998

48. Office of National Drug Control Policy, *Treatment Protocol Effectiveness Study*, US Government, Washington, 1996; Gossop, M., Marsden, J., Stewart D., NTORS at One Year. The National Treatmant Outcome Research Study. Changes in Substance Use, Health and Criminal Behaviour One Year after Intake

49. ONDCP, *The National Drug Control Strategy: 1996*, Washigton, 1996, p.46

50. National Addiction Centre, '*The National Treatment Outcome Research Study: Changes in Substance Use, Health and Criminal Behaviours One year after Intake*', Bulletin 3, London 1993.

51. NIDA, *Drug Abuse Treatment Outcome Studies, Background*, (http://www.datos.org/background.html#DARP and TOPS Findings.)

52. SAMHSA, *Treatment Episode Data Set (TEDS), 1992-1997*, pp. 92-97.

53. Rajkuman, A.S., French, M.T., 'Drug Use, Crime Costs, and the Economic Benefits of Treatment,' *Journal of Quantitative Criminology*, 13, pp. 291-323; Simpson, D. & Brown, B. 'Special Issue on Treatment Process and Outcome Studies from DATOS', *Drugs and Alcohol Dependence*, 1999, [Summary]; Simpson, D.k Joe Gl., Fletcher, Bl, Hubbard, R. & Anglin, D., 'A National Evaluation of Treatment Outcomes for Cocaine Dependence', *Archives of General Psychiatry*, 56, pp. 507-514 [Abstract].

54. Rydell, C.P. Caulkins, J.P., Everingham, S. 'Enforcement or Treatment? Modeling the Relative Efficacy of Alternatives for Controlling Cocaine'. *Operations Research* Vol.44, No.5, September-October 1996: 687-695

55. Toteva, S. and I. Milanov, 'The Use of Body Acupuncture for Treatment of Alcohol Dependence and Withdrawal Syndrome: A Controlled Study'. *American Journal of Acupuncture*, 1996, 24(1): p. 19-25.

56. Bearne, J., M. Gossop, and J. Strang, 'Rapid opiate detoxification treatments'. *Drug and Alcohol Review*, 1999, 18(1): p. 75-81;Cucchia, A., *et al.*, 'Ultra rapid opiate detoxification using deep sedation with oral midazolam: short and long term results'. *Drug and Alcohol Dependence*, 1998, 52: p. 243- 250.

57. Seoane, A., *et al.*, 'Efficacy and safety of two new methods of rapid intravenous detoxification in heroin addicts previously treated without success'. *British Journal of Psychiatry*, 1997, 171: p. 340-345; Simon, D., 'Rapid opioid detoxification using opioid antagonists: history, theory and the state of the art'. *Journal of Addictive Diseases*, 1997, 16: p. 103-122.

58. Bearne, J., Gossop, M., and Strang, J., *Drug and Alcohol Review*, 1999, 18(1): p. 75-81

59. Silverman, K., *et al.*, 'Increasing opiate abstinence through voucher-based reinforcement therapy'. *Drug and Alcohol Dependence*, 1996, 41: p. 157-165.

60. Marsden, J., Gossop, M., Farrell, M., Strang, J., 'Opioid Substitution: Critical Issues and Future Directions'. *Journal of Drug Issues*, 1998; 28(2): 243-264 ; Kreek, M.J., 'Long-term pharmacotherapy for opiate (primarily heroin) addiction: Opioid agonists', in *Pharmacological aspects of drug dependence: Towards an integrated neurobehavioral approach*, C.R. Schuster and M.J.Kuhar, Editors, 1996, Springer: Berlin. p. 487-562.

61. Ball, J.C., Ross, A. *The Effectiveness of Methadone Maintenance Treatment: Patients, Programs, Services, and Outcome*, 1991, Springer-Verlag, New York ; Marsch, L., 'The efficacy of methadone maintenance interventions in reducing illicit opiate use, HIV risk behaviour and criminality: a meta-analysis', *Addiction* 1998; 93(4): 515-532; Ghodse, H., Clancy, C., Oyefeso, A., *Methadone Substitution Therapy. Policies and Practices*. 1998, European Collaborating Centres in Addiction Studies, Monograph Series No.1, London; Newman, R.G., 'Methadone: prescribing maintenance, pursuing abstinence', *The International Journal of Addictions*, 1995, 30(10): 1303-1309

62. Ling W., Rawson R.A., Compton M.A., 'Substitution Pharmacotherapies for Opioid Addiction: From Methadone to LAAM and Buprenorphine'. *Journal of Psychoactive Drugs*, 1994, 26(2): 119-128; Johnson, R.E., Strain, E.C., 'Other medications for opioid dependence', in *Methadone Treatment for Opioid Dependence*, S. E.C. and M. Stitzer, Editors, 1999, The Johns Hopkins University Press: Baltimore; Glanz, M., Klawansky, S., McAullife, W., Chalmers, T., 'Methadone vs. L-alpha- acetylmethadol (LAAM) in the treatment of opiate addiction. A meta-analysis of the randomized, controlled trials'. *American Journal of Addictions* 1997, Fall; 6(4):339-349

63. Johnson, R.E., J.H. Jaffe, and P.J. Fudala, 'A controlled trial of Buprenorphine treatment for opioid dependence'. *Journal of the American Medical Association*, 1992, 267:

p. 2750-2755; Strain, E.C., *et al.*, 'Comparison of buprenorphine and methadone in the treatment of opioid dependence'. *American Journal of Psychiatry*, 1994, 151: p. 1025-1030.

64. Washton, A.M., M.S. Gold, and A.C. Pottash, 'Successful use of Naltrexone in addicted physicians and business executives'. *Advances in Alcohol and Substance Abuse*, 1984, 4: p. 89-96.

65. Brewer, C., 'Recent developments in maintenance prescribing and monitoring in the United Kingdom'. *Bulletin of the New York Academy of Medicine*, 1995, 72(3): p. 359.

66. Uchtenhagen, A., F. Gutzwiller, and A. Dobler-Miklos, *Medical Prescription of Narcotics Research Program Final Report of the Principal Investigators*, 1996, Institut fur Sozial-und Praeventivmedizin der Universitat Zurich, Zurich.

67. External Evaluation Panel, *Report of the External Evaluation Panel on the Evaluation of the Swiss Scientific Studies of Medically Prescribed Narcotics to Drug Addicts*, 1999, Unpublished Report to the WHO.

68. Uchtenhagen, A., Gutzwiller, F., and Dobler-Miklos, A., *Medical Prescription of Narcotics Research Program Final Report of the Principal Investigators*, Zurich, 1996.

69. Brewer, C., *Bulletin of the New York Academy of Medicine*, 1995, 72(3): p. 359

70. Levin, R.R. and A.F. Lehman, 'Meta-analysis of desipramine as an adjunct in the treatment of cocaine addiction'. *Journal of Clinical Psychopharmacology*, 1991, 11: p. 374-378; Pollack, M.H. and J.F. Rosenbaum, 'Fluoxetine treatment of cocaine abuse in heroin addicts'. *Journal of Clinical Psychiatry*, 1991, 52: p. 31-33; Grabowski, J., *et al.*, 'Fluoxetine is ineffective for treatment of cocaine dependence or concurrent opiate and cocaine dependence: two placebo-controlled double-blind trials'. *Journal of Clinical Psychopharmacology*, 1995, 15: p. 163-174; Small, G.W. and J.J. Purcell, 'Trazodone and cocaine abuse'. *Archives of General Psychiatry*, 1985, 42: p. 524; Margolin, A., *et al.*, 'A multicentre trial of Bupropion for cocaine dependence in methadone maintained patients'. *Drug and Alcohol Dependence*, 1995, 40: p. 125-131.

71. Giannini, A., P. Baumgartel, and L. DiMarzio, 'Bromocriptine therapy in cocaine withdrawal'. *Journal of Clinical Pharmacology*, 1987, 27: p. 267-270; Alterman, A., *et al.*, 'Amantadine may facilitate detoxification of cocaine addicts'. *Drug and Alcohol Dependence*, 1992, 31: p. 19-29; Kosten, T., *et al.*, 'Pharmacotherapy for cocaine-abusing methadone-maintained patients using amantadine or desipramine'. *Archives of General Psychiatry*, 1992, 49: p. 894-898.

72. Weddington, W., Jr., *et al.*, 'Comparison of amantadine and desipramine combined with psychotherapy for treatment of cocaine dependence'. *American Journal of Drug and Alcohol Abuse*, 1991, 17: p. 137-152; Handelsman, L., *et al.*, 'Bromocriptine for cocaine dependence. A controlled clinical trial'. *American Journal of Addiction*, 1997, 6: p. 54-64.

73. Platt, J.J., *Cocaine addiction, Theory research and Treatment*, 1997, Cambridge: Harvard University Press.

74. Fox, B.S., 'Development of a therapeutic vaccine for the treatment of cocaine addiction'. *Drug and Alcohol Dependence*, 1997, 48: p. 153-158; Pentel, P.R., *et al.*, 'A nicotine conjugate

vaccine reduces nicotine distribution to the brain and attenuates its behavioural and cardiovascular effects in rats'. *Pharmacology Biochemistry and Behavior*, 2000, 65: p. 191-198.

75. Toteva, S. and I. Milanov, *American Journal of Acupuncture*, 1996, 24(1): p. 19-25.

76. National Institute on Drug Abuse, *Principles of Drug Addiction Treatment: A research- based guide*, National Institutes of Health, Washington D.C., 1999.

77. WHO Programme on Substance Abuse, *Approaches to Treatment of Substance Abuse*, World Health Organization: Geneva, 1993.

78. Marsch, L.A. , 'The efficacy of methadone maintenance interventions in reducing illicit opiate use, HIV risk behavior and criminality: a meta-analysis', *Addiction*, 93, 515-32, 1998.

79. Hubbard, R.L., Craddock, G., Flynn, P., Anderson, J. & Etheridge, R. (1997) 'Overview of 1-year outcomes in the Drug Abuse Treatment Outcome Study (DATOS)', *Psychology of Addictive Behaviour*, 11, 261-278.

80. Gossop, M., Marsden, J., & Stewart, D. *National Treatment Outcome Research Study (NTORS) at one-year.* London: Department of Health, 1998.

81. MacDonough, T., 'Evaluation of the effectiveness of intensive confrontation in changing the behavior of alcohol and drug users'. *Behavior Therapy*, 1976, 7: p. 408-409; Miller, W.E. and R.K. Hester, *The effectiveness of treatment techniques: what works and what doesn't*, in *Treating addictive behaviors: processes of change*, W.E. Miller and N. Heather, Editors,1986, Plenum Press: New York; Annis, H.M., 'Group treatment of incarcerated offenders with alcohol and drug problems: a controlled trial'. *Canadian Journal of Criminology*, 1979, 21: p. 3-15.

82. Miller, W.R., 'Motivational interviewing: Research, practice and puzzles'. *Addictive Behaviors*, 1996, 6: p. 835-842.

83. National Institute on Drug Abuse. *Therapy Manuals for Drug Addiction. Manual 1. A Cognitive-Behavioral Approach: Treating Cocaine Addiction.* U.S. Government Printing Office, 1998.

84. National Institute on Drug Abuse, *Principles of Drug Addiction Treatment: A research- based guide*, National Institutes of Health, Washington D.C., 1999; National Institute on Drug Abuse. *Therapy Manuals for Drug Addiction. Manual 2. A Community-Reinforcement Approach: Treating Cocaine Addiction*, U.S. Government Printing Office, Washington D.C., 1998.

85. Milby, J.B., *et al.*, 'Sufficient conditions for effective treatment of substance abusing homeless'. *Drug and Alcohol Dependence*, 1996, 43: p. 39-47.

86. Miller, W.E. and R.K. Hester, 'The effectiveness of treatment techniques: what works and what doesn't', in *Treating addictive behaviors: processes of change*, W.E. Miller and N. Heather, Editors,1986, Plenum Press: New York; Scott, S.G. and R.A. Bruce, 'Determinants of innovative behavior: A path model of individual innovation in the workplace'. *Academy of Management Journal*, 1994, 37: p. 580- 607.

87. Landry, M., *Overview of Addiction Treatment Effectiveness*, 1995, Rockville, MD: SAMHSA, Office of Applied Studies. 116.

88. WHO Programme on Substance Abuse, *Approaches to Treatment of Substance Abuse*, World Health Organization: Geneva, 1993.

89. Poshyachinda, V., *Indigenous Drug Dependence Treatment in Thailand*, Bangkok: Drug Dependence Research Center, Institute of Health Research, Chulalongkorn University, 1992.

90. Spencer, C.P., H.K. Heggenhougen, and V. Navaratnam, 'Traditional Therapies and the Treatment of Drug Dependence in South East Asia'. *American Journal of Chinese Medicine*, 1980, 8: p. 230-238.

91. Costello, R.M., 'Alcoholism aftercare and outcome: cross-lagged panel and path analysis'. *British Journal of Addiction*, 1980, 75: p. 49-53; Ito, J.R. and D.M. Donovan, *Aftercare in alcoholism treatment: a review*, in *Treating Addictive Behaviors: processes of change*, W.E. Miller and N. Heather, Editors, 1986, Plenum Press: New York; Ahles, T.A., *et al.*, 'Impact of aftercare arrangements on the maintenance of treatment success in abusive drinkers'. *Addictive Behaviors*, 1983, 8: p. 53-58.

92. WHO Programme on Substance Abuse, *Approaches to Treatment of Substance Abuse*, World Health Organization, Geneva, 1993.

93. Leshner, A.I., 'Science-based views on drug addiction and its treatment'. *JAMA*, 1999, 282(14).

94 . Hunt, G., Barker, J.C., 'Drug treatment in contemporary anthropology and sociology'. *European Addiction Research* 1999; 5(3):126-132; Bergmark, A., 'The contextualization of drug treatment- future research perspectives'. *European Addiction Research* 1999; 5(3):153-158.

95. Hubbard, R.L., *et al.*, *Drug Abuse Treatment: A national study of effectiveness*, University of North Carolina Press: Chapel Hill, N.C., 1989.

CHAPTER 3
ALTERNATIVE DEVELOPMENT

INTRODUCTION

Today the possibility of any sustained eradication of illicit crops is usually met with a sceptical response. Actual experience, however, belies this scepticism. There are many examples of sustained crop eradication which should strengthen our confidence in what is known as alternative development. Since the 1920s, when an international drug control system was established under the rubric of the League of Nations, the elimination of illicit crops has been both achieved and maintained in many producing countries. At the beginning of the twentieth century, for example, global production of opium was estimated at approximately 20,000 tonnes per year. Today it is less than a third of that: global licit production of opium is about 1,300 tonnes and illicit production around 4,800 tonnes. Within this large global picture, there is an even more interesting example of successful, sustained crop elimination. The bulk of the 20,000 tonnes produced annually at the beginning of the twentieth century was produced in China. Licit opium production in China today is almost negligible, at about 20 tonnes, and illicit cultivation has been virtually non-existent for the last fifty years. Similarly, once widely grown in Formosa (now Taiwan, Province of China) and Indonesia, the coca bush has not been cultivated in either country for half a century.

The history of drug control has many such examples. Other cases of successful and sustained eradication, to name a few, are Iran, Thailand, Pakistan, Lebanon and Guatemala. The very fact that the elimination of illicit cultivation has been sustained in these countries has a odd result: it is often forgotten that some of them were once major illicit producers of narcotic drugs.

For example, in 1934, officially reported world production of opium was 7,023 tonnes. Of this, China produced 83%, Iran 7%, India 5% and Turkey 2%. Though Chinese production decreased over the next two decades, it was still substantial in 1949. Between 1950 and 1952, the new People's Republic of China instituted a massive campaign to extinguish opium production and consumption. By 1952, China was considered to be virtually drug-free.

Alternative development
© UNDCP

Similar successes were achieved in India in the middle of the twentieth century. In 1949, the newly independent state of India drew up a ten year plan to prohibit the non-medical use of opium. In 1950, the cultivation and manufacture of opium throughout the country was brought entirely under government supervision and control. By 1954, production had decreased, prices increased, and consumption was down by 45%. The end of the decade saw the achievement of a total prohibition on the sale of opium. Thereafter the government supervised control system was further rationalized, in accordance with international obligations. Today, India is the world's largest producer of licit opium for medical purposes. It also has in place a control system which prevents any significant diversion of this licit opium into illicit markets.

Illicit cultivation has also been successfully eliminated in Iran. By the law of 30 October 1955, opium production and consumption were prohibited in the country. In 1969, however, pressure from influential landowners and farmers led to the law being rescinded. A decade later, the Islamic revolution of 1979 brought a total prohibition on opium poppy cultivation. For more than 20 years, this has been maintained and today there is no opium poppy cultivation in Iran.

In Turkey, illicit cultivation emerged as a major problem only in the 1960s. Clandestine exports of heroin to Europe and the USA became a serious problem, leading to the complete transformation of illicit cultivation into strictly controlled licit cultivation. This was achieved in the 1970s by means of the government's firm commitment and resolute policy, supported by the United Nations and the U.S.A. The initiation of controlled cultivation was accompanied by rigorous law enforcement action to ensure the elimination of illicit cultivation by farmers. The success of these actions has been maintained; in Turkey no illicit cultivation takes place today.

Past experience demonstrates that although elimination of illicit cultivation may be difficult to achieve and sustain, it is by no means impossible. It does, however, require a number of prerequisites. These include resolute political commitment from the government and from bilateral and multilateral partners working together within the framework of the international drug control system. Effective sovereignty over the areas of illicit cultivation is also a prerequisite. In all four of the cases noted above, elimination was achieved and sustained because governments were able to exercise control over the areas where illicit crops were grown.

Today, the situation is different, and the majority of illicit crops are grown in different circumstances. This cultivation puts parts of the rural population into an extremely precarious and insecure situation. Because of their geographical remoteness or because of political instability or civil war, there is often a lack of effective government control in the illicit crop producing areas. Since these marginal areas are frequently outside the control of the national government, the people living there have little or no access to even the most basic of services, such as education, sanitation and healthcare, which are normally provided by the government. Communities also may find themselves in the very vulnerable situation of being outside the protection of the law, either because of the lack of government control or because they make a necessary economic decision to remove themselves from the rule of law in order to engage in an illicit activity. Once outside the rule of law, they become vulnerable to exploitation by criminal groups and lose some of their most basic human rights.

These differences are now better understood and appreciated. Since the late 1960s and early 1970s there has been a growing recognition in the international community that the programmes designed to eliminate illicit cultivation can only be sustained if they respond to the complex factors which lead to the peasant household's decision to engage in an illicit activity and grow an illicit crop in the first place.

Based upon the recognition that economic necessity often plays a key role in the decision to cultivate illicit crops, there is now a consensus in the international community that the economic reliance on narcotic crop cultivation can only be removed when viable, sustainable income-generating alternatives are available in in the legal sector. "Alternative development" has been the method used by the United Nations to achieve this objective since the late 1970s. In practice, alternative development is simply the implementation of a coordinated set of programmes with the intended objective of addressing the factors which are at the heart of the drug problem. Emphasizing human development, the security of the individual and the community, rural agricultural and industrial development, these programmes are intended to achieve not only a viable eradication of narcotic crops in the near term, but to sustain the elimination of these crops and the violence and insecurity that are almost always attendant to their cultivation.

3.1 THE INTERNATIONAL LEGAL FRAMEWORK

In 1961, the first international agreement with binding force and direct reference to the problem of illicit drug cultivation was adopted. The 1961 Convention on Narcotic Drugs, consoli-

dated most of the earlier international instruments in drug control. It entered into force on 13 December 1964, and was amended by the 1972 Protocol. The United Nations had three objectives in adopting the Single Convention. First, the convention was meant to codify all existing multilateral treaty laws in this field as a primary goal. The new treaty also simplified and streamlined the control machinery, another important step in enhancing the potential impact of the international community's efforts. The third goal was to extend the international control system then in place to include the cultivation of plants that were grown as the raw material of natural narcotic drugs. In this regard, the 1961 Convention had immediate legislative ramifications for State Parties where illicit crop cultivation was taking place. It placed a specific obligation on states to limit production of narcotic plants exclusively to the amount needed for medical and scientific purposes. It also prohibited the use of the cannabis plant for any non-medical purposes.

The 1972 Protocol, which amended the Single Convention, came into force on 8 August 1975. It underscored the necessity for increasing efforts to prevent illicit production of, traffic in and use of narcotics. The Protocol also strengthened the role of the International Narcotics Control Board (INCB) in drug control matters, giving it additional responsibility for ensuring a balance between supply and demand of narcotic drugs for medical and scientific purposes.

The key articles of significance in the context of alternative development are articles 21-28, which cover such topics as the limitation of production of opium (Article 21bis), control of poppy straw (Article 25), the control of coca leaf and bush (Articles 26-27), and the control of cannabis (Article 28). Article 21bis begins by stating that "The production of opium by any country or territory shall be organized and controlled in such manner as to ensure that, as far as possible, the quantity produced in any one year shall not exceed the estimate of opium to be produced as established under paragraph 1 (f) of article 19."

The global framework intended to influence state-level legislative development continued to take shape into the 1970s, with the passage of the 1971 Convention on Psychotropic Substances. Until 1971, only the plant-based drugs had been subject to international control. Growing concern over the harmful effects of psychotropic substances, amphetamine-type stimulants and hallucinogens led in 1971 to the adoption of the Convention. It came into force on 16 August 1976, thus reinforcing the international drug control system, which would henceforth cover hallucinogens, such as LSD, stimulants and sedative-type hypnotics such as barbiturates.

An important milestone, the International Conference on Drug Abuse and Illicit Trafficking (ICDAIT), took place in Vienna from 17-26 June 1987. The conference, convened by the-Secretary-General of the United Nations, was attended by representatives of 138 States. Guidelines for dealing with the reduction of illicit supply were adopted by the Conference under the title A Comprehensive Multidisciplinary Outline of Future Activities relevant to the Problems of Drug Abuse and Illicit Trafficking (CMO). The CMO succinctly describes the various dimensions of the illicit drug problem, and gives specific, suggested courses of action at the national level. Chapter II of that document advocated the reinforcement of measures for the control of illicit drug supply. In particular, the CMO has specific targets on the "Identification of Illicit Narcotic Plant Cultivation," the "Elimination of Illicit Plantings," and the "Redevelopment of Areas Formerly under Illicit Drug Crop Cultivation." With regard to the latter, the CMO makes the following suggestions for national authorities:

The national authorities concerned could:
(a) Carry out market surveys followed by in-depth studies, where necessary, aimed at identifying domestic and export markets for substitute crops...
(b) Strengthen agricultural research and extension in areas growing illicit drug crops with a view to determining the short-term and long-term requirements of any crop substitution programmes envisaged...
(c) Develop the infrastructure with a view to creating an improved living environment for the farmer, in support of government efforts to eliminate illicit cultivation...

The CMO includes a range of recommendations for action at the regional and international levels as well. For example, the above group of recommendations at national level are complemented by suggestions for action at the regional and international levels which include: regional efforts aimed at identifying areas formerly under illicit cultivation which are now ready for redevelopment (paragraph 213); UN-led campaigns aimed at increasing the flow of resources to crop substitution programmes (paragraph 214); contributions from international financing institutions in support of integrated rural development and in support of the eradication of illicit plantings (paragraph 218).

The two major UN conventions of 1961 and 1971 focused primarily on the control of licit activities, mainly those related to the markets of controlled substances. In contrast, the UN Convention against Illicit Traffic in Narcotic Drugs and Psychotropic Substances, agreed in 1988, deals specifically with illicit activities. The convention entered into force on 11 November 1990. It is designed to allow governments the legal force to deprive drug traffickers of ill-gotten financial gains and freedom of movement. One of the more innovative provisions of the 34-article convention concerns the tracing, freezing and confiscation of proceeds and property derived from drug trafficking. In addition, the 1988 convention bars all havens to drug traffickers, particularly through its provisions for: extradition of major drug traffickers; mutual legal assistance between states on drug-related investigations; and the transfer of proceedings for criminal prosecution. Insofar as it has implications for alternative development, the convention strengthens international drug control by calling for strict monitoring of the chemicals used in illicit production.

The convention is unequivocal in its support for eradication efforts but it also gives due regard to the communities whose livelihood could be jeopardized. The convention's most significant articles in this regard begin with Article 14, which cites "Measures to eradicate illicit cultivation of narcotic plants and to eliminate illicit demand for narcotic drugs and psychotropic substances," which states that

"Each Party shall take appropriate measures to prevent illicit cultivation of and to eradicate plants containing narcotic or psychotropic substances, such as opium poppy, coca bush and cannabis plants, cultivated illicitly in its territory. The measures adopted shall respect fundamental human rights and shall take due account of traditional licit uses, where there is historic evidence of such use, as well as the protection of the environment...The Parties may co-operate to increase the effectiveness of eradication efforts. Such co-operation may, *inter alia*, include support, when appropriate, for integrated rural development leading to economically viable alternatives to illicit cultivation. Factors such as access to markets, the availability of resources and prevailing socio-economic conditions should be taken into account before such rural development programmes are implemented. The Parties may agree on any other appropriate measures of co-operation."

The UN General Assembly, at its seventeenth special session, adopted on 23 February 1990 a Political Declaration and Global Programme of Action, the latter setting forth the actions which governments carry out in fulfilling the commitment of the former. The General Assembly also proclaimed the period from 1991-2000 the United Nations Decade against Drug Abuse, a period which would thus give rise to national, regional and international actions to promote the implementation of the

Global Programme of Action. Later that year, in December 1990, the General Assembly, in its resolution 45/179, established the UN International Drug Control Programme(UNDCP), thus integrating the previous institutional structures and functions in this field.

Upper Xienkhouang development project, Laos PDR
© T.Haley/UNDCP

By adopting the Political Declaration, Member States committed themselves to a number of objectives in reducing illicit supply. For example, they urged one another "to increase economic and technical cooperation to developing countries and to facilitate trade flows in support of viable alternative income schemes, such as crop-substitution programmes, by means of integrated rural development strategies, including facilitation of appropriate efficient marketing and sound economic policies, so as to eliminate illicit cultivation and production of narcotic drugs." In the Global Programme of Action, the General Assembly outlined an extensive range of measures with which they would pursue the objectives set out in the Declaration. One set of measures focuses on eradication and substitution of illicit production of narcotic drugs.

As of October 2000, a total of 171 States were parties to the Single Convention on Narcotic Drugs of 1961 or parties to that Convention as amended by the 1972 Protocol. With regard to the 1971 Convention, 164 States were parties. No fewer than 156 States were parties to the United Nations Convention against Illicit Traffic in Narcotic Drugs and Psychotropic Substances of 1988.

It is clear that with the passing of time, the normative influence of international agreements, many drafted under the auspices of the UN system, has grown. One authority has recently written that national drug policies "are the outgrowth and the legal follow-on to a system of international control of drugs which was established in the early years of the present [twentieth] century. This was one of the earliest examples of an international legal system as distinct from the general spirit of international cooperation in many health areas (alcohol, for example) which marked the end of the 19th and beginning of the 20th centuries."[1]

The evolution of the international drug control system took a major step forward in June 1998, with the convening of the UN General Assembly's twentieth special session (UNGASS) on the international drug problem. Although UNDCP, together with local and regional partners, has

Crop monitoring
© UNDCP

been implementing alternative development programmes for many years, it was not until the General Assembly special session of 1998 that the pluralistic approach to illicit crop reduction by means of alternative development, law enforcement and eradication received formal endorsement in the form of a resolution. The Action Plan on eradication and alternative development adopted at the session[2] was significant in several respects. First, governments demonstrated an apparently genuine commitment and willingness to design time-bound strategies for the elimination or significant reduction of illicit crops. Secondly, governments highlighted the importance of monitoring mechanisms, considered to be indispensable to assess the extent of and the trends in illicit cultivation. Finally, the action plan approved by UNGASS calls for specific action in the areas of economic and social development, to support the elimination of illicit cultivation.

A prerequisite for being able to monitor crop reduction and eradication levels is, naturally, the existence of instruments to measure these, but to date, no international mechanism for the collection and analysis of data on illicit narcotic crops has been available. Ideally, monitoring of illicit crop cultivation is done by means of four basic survey methodologies, used in combination where appropriate – ground surveys, rapid assessment techniques, aerial surveys and satellite monitoring. The Action Plan points out that, despite 'valiant efforts' by States to eliminate illicit cultivation,

> [..] the potential of such efforts has not been fully exploited because of insufficient information and cooperation at policy and operational levels. [..] Governments in the producing areas should design efficient and accurate monitoring and verification mechanisms using the most efficient, cost-effective and accessible data collection methods available. [..] Governments should implement follow-up and evaluation systems that will enable them to monitor the qualitative and quantitative impact of alternative development programmes. [..] Governments should share information on illicit drug crop assessment with

UNDCP and reciprocally with other Governments in order to increase cooperation to eliminate such cultivation. Assessments should also include information about the causes and effects of narcotics production, including linkages to other development problems.

In response to this, UNDCP has developed an International Crop Monitoring Programme (ICMP). It aims to have all elements of the monitoring system functioning by 2001, and thus to have benchmarks by which to measure progress in 2008.

In the aftermath of the special session, Bolivia, Peru and Colombia each formulated "business plans" that combine illicit crop eradication with a full range of alternative development measures. Collectively, the three plans involve 15 projects calling for investments essential to achieving alternative development goals: to generate agro-industries with proven markets, producing cash and food crops, wood pulp, timber and livestock; and, accompanied by the necessary infrastructure development and training, to modernize existing producers' associations. The projects attach much importance to the effective promotion of competitive business practices in production and marketing as well as to environmental protection.

3.2 MOVING TOWARD ALTERNATIVE DEVELOPMENT AS A DRUG CONTROL STRATEGY

Many differences remain among the various national approaches to reducing illicit supply; this divergence is due to different nuances of the supply problem, varying rates of policy adaptation at the national level, as well as the conditions which are unique to each major producing country.

One reason for the diversity in country-level approaches to reducing illicit supply is that alternative development has itself undergone various stages of technical refinement and experimentation throughout the past four decades. Only in recent years has the approach reached a state of universal acceptance.

In the 1960s, growing recognition that heroin consumption was posing a major problem compelled governments to begin considering new ways to reduce the supply of the raw materials for illicit drug production, in this case, opium poppy. Thus, drug control authorities considered introducing development-oriented measures into the range of technical options for reducing the illicit supply of opium.

As described in the previous section, in 1961 a key international agreement with binding force and direct reference to the problem of illicit drug cultivation was adopted. The 1961 Convention on Narcotic Drugs codified States' obligations to eliminate illicit cultivation of drug crops irrespective of economic and social conditions and style of governance. It was clear at the outset that fulfilling this obligation would depend on the ability of State Parties to extend the reach of legal controls into cultivation sites, which were invariably located in detached, rural areas.

With the passing of time, countries such as Turkey, Iran, and India succeeded in eliminating illicit cultivation. Their success, however, created a vacuum in the global supply of opiates, with one result being an increase in production in two developing countries which had hitherto played a relatively minor role in global drug supply: Afghanistan and Pakistan. It was clear that of the various incentives which underpinned illicit production, the profit motive played an important role in fuelling the outward expansion of the drug trade. This dynamic, with reductions in some countries triggering increases in others, focused further attention on the need to situate drug control efforts in the broader realm of economics and development.

It is in this context significant that the 1970s also witnessed the emergence of refreshing new perspectives in development theory. There was a widely supported global campaign to bring about a "New International Economic Order" which would presumably right the economic wrongs that had defined North-South relations throughout the twentieth century. Support for the NIEO turned out to be short-lived but the movement did succeed in focusing attention on the grievances of developing countries which had too often been seen solely as sources of raw materials and cheap labour. The interests and needs of developing countries themselves would subsequently always be seen differently in the eyes of the international donor community.

Training in agro forestry, Bolivia
© UNDCP

In the UN system, the new perspective led to tangible results in 1971, in the establishment of what would thereafter act as the leading proponent of a more development-oriented approach in supply reduction, the UN Fund for Drug Abuse Control (UNFDAC). Reminiscent of the powerful political impetus that gave rise to the Shanghai commission more than half a century earlier, public awareness had once again played a key role in the creation of UNFDAC.

The first UNFDAC crop substitution project targeting poppy cultivation began in Thailand

in 1971. It was followed by similar projects in other growing areas in Thailand, Myanmar and Pakistan. These projects had several objectives in common: first and foremost, they all sought to mitigate the economic appeal of drug crops by making other crops, in the licit sector, more financially rewarding. By focusing on small-scale production sites, success could more easily be assured. Once entrenched in the immediate production site, the logic went, the newly introduced economic activities and products could then spread to adjoining growing areas, eventually covering, and replacing the entire zone of illicit cultivation. The areas for which this approach was deemed appropriate were traditional growing areas, where communities were earning bare minimum subsistence wages for their efforts.

Thailand provides a good example of this. For over 700 years, Thailand and its predecessor the Kingdom of Siam, had been cultivating and periodically banning opium and its non-medical use.[3] While the country brought its national legislation and mechanisms consistently into line with the developing international drug control system, efforts at control were made increasingly difficult by a concentration of production in geographically remote areas in the Burmese and Thai hills. While the Government moved quickly to control this concentration of cultivation, it soon realized that its geographical remoteness and political complexity required a more holistic approach. The Government's commitment was strengthened by the fact that opium addiction was increasingly spreading outside of this relatively contained area and into the cities. What had previously been considered a problem of selected ethnic minorities based in these remote hills was, by the 1960s becoming entrenched in the mainstream population, which included students and urban youth. The Government thus commited itself to an innovative set of integrated rural development programmes.[4] Cultivation then declined from approximately 12,000 hectares (ha) in 1961–1962 to about 3,000ha in 1987. Cultivation in Thailand currently is a mere 700ha.[5]

There was the question of which crops could serve as viable alternatives; if the legal crops were so appealing, why hadn't the rural producers opted for them in the first place? During the second half of the 1970s, governments together with drug control specialists, agronomists, and development experts went about seeking answers to this question. Several plant species likely to be successful as substitute crops were identified on the basis of their suitability to soil and climatic conditions and the feasibility of introducing them into these opium growing areas. It turned out that the near-total isolation of the peasant communities was the main obstacle to introduction of alternative crops. First of all, in physical terms, isolation made the transportation of perishable produce to markets impossible. Also, isolation was significant in terms of impeding communication with other farming communities. Many of the illicit crop- producing communities were in effect cut off from outside information sources that could have called attention to other options. With improved access to

markets and a greater range of crop selection, substitution efforts in Northern Thailand have demonstrated that farmers' annual earnings can be increased considerably by replacing opium with cabbage, tomatoes, potatoes or apricot (see Table 1). In Ucayali, Peru, palm oil has been found to be 50% more profitable than coca. In South West Asia, including Afghanistan, alternative crops now range from wheat to onions, cumin, saffron, and various fruits. In Laos, income from coffee, chili and sericulture exceeds income from opium. On a per hectare basis in 1995, coffee exceeded opium by almost 300% and chili exceeded opium by 370% in income.

In the 1970s, however, there was considerable learning still to be done before this discovery process led to the identification of economically-competitive crops in the licit sector. It soon became clear, in any case, that focusing solely on the crops was, in itself, insufficient. Modern-day concepts such as marketing, as well as technical advances in the area of food

Table 1: Comparison of income/ha for different crops as a percentage of gross income/ha for opium, Thailand, 1992-1993 (gross income for opium = 100 per cent)

Product	Gross income/ha as % of opium gross income/ha	Net income/ha [a] as % of opium gross income/ha
Opium	100	67
Red kidney beans	17	10
Upland rice [b]	11	10
Maize (improved)	17	16
Red cabbage	180	150
Lettuce	86	66
Tomatoes	240	166
Potatoes	400	250
Coffee Arabica [c]	64	44
Japanese apricot (rainfed) [d]	400	390

Sources: Office of the Narcotics Control Board (ONCB), Thailand; Thai-German Highland Development Project

a) Difference between gross and net income includes costs for labour, fertilizer, etc.
b) For crop year 1991-1992
c) 2 years to maturity
d) 5 years to maturity

processing, had yet to trickle down to the rural peasant communities; in a sense, time had left the illicit crop cultivators behind. The only business savvy actors on the scene were the traders, the drug traffickers. They demonstrated a clear affinity for quickly adjusting the price paid for opium as market conditions fluctuated. Their involvement imposed clear limits on the long term sustainability of crop substitution efforts which failed to take into account the full range of social and economic concerns of the community.

By the end of the 1970s, the crop substitution approach was broadened to include programmes of complementary measures aimed at improving quality of life. This strategy, known as integrated rural development, addressed issues such as infrastructure, health, and education. Various agricultural inputs – improved seeds, livestock breeds, irrigation facilities, fertilizers, credit, storage, transport and marketing services – and complementary measures were implemented simultaneously so as to correspond more closely to the basic needs as expressed by the communities themselves. This approach also came to be identified with specific geographic areas – it was at this time that the term "area development" came into use. By recognizing the unique constraints (geographical, level of political stability) of individual communities the approach proved successful in traditional growing areas in several Asian countries. For example, an integrated rural development project in Chiangmai Province, Thailand emphasized agricultural extension as well as the introduction of new cash crops. At the end of the project, the cash crop area per household had doubled and opium cultivation was almost eliminated. Further, the project was successful in improving health and education in the target areas[6].

However, integrated rural development projects, as they were then designed, still failed to meet expectations. They were costly and administratively complex. Reductions in illicit crop cultivation were invariably short lived. One key

flaw was that local communities participated little, if at all, in the actual design of the programmes themselves. This drawback led, predictably, to inappropriate – or at the very least, sub-optimal – project design. Also, by not placing enough emphasis on the level of illicit activity in all aspects of community life i.e. the level to which trafficking organisations were providing other administrative or municipal services in communities – central elements in the decision to engage in illicit cultivation – which went beyond simple crop profitability – were ignored. It also became evident that cultivation could be introduced by traffickers into new, non-traditional areas to meet a growing market, thereby offsetting gains made in the traditional area. While traffickers had a very clear financial incentive in keeping illicit crop cultivators in the dark about legal crops, they had few qualms about encouraging the cultivation of drug crops in communities that had hitherto been involved solely in legal activities. This sometimes meant encouraging consumption of the drugs themselves in new markets.

Also around this time, the concept of rural development expanded into the demand side when it became evident that opiate addiction was spreading to neighbouring populations that were not ostensibly involved in poppy cultivation. The spread of heroin addiction in such non-producing locations was particularly shocking in Pakistan. With this unfolding scenario, it became clear that demand reduction policies would have to be elevated on equal terms with supply reduction, not least as support to rural development initiatives which targeted supply.

With the arrival of the 1980s, the production of opium skyrocketed in Asia and that of coca leaf in Latin America. In Latin America, governments began to posit that, given that most consumers were in the developed countries, the wealthy nations were clearly the principal beneficiaries of the fight against production and trafficking of drugs; as such, they should bear most of the costs of crop substitution and rural development initiatives, either through bilateral aid or through the UN. With the passing of time, this distinction between drug producer and consumer countries was blurred by the continuing rise in consumption in the developing countries. Drug abuse was also on the rise in the urban centers of Latin America. The question, however, of who would be the lead financiers of alternative development activities was left unanswered.

It was therefore inevitable that the growing worldwide acceptance of alternative development in the 1990s would run up against the cold reality of limits on funding. The UN certainly could not undertake on its own the financing of the overall socio-economic development of communities involved in drug production. The governments of the countries in question had limited resources at their disposal, and few industrialized nations could justify to often skeptical publics how funding economic development in far-away lands served their national interests.

Because of this situation, there followed a process of strategic and technical streamlining. Rather than sounding the death knell for alternative development, the consequent narrowing of aims resulted in an improved, more focussed strategy that was far better placed to achieve the supply-side aims stated in the international agreements. By the end of the 1980s the technical content of programmes began to change accordingly. Already beginning in the late 1980s, projects were streamlined, with fewer and more focussed, objectives. The idea of substituting one crop for another was abandoned completely as practitioners became committed to "income substitution" which was broader, more realistic and concentrated on sustainability. Thereafter, alternative development projects addressed the specific economic and agricultural realities of the immediate project location. Greater emphasis was placed on the local as well as regional economic factors that influenced farming decisions. And a concerted effort was made to bring producing communities back into the mainstream

of national development programmes, thus creating economies of scale with the resources made available by national governments.

Erradication Afghanistan
© UNDCP

In recent years, the full range of concepts that constitute alternative development as we know it today have been introduced one by one. Emphasis is today placed on community-based approaches to natural resource management in sustainable production systems. Project planning involves participatory, people-centred methods that rely on local knowledge, skills, interests and needs as a basis for appropriate interventions. While the emphasis on participatory planning has been in place for over a decade, what is different now is the newfound recognition of the need for training and human resource development in the immediate project area. Alternative development projects today include institution-building components at all levels of project design and implementation; one key goal, the achievement of which influences the overall outcome of alternative development projects, is to promote the development of local institutions.

As described above, various experiments carried out in the field, in different contexts and

151

conditions, have led to the gradual acquisition of know-how and a precise formulation of the concept of alternative development. There is today an officially recognized definition of alternative development, endorsed by the General Assembly special session (UNGASS), 1998. In the Action Plan on International Cooperation on the Eradication of Illicit Drug Crops and on Alternative Development, adopted by the General Assembly and described above, the concept was expressed as follows:

> Defining alternative development as a process to prevent and eliminate the illicit cultivation of plants containing narcotic drugs and psychotropic substances through specifically designed rural development measures in the context of sustained national economic growth and sustainable development efforts in countries taking action against drugs, recognizing the particular socio-cultural characteristics of the target communities and groups, within the framework of a comprehensive and permanent solution to the problem of illicit drugs.

3.3 SUCCESS IN ALTERNATIVE DEVELOPMENT[7]

Although the media sometimes likes to focus on the disappointments in drug control, the fact is that most alternative development projects have been successful. In Bolivia, the area of coca bush cultivation was estimated at about 50,000 hectares in 1997, of which 12,000 hectares in the Yungas area considered licit cultivation. In 1999, the government eliminated 14,000 hectares of illicit coca, surpassing its own record from the previous year. The country began year 2000 with barely 10,000 hectares of illicit cultivation remaining which is a 78% decrease in only three years. Income from illegal coca has fallen from US$ 425 million in 1988 (8.5% of GDP) to 86 million in 1999, which is equivalent to about 1% of the country's legitimate GDP.[8] This is an unprecedented achievement and deserves worldwide recognition. Similarly,

coca cultivation in Peru decreased from a peak of 129,000 hectares in 1992 to 38,000 hectares in 1999. In Pakistan opium poppy cultivation has been reduced from approximately 800 tonnes in 1980 to about 9 tonnes in 1999. In Laos, Thailand, Bolivia and others, success stories are many. Positive results from different countries highlight the importance of locally adapted alternative development interventions.

The progress achieved thus far has come about despite the paucity of investment in alternative development. These investments are small even when compared to Official Development Assistance (ODA) received by the countries under consideration. For example in 1995, total investment in alternative development was US$ 71.8 million which was equivalent to 1.6% of ODA in the countries concerned (see Table 2). Furthermore, alternative development activities are often the only institutionalized intervention in isolated or difficult regions. These marginalized areas, despite substantial income from narcotic crops, rarely have the social or economic infrastructure which would facilitate sustainable development.

Upper Xienkhouang development project, Laos PDR
© T.Haley/UNDCP

152

Table 2: Investment in Alternative Development compared with Official Development Assistance

Country	Annual investment in alternative development (million US$) [a]	Total net ODA from DAC [b] countries, Multilateral Organisations and Arab countries in 1995 (million)	Investment in alternative development as % of 1995 ODA
Myanmar	1.4	n.a.	n.a.
Thailand	9.5	863	0.1
Viet Nam	0.4	826	0.05
Lao PDR	2.9	311	0.9
Colombia	3.3	231	1.4
Bolivia	18.2	692	2.6
Peru	19	428	4.4
Pakistan	15.2	805	1.9
Afghanistan	1.9	214	0.9
Total	**71.8**	**4370**	**1.6**

a) Annual average based on 1987-1996 figures, including UNDCP and other international assistance
b) DAC = Development Assistance Committee of the Organization for Economic Cooperation and Development (OECD)

The examples cited in the previous section showed that in order to be effective, alternative development must link closely with national development policy. Past experience has also made clear that the viability of alternative development programmes depends on: (a) a sustainable economic environment that makes illicit cultivation less attractive; (b) effective control of the area by central government and an absence of counter-pressures from insurgent groups; and (c) consistently applied disincentives through law enforcement and eradication.

Another key lesson learned in recent years is that alternative development programmes must take into account the particular needs of women. In almost all coca and opium producing areas, women are involved in the cultivation the illicit drug crop and other crops. Incorporation of the gender perspective in alternative development projects in Peru has increased effectiveness and sustainability of the activities. Access of women to training as rural promoters has been improved, especially in areas of traditional female work in agricultural

production. Also, the statutes of producers' cooperatives were adjusted to allow better participation of women i.e. those who were not landholders themselves; the reservation of one board position in the sectoral committees for a female social delegate proved to be instrumental in getting women board members. Under this approach, 6,500 women are today actively participating in farmers organizations. The organizations have contributed positively to a long process of change in existing gender relations and the new organizations have helped to create women leaders in local communities and districts. With their new political status, women are better able to deal with the drug subculture, which is increasingly becoming a problem in rural areas.

Even with today's refined concept of alternative development, the many local nuances of illicit crop cultivation necessitate initial adjustments and fine-tuning so that large scale investments can be optimally cost effective. A UNDCP sponsored project in Palavek, Laos is an example of a so-called "pilot" project which served as a model for further alternative development interventions in the country. In the Palavek area annual opium production was 3.5 tonnes in 1989. From then, UNDCP invested US$ 6.6 million in the area over the next six years. The project was able to make the area accessible (from 3-days travel by foot, ferry and car to three hours by road), open it up to trade (the number of shops increased from two to more than 60), provide better health care and food security, transforming Palavek from a rice importing district into an exporting one. Dependency on opium was reduced because the project addressed opium in each of its three main roles: as cash crop, source of credit and medicine. At the end of the project, annual opium production had decreased from 3.5 tonnes to less than 100 kg. This project demonstrated to the Lao Government and other donors the merits of the approach; it served as a model for expanding alternative development in other opium producing areas. The project was also used to raise awareness of the need to incorporate drug control components in rural development assistance programmes.

A UNDCP sponsored project in Dir District, Pakistan demonstrated the extent to which alternative development interventions could have multiplier effects well beyond the project area. The project was in operation from 1985 to 2000; its expenditure for this period was US$ 38 million. The project was based on a series of sub-projects designed to improve the infrastructure and economic and social services of the district in support of a phased programme of poppy eradication carried out by the government.

One of the main lessons learned in the first phase of project implemetation was that community participation in the selection of activities as well as in construction, operation and maintenance was essential for success. In line with this finding, the second phase of the project helped establish 429 Village Development Committees which were actively involved in construction of roads and bridges, extension and improvement of 150 irrigation facilities,

social forestry projects, agriculture development and animal husbandry activities, construction of more than 70 drinking water schemes and the establishment of basic health units.

This approach proved to be extremely successful. At the time of the project launch, 50% of the Dir's population lived below the poverty line and opium poppy cultivation was at its peak in 1992 with 3670 ha. Today, the district is the third-wealthiest district of the Northwest Frontier Province and poppy cultivation has been effectively eliminated. But apart from this noteworthy success in the immediate project area, adjoining districts have been selected by IFAD and the Government of Pakistan for investment through loans amounting to US$ 22 million for the period 1997-2003. Having simultaneous projects in all the main poppy areas will help to contain the displacement of poppy cultivation and will sustain the reduction of opium poppy cultivation achieved so far.

3.4 POLITICAL CONSIDERATIONS

In addition to the international policy framework and the technical intricacies of alternative development, it cannot be overlooked that progress in reducing illicit crop cultivation depends on the political environment in which central governments and local communities interact. Indeed, a key factor is the ability of the state to generate a shared sense of urgency from the local community. The readiness of the local community to work with the state is, however, influenced by a range of political factors. This section focuses on some of those which have influenced local communities' relationship with national governments insofar as this relationship has a bearing on the outcome of alternative development programmes.

As discussed earlier, one basic tenet of the international legal framework for drug control is that policies agreed at the international level should be adapted and ultimately implemented at the individual country level. However, the process of normative adaptation and implementation should not be seen in isolation of other country-level political processes that influence the state's ability to achieve its aims in drug control. One development which has in recent years transformed the context in which governments must work with local communities in the area of alternative development is the ongoing process of democratization.

Illicit crop cultivation, whether in Myanmar, Afghanistan or Peru, is often driven by specific groups that have a common ethnicity, or language, or socio-economic profile. The stigma attached to involvement in such activities is such that, should the ruling powers be associated with the same groups, there is the risk that no significant action will be taken due to reluctance of representatives to alienate their so-called "in-group." In other words, the close relationship between political representatives in the national capital and those they represent in far-away, rural, drug producing localities, may contribute to inconsistent or selective application of the legal controls designed to eliminate reliance on illicit crop cultivation.

The introduction of pluralistic, democratic governance dilutes this risk of selective application, for it devolves decision-making power to a broader cross-section of a country's ethnic and regional interests. While an elected official from one part of a country known for illicit poppy cultivation may be reluctant to call attention to the region's top, albeit illegal, income earner, there may be other representatives, or a free press, that is willing to do so out of competing self-interest. Conversely, parliamentary debate in a functioning democracy can act as a powerful safeguard against the scapegoating of particular ethnic minorities for political ends. In other words, the success of alternative development depends to a great extent on the quality of governance and the rule of law.

Unfortunately, the importance of good governance often goes unrecognised in the context of

Alternative development – Dir District, Pakistan
© UNDCP

alternative development, as though drug control norms could in themselves meet with their intended outcome despite the obstacles and constraints that the state must often overcome when reaching out to local communities. Activities such as illicit drug production are often classified as "victimless" crimes; thus, reporting often depends more on moral, egalitarian considerations rather than a sense of personal loss or harm. However, there is a problem when police and state conduct give grounds for counterbalancing moral consideration: when the state is seen as foe rather than friend, the obvious result is that no voluntary reporting will take place. In the case of countries where past eras of political oppression and internal strife have weakened the ties that bind state to civil society, the information flow on illicit drug activity both within the community and between the community and the police may be especially sparse.

Armed conflict is another important political dynamic with implications for alternative development activities. Illicit drug production in Afghanistan and Myanmar, for example, has evolved alongside military conflict: in Afghanistan, sudden economic upheaval has forced many farmers to search for new income sources; in Myanmar, opium poppy cultivation has provided ethnic insurgents with a source of military financing. The cases of Afghanistan and Myanmar, in particular, demonstrate with unusual clarity that wartime may under certain conditions minimize the costs while raising the benefits of illicit drug production; conflict can act as a catalyst which converts traditional, small-scale drug production into a large-scale, income-generating enterprise.

Cultivation of exotic flowers for export
© UNDCP

The problem is that all too often the political, economic and social factors, which have skewed the costs and benefits in this way, are ignored. It is assumed that the drug problem can be eliminated solely on the basis of calculations which take into account the volume of illicit drug produced. As this chapter has sought to demonstrate, such assumptions are no longer valid. More recognition of the economic, political and social environment is required in order to successfully reduce illicit drug supply. The most successful alternative development projects have met with success precisely because they have been designed with a focus not only on economics, but on the socio-political structures in which members of peasant communities interact, exchange information and arrive at collective decisions.

The number of countries and regions where illicit crop cultivation poses a serious international problem has been reduced substantially in recent years. Today, the "major producing countries" can be counted on the fingers of one hand. On the negative side, however, those that remain - Afghanistan, Myanmar and Colombia being the most obvious - are also the most problematic. The international community's efforts in assisting these countries must go hand-in-hand with a convergence of political, economic and social factors. Economic support and political commitment are essential prerequisites for successful alternative development; sensitivity to the political scenario in each country, as well as a sustained willingness to support initiatives that can make a difference, are likely to prove the most important guiding principles during the next phase of the international community's efforts to rid the world of illicit drugs.

Social institutions at grass-roots level are likely to play an increasingly important role in alternative development activities. Sustained economic growth entails a transformation of social institutions. Conversely, social groups play a key role in placing rural economies on new economic footings. In future, it will be essential that stronger links be established between the social networks at local level and those in national government. The subject of social capital, in this regard, has considerable significance in the context of alternative development, for it highlights the key role played by trust: trust between peasants and government workers, trust between national governments and multilateral institutions. Over and above the historical, technical and economic complexities that define alternative development, global efforts to reduce current levels of illicit drug production are likely to hinge on this one, rather straightforward, requirement.

ENDNOTES

1. Virginia Berridge, 'European Drug Policy: The Need for Historical Perspectives,' *European Addiction Research*, 1996, 2, p. 222.

2. General Assembly Resolution S-20/4, Action Plan on International Cooperation on the Eradication of Illicit Drug Crops and on Alternative Development, June 1998

3. Tullis, LaMond, *Unintended Consequences: Illegal Drugs and Drug Policies in Nine Countries*, Lynne Rienner Publishers, Boulder, 1995, p. 107.

4. *ibid*, p. 110.

5. ODCCP, *Global Illicit Drug Trends 2000*, Vienna, 2000.

6. UNDCP, 'Evaluation of Assistance in Alternative Development in Thailand', May 1993.

7. This section draws on several project progress and evaluation reports prepared by the United Nations International Drug Control Programme, in particular, UNDCP, Report on the Thematic Evaluation of Alternative Development in Peru, March 1997; UNDCP, Report on Guidelines for Best Practices on Gender Mainstreaming in Alternative Development, January 2000.

8. *Bolivia's, Coca/Cocaine Economy in 1988, A Computer Model*, USAID/Bolivia, July 1999.

TABLES

GLOBAL ILLICIT CULTIVATION OF OPIUM POPPY AND PRODUCTION OF OPIUM, 1994-1999
(Source: UNDCP Global Illicit Drug Trends 2000)

	1994	1995	1996	1997	1998	1999
Cultivation(1) in hectares						
SOUTH-WEST ASIA						
Afghanistan	71,470	53,759	56,824	58,416	63,674	90,583
Pakistan	5,759	5,091	873	874	950	284
Subtotal	77,229	58,850	57,697	59,290	64,624	90,867
SOUTH-EAST ASIA						
Lao PDR	18,520	19,650	21,601	24,082	26,837	22,543
Myanmar	146,600	154,070	163,000	155,150	130,300	89,500
Thailand	478	168 3	68	352	716	702
Viet Nam	3,066	1,880	1,743	340	442	442
Subtotal	168,664	175,768	186,712	179,924	158,295	113,187
OTHER ASIAN COUNTRIES						
Combined	5,700	5,025	3,190	2,050	2,050	2,050
Total Asia	251,593	239,643	247,599	241,264	224,969	206,104
LATIN AMERICA						
Colombia	15,091	5,226	4,916	6,584	7,466	7,500
Mexico	5,795	5,050	5,100	4,000	5,500	3,600
Total Latin America	20,886	10,276	10,016	10,584	12,966	11,100
GRAND TOTAL	**272,479**	**249,919**	**257,615**	**251,848**	**237,935**	**217,204**
Production in metric tons						
SOUTH-WEST ASIA						
Afghanistan	3,416	2,335	2,248	2,804	2,693	4,565
Pakistan	128	112	24	24	26	9
Subtotal	3,544	2,447	2,272	2,828	2,719	4,574
SOUTH-EAST ASIA						
Lao PDR	120	128	140	147	124	124
Myanmar	1,583	1,664	1,760	1,676	1,303	895
Thailand	3	2	5	4	8	8
Viet Nam	15	9	9	2	2	2
Subtotal	1,721	1,803	1,914	1,829	1,437	1,029
OTHER ASIAN COUNTRIES						
Combined	90	78	48	30	30	30
Total Asia	5,355	4,328	4,234	4,687	4,186	5,633
LATIN AMERICA						
Colombia	205	71	67	90	102	102
Mexico	60	53	54	46	60	43
Total Latin America	265	124	121	136	162	145
GRAND TOTAL	**5,620**	**4,452**	**4,355**	**4,823**	**4,348**	**5,778**
Potential HEROIN	562	445	436	482	435	578

(1) Potentially harvestable, after eradication.

**GLOBAL ILLICIT CULTIVATION OF COCA BUSH AND PRODUCTION OF COCA LEAF AND COCAINE, 1994-1999
(Source: UNDCP Global Illicit Drug Trends 2000)**

	1994	1995	1996	1997	1998	1999
Cultivation[1] of coca bushes in hectares						
Bolivia[2]	48,100	48,600	48,100	45,800	38,000	21,800
Colombia	44,700	50,900	67,200	79,436	101,800	122,500
Peru	108,800	106,500	75,000	65,338	51,000	38,700
Total	201,600	206,000	190,300	190,574	190,800	183,000
Production of coca leaves in metric tons						
Bolivia	89,800	85,000	75,100	70,100	52,900	22,800
Colombia	67,497	80,931	108,864	129,481	165,934	195,000
Peru	162,003	159,750	131,003	117,726	95,600	72,500
Total	319,300	325,681	314,967	317,307	314,434	290,300
Potential manufacture of cocaine in metric tons						
Bolivia	255	240	215	200	150	70
Colombia	201	230	300	350	435	520
Peru	421	399	328	294	239	175
Total	877	869	843	844	824	765

(1) Potentially harvestable, after eradication
(2) Annual estimates include 12,000 hectares authorized by Bolivian law 1008

Annual Prevalence of abuse by substance, as percentage of the population aged 5 and above (unless otherwise indicated)

AFRICA	Cannabis		Opiates		Cocaine*		ATS [1]	
	%	Year	%	Year	%	Year	%	Year
East and Southern Africa								
Kenya	4.0	1994[a]	0.1	[aa]	0.1	[aa]	0.6	[aa]
Namibia	3.9	1997	0.1	1998	0.2	1998	(0.1)	1998
South Africa	7.1	1996[a]	0.1	1998	0.3	1996[a]	0.6	[aa]
Zimbabwe	6.3	1998	0.01	[a]	0.03	1998	0.01	1998
North and Eastern Africa								
Egypt	5.1	[aa]					0.5	[aa]
Ethiopia			0.04	[aa]			0.3	[aa]
Libyan Arab Jamahiriya	0.05	1998						
Mauritius	0.7	1998	0.8	1998				
Morocco	7.4	[aa]	0.2	[aa]				
Rwanda			0.04	[aa]				
Tanzania, United Rep.	2.0	1998[a]	0.02	1998				
Uganda	1.4	[aa]	0.04	[aa]				
West and Central Africa								
Cameroon							0.9	[aa]
Chad	0.9	1995	0.2	1995	0.01	1995	0.01	1996
Congo	0.01	1994						
Cote d'Ivoire	0.01	1997						
Ghana	21.5	1998	0.7	1998	1.1	1998	1.0(0.01)	[aa]
Mali	7.8	1995[a]						
Nigeria (11-61)	8.7	[aa]	0.3	[aa]	1.0	[aa]	1.2	[aa]
Sao Tome Principe	0.01	1997			0.02	1997		
Senegal			0.03	[aa]				
Sierra Leone	16.1	1996	0.01	1997	0.02	1996		

AMERICAS	Cannabis		Opiate		Cocaine*		ATS [1]	
	%	Year	%	Year	%	Year	%	Year
Central America								
Belize	0.1	1994			0.4	1994		
Costa Rica	0.5	1997	0.1	[a]	0.3	1995[a]		
El Salvador	9.2	[aa]	0.06	[aa]	0.6	[aa]		
Guatemala (12-18)	3.2	[aa]			1.6	1998	1.7	1998
Honduras	5.9	1997	0.1	1995	2.0	1997	2.5	1997
Nicaragua	2.6	[aa]						
Panama			0.04	[aa]	1.0	[aa]	1.2	1991
North America								
Canada	7.4	[aa]	0.2	[a]	0.7	[a]	0.7(0.5)	1993[a]
Mexico	1.1	1998	0.1	[aa]	0.3	1998[a]	0.3(0.01)	1997[a]
USA (12 and above)	12.3	1998	0.5	1998	3.2	1998	0.7(0.5)	1998

AMERICAS (cont.)	Cannabis		Opiate		Cocaine*		ATS [1]		
	%	Year	%	Year	%	Year	%	Year	
South America									
Argentina	2.3	1998	0.03	1995	1.2	aa			
Bolivia (12-50)	2.2	1998	0.04	aa	1.7	1998	0.5	1999	
Brazil	7.7	aa	0.1	aa	0.8	a	0.9	aa	
Chile (12-69)	4.7	1998	0.3	1995	1.3	1998	1.1	1997	
Colombia (12 and above)	5.6	1998	0.3	a	1.6	1998	0.5	1997	
Ecuador	1.2	aa	0.4	1999	1.5	1999	0.3	1995	
Paraguay	0.6	aa							
Peru	2.1	a			1.5	a			
Suriname	1.3	1998	0.02	1998	0.3	1998			
Uruguay (15-65)	1.2	aa			0.4	1998ª	0.2	1994	
Venezuela (12 and above)	1.0	a	0.1	aa	1.2	aa	0.6	a	
The Caribbean									
Bahamas (16-59)	3.3	1997ª			0.3	1998			
Dominica	0.1	1996			0.01	1996			
Dominican Rep.	6.9	1997	0.02	aa	2.5	1997			
Grenada	0.01	1998			0.02	1998			
Jamaica					0.9	aa			
Montserrat	0.8	1997			0.01	1997			
St. Lucia					0.1	1994			
St. Vincent Grenadines	18.6	aa							

ASIA	Cannabis		Opiate		Cocaine*		ATS [1]		
	%	Year	%	Year	%	Year	%	Year	
Central Asia and Transcaucasia									
Armenia	0.8	1998ª	0.3	aa					
Azerbaijan	1.1	1998ª	0.3	aa					
Georgia			1.2	aa					
Kazakhstan	3.2	1998ª	0.9	aa					
Kyrgyzstan	1.7	aa	0.4	aa					
Tajikistan	3.4	1998ª	2.0	aa					
Turkmenistan	0.3	aa							
Uzbekistan	1.3	1998ª	0.7	aa			0.01	1997ª	
East and South-East Asia									
Brunei Darussalam	0.02	1996	0.01	1998			0.03	1998	
Cambodia	1.3	aa							
China	0.5	aa	0.1	1998					
China (Hong Kong SAR)	0.6	aa	0.3	1998			0.02	1998	
China (Macao SAR)	0.2	aa	0.2	1998					
Indonesia	0.1	aa	0.01	1998	0.1	aa			
Japan*	0.05	aa	0.02	a			0.3	aa	
Korea, Rep.	0.05	aa					0.5	aa	
Lao People's Dem. Rep.	1.0	aa	2.1	aa					
Malaysia	0.04	1997	0.2	1998			0.01	1998	
Myanmar	0.1	aa	0.9	aa					

ASIA (cont.)	Cannabis		Opiate		Cocaine*		ATS [1]	
	%	Year	%	Year	%	Year	%	Year
Philippines	3.5	aa					2.2	aa
Singapore	0.03	1998	0.3	1998	0.01	1993	0.04(0.01)	1998a
Taiwan, Province of China	0.5	aa	0.4	a	1.5	aa		
Thailand	0.7	aa	0.6	aa	1.1	aa		
Viet Nam	1.0	aa	0.4	1999				
Near and Middle East / South-West Asia								
Afghanistan	3.0	aa						
Bahrain	0.4	aa	0.3	1998	0.1	aa		
Iran, Islamic Republic	0.4	aa	2.8	1999				
Israel	0.9	aa	0.8	1995	0.3	1995	0.4(0.4)	1998
Jordan	0.2	1998	0.5	1998	0.03	1998	0.1	1998
Kuwait			0.01	1998				
Lebanon	0.5	aa	0.01	1998			0.02	1998
Oman	0.01	1994	0.01	1994			0.1 1	998
Pakistan	1.2	1998a	1.7	1999a				
Qatar	0.1	1996	0.01	1996			0.02	1996
Saudi Arabia							0.01	1998
Syrian Arab Rep.	0.01	1998	0.02	1998			0.07	1998
South Asia								
Bangladesh	3.2	**	0.6	a				
India	3.2	aa	0.5	a				
Maldives	0.5	1994	0.9	1994				
Nepal	2.8	aa	0.3	1996				
Sri Lanka	1.4	1998	0.3	1997				

EUROPE	Cannabis		Opiates		Cocaine*		ATS		Ecstasy	
	%	Year	%	Year	%	Year	%	Year	%	Year
Central and Eastern Europe										
Belarus	0.1	aa	0.08	1998			0.01	1998	0.01	1997a
Bulgaria	1.2	1998	0.7	1998	0.04	1998	0.2	1998	0.1	1998
Croatia	2.6	1997	0.8	1997	0.1	1997	0.2	1997	0.01	1997
Czech Rep.	3.6	1998	0.1	1997	0.01	1998	0.3	1998	0.01	1998
Estonia	2.8	a			0.1	1998	0.01	1998		
Hungary	1.4	aa	0.3	1999	0.01	1997	0.3	a		
Latvia	0.5	aa	0.3	a			0.2	a	0.01	1997
Lithuania	0.3	aa	0.3	a			0.6	a		
Macedonia	0.7	1998	0.3	1998			0.01	1995		
Moldova, Rep.	1.8	1998a	0.04	1997			0.01	1998		
Poland	3.4	1997	0.3	a			0.3	aa		
Romania			0.03	a						
Russian Federation	0.9	aa	0.9	a						
Slovakia (18 and above)	1.7	a	0.5	a			0.3	1996		
Slovenia	3.1	aa	0.3	1993			0.2	a		
Ukraine	0.6	1998	0.3	1992	0.04	1997	0.01	1998		

EUROPE	Cannabis		Opiates		Cocaine*		ATS		Ecstasy	
	%	Year	%	Year	%	Year	%	Year	%	Year
Western Europe										
Austria	3.0	1996[a]	0.2	1998	0.5	1996[a]	0.2	1996[a]	0.8	[a]
Belgium (18-65)	5.0	[a]	0.2	[aa]	0.5	[aa]	0.5	[aa]	0.7	1998[a]
Denmark (18-69)	4.0	1995[a]	0.3	1995	0.3	1995	0.9	1995[a]	0.7	[a]
Finland	2.5	1998[a]	0.05	1997[a]	0.2	1998	0.1	1998[a]	0.2	1998[a]
France (18-69)	4.7	1995	0.3	1997[a]	0.2	1995	0.3	1995[a]	0.3	[a]
Germany (18-59)	4.1	1997	0.2	1998	0.6	1997	0.4	[aa]	0.8	1997[aa]
Greece (12-64)	4.4	1998[a]	0.4	[a]	0.5	[aa]	0.06	1998[a]	0.01	1998[a]
Ireland	7.9	1995[a]	0.3	1997[a]	0.6	[aa]	0.6	[aa]	1.0	[aa]
Italy	4.6	[aa]	0.5	1997[a]	0.6	1996[a]	0.5	[aa]	0.5	[a]
Liechtanstein	0.8	1996	0.1	1998	0.4	1998	0.02	1997	0.2	1998
Luxembourg	4.0	1998[a]	0.5	1997[a]	0.4	[aa]	0.3	1998	0.2	[a]
Malta	2.2	[aa]	0.2	1998	0.1	1996	0.01	1997	0.2	[a]
Monaco	0.4	1996	0.1	1995	0.01	1994	0.01	1993	0.4	[a]
Netherlands (12 and above)	5.2	1998	0.2	1998	0.7	1998[a]	0.4	1997[a]	0.8	1998[a]
Norway	3.8	1998[a]	0.2	1994	0.3	1997[a]	0.5	1997[a]	0.1	[aa]
Portugal	3.7	[aa]	0.9	1998	0.5	1998[a]	0.2	[aa]	0.1	[a]
San Marino	4.0	1997[a]	0.02	1997	0.04	1994	0.3	1994	0.3	[a]
Spain	7.6	1997[a]	0.6	1999	1.7	1997	0.8	[a]	1.0	1997[a]
Sweden (15-75)	0.1	1998	0.1	1997	0.2	1998[a]	0.2	1997	0.1	1998[a]
Switzerland (18-45)	8.5	1998[a]	0.5	1998	0.5	1998[a]	0.7	[aa]		
Turkey			0.01	1998						
United Kingdom	9.0	1998[a]	0.5	[aa]	1.0	1998[a]	1.3	[aa]	1.0	1998[a]

OCEANIA	Cannabis		Opiates		Cocaine*		ATS [1]	
	%	Year	%	Year	%	Year	%	Year
Australia (14 and above)	17.9	1998	0.7	1 998	1.4	1998	3.6(2.4)	1998
Fiji	0.2	1996						
Micronesia Fed.State.	29.1	1995						
New Caledonia	1.9	[aa]						
New Zealand	15.0	1998	0.6	1998	0.04	1998	2.0	1998
Papua New Guinea (6-45)	29.5	1995			0.01	1995		
Vanuatu	0.1	1997						

[a] UNDCP estimate
[aa] Tentative estimate for the late 1990s
* Includes *basuco*
(1) Where available Ecstasy prevalence in brackets
Source: Global Illicit Drug Trends 2000

GLOBAL ILLICIT SUPPLY OF OPIATES(*) 1994-1998
Source: UNDCP Global Illicit Drug Trends 2000

	1994	1995	1996	1997	1998
Potential opiate production					
metric tons	562	445	436	482	435
Opiates seized					
metric tons	56	69	58	73	74
as a % of production	10%	15%	13%	15%	17%
Opiates available for consumption					
metric tons	506	377	378	410	360
as a % of production	90%	85%	87%	85%	83%

(*) Opiates = opium, heroin and morphine combined, in heroin equivalent

GLOBAL ILLICIT SUPPLY OF COCAINE 1994-1998
Source: UNDCP Global Illicit Drug Trends 2000

	1994	1995	1996	1997	1998
Potential cocaine production					
metric tons	877	869	843	844	824
Cocaine seized					
metric tons	326	295	324	332	380
as a % of production	37%	34%	38%	39%	46%
Cocaine available for consumption					
metric tons	551	574	519	512	444
as a % of production	63%	66%	62%	61%	54%

Remark: While 1999 production data was available at the time of preparation of the present report, statistics on seizures for 1999 were not, as the compilation/reporting process by national law enforcement agencies and international institutions takes longer than for production data.

SEIZURES OF OPIUM BY SUBREGION, IN KILOGRAMS, 1994-1998
In descending order from largest seizures, 1998

	1994	1995	1996	1997	1998
Near and Middle East / South-West Asia	132,036	236,232	157,140	169,793	159,508
East and South-East Asia	5,898	4,096	4,541	11,331	8,628
Central Asia and Transcaucasian countries	1,450	2,071	7,318	10,015	5,055
South Asia	2,270	1,349	2,877	3,316	2,032
Western Europe	271	159	349	213	492
North America	166	266	259	393	210
South America	709	168	103	122	111
North Africa	50	30	16	31	26
Eastern Europe	1,668	1,284	1,600	255	24
Southern Africa	0.2	2	0.1	7	
Oceania	0.03	0.3	8	2	0.01
Central America	6				
World total	**144,517**	**245,663**	**174,213**	**195,470**	**176,094**

Source: UNDCP Global Illicit Drug Trends 2000, UNDCP DELTA

SEIZURES OF OPIUM BY COUNTRY, IN KILOGRAMS, 1994-1998
In descending order from largest seizures, 1998, for first 15 countries

	1994	1995	1996	1997	1998
Iran (Islamic Republic of)	117,095	126,554	149,577	162,414	154,454
Myanmar	1,689	1,061	1,300	7,884	5,706
Pakistan	14,663	109,420	7,423	7,300	5,022
India	2,256	1,349	2,876	3,316	2,031
Uzbekistan	226	835	1,865	2,364	1,935
Thailand	606	927	381	1,151	1,631
Turkmenistan	650			1,410	1,412
China	1,778	1,110	1,745	1,880	1,215
Tajikistan	120	3,405	3,516	1,190	
Kazakhstan	435	245	500	1,000	297
Germany	36	15	45	42	286
Kyrgyzstan	727	1,490	1,639	172	
Mexico	149	223	196	342	149
Turkey	91	122	233	93	142
Colombia	128	144	103	122	100

Source: UNDCP Global Illicit Drug Trends 2000, UNDCP DELTA

SEIZURES OF HEROIN AND MORPHINE COMBINED BY SUBREGION, IN KILOGRAMS, 1994-1998
In descending order from largest seizures, 1998

	1994	1995	1996	1997	1998
Near and Middle East /South-West Asia	20,534	24,752	17,889	27,444	28,912
Western Europe	8,662	9,865	11,386	9,408	12,181
East and South-East Asia	6,529	3,826	6,397	8,309	9,249
Eastern Europe	2,303	1,217	869	999	2,235
North America	1,692	1,650	1,813	1,754	1,725
Central Asia and Transcaucasian countries	15	19	55	2,126	1,019
South Asia	1,114	1,733	1,328	1,526	741
South America	211	553	312	325	409
Oceania	249	50	49	369	311
Central America	29	40	25	56	41
North Africa	91	60	54	52	32
West and Central Africa	182	62	73	458	30
East Africa	45	39	54	56	29
Southern Africa	32	160	2	3	10
Caribbean	12	8	15	16	7
World total	**41,699**	**44,035**	**40,319**	**52,900**	**56,930**

Source: UNDCP Global Illicit Drug Trends 2000, UNDCP DELTA

SEIZURES OF HEROIN AND MORPHINE COMBINED BY COUNTRY, IN KILOGRAMS, 1994-1998
In descending order from largest seizures, 1998, for first 15 countries

	1994	1995	1996	1997	1998
Iran (Islamic Republic of)	13,767	13,121	11,235	20,936	25,186
China	4,086	2,488	4,525	5,835	7,504
Turkey	2,474	4,396	5,579	4,173	5,406
Pakistan	6,444	10,760	5,872	6,156	3,364
Netherlands	246	351	361	190	2,072
United States	1,333	1,337	1,366	1,542	1,581
United Kingdom	776	1,397	1,072	2,235	1,386
Italy	1,152	940	1,251	470	706
Germany	1,590	933	898	722	686
India	1,062	1,685	1,261	1,460	674
Hungary	812	574	319	207	635
Thailand	1,295	518	598	323	508
Myanmar	233	73	505	1,447	499
Turkmenistan	12			1,948	495
Spain	824	546	537	479	444

Source: UNDCP Global Illicit Drug Trends 2000, UNDCP DELTA

SEIZURES OF COCAINE BY REGION, IN KILOGRAMS, 1994-1998
In descending order from largest seizures, 1998

	1994	1995	1996	1997	1998
South America	114,167	113,658	100,339	97,417	154,563
North America	160,017	137,148	155,684	139,042	140,160
Western Europe	29,413	20,979	31,194	38,807	34,928
Central America	10,898	12,121	18,934	36,036	34,449
Caribbean	7,702	9,330	16,455	11,511	13,758
Eastern Europe	596	553	885	1,437	1,152
Southern Africa	74	202	192	731	681
East and South-East Asia	55	53	54	75	201
Near and Middle East /South-West Asia	146	36	295	51	115
Oceania	632	348	2	82	103
West and Central Africa	108	43	97	396	43
North Africa	4	7	92	6,057	32
Central Asia and Transcaucasian countries			0.01		21
East Africa	0.1	0.4	11	1	1
South Asia	2	40	3	48	1
World total	323,814	294,519	324,236	331,689	380,209

Source: UNDCP Global Illicit Drug Trends 2000, UNDCP DELTA

SEIZURES OF COCAINE BY COUNTRY, IN KILOGRAMS, 1994-1998
In descending order from largest seizures, 1998, for first 15 countries

	1994	1995	1996	1997	1998
United States	129,543	110,842	128,725	102,000	117,000
Colombia	69,592	59,030	45,779	42,044	107,480
Mexico	22,117	22,708	23,835	34,952	22,597
Panama	5,177	7,169	8,618	15,177	11,828
Spain	4,016	6,897	13,743	18,419	11,688
Netherlands	8,200	4,896	8,067	6,744	11,452
Bolivia	10,021	8,497	8,305	13,689	10,102
Peru	10,634	22,661	19,695	8,796	9,937
Guatemala	1,900	956	3,951	5,098	9,217
Venezuela	6,035	6,650	5,906	16,741	8,159
Costa Rica	1,411	1,170	1,873	7,857	7,387
Brazil	12,028	5,815	4,071	4,309	6,560
Nicaragua	1,338	1,507	398	2,790	4,750
Ecuador	1,790	4,284	9,534	3,697	3,854
Bahamas	492	392	115	2,579	3,343

Source: UNDCP Global Illicit Drug Trends 2000, UNDCP DELTA

SEIZURES OF CANNABIS HERB BY REGION, IN KILOGRAMS, 1994-1998
In descending order from largest seizures, 1998

	1994	1995	1996	1997	1998
Western Europe	1,100,536	1,557,381	1,831,090	1,773,839	1,888,444
Near and Middle East/					
South-West Asia	283,018	290,523	239,513	222,315	241,230
North Africa	254,306	359,727	318,348	288,594	235,209
Central Asia and					
Transcaucasian countries	273,301	362,339	243,563	199,189	169,463
North America	29,870	311,406	65,433	36,793	92,974
South Asia	194,971	135,392	85,718	146,246	78,081
Eastern Europe	34,241	37,287	46,333	38,160	68,300
Caribbean	22,057	25,996	43,982	27,060	62,031
East and South-East Asia	2,986	2,473	37,061	15,880	19,397
East Africa	914	2,110	2,498	4,818	16,386
Southern Africa	29,377	31,606	37,385	93,019	14,660
South America	23,768	9,226	6,116	19,192	13,416
Oceania	13,153	9,434	11,828	112,870	12,860
West and Central Africa	60,177	61,267	66,191	57,698	12,340
Central America	7,543	1,099	8,704	13,288	2,166
World total	**2,330,217**	**3,197,265**	**3,043,762**	**3,048,962**	**2,926,956**

Source: UNDCP Global Illicit Drug Trends 2000, UNDCP DELTA

SEIZURES OF CANNABIS HERB BY COUNTRY, IN KILOGRAMS, 1994-1998
In descending order from largest seizures, 1998, for first 15 countries

	1994	1995	1996	1997	1998
Mexico	529,933	780,170	1,015,756	1,038,470	1,062,143
United States	474,972	627,946	638,661	684,745	799,001
South Africa	268,652	238,813	203,354	171,929	197,116
Paraguay	12,756	97,566	43,325	17,218	80,078
Colombia	207,712		238,943	178,132	70,025
Senegal	1,392	84,392	24,803	13,627	69,652
India	187,896	121,873	62,992	80,866	68,221
Netherlands	190,477	275,035	82,232	31,513	55,463
Italy	803	473	5,722	45,011	38,786
Morocco	34,200	35,808	38,521	27,956	37,161
Egypt			6,609	10,186	31,078
Brazil	18,837	11,731	22,431	31,828	28,982
Canada	95,631	149,265	176,673	50,624	27,300
Russian Federation	19,936	20,142	18,968	22,976	23,511
United Kingdom	11,579	13,872	34,189	31,120	21,658

Source: UNDCP Global Illicit Drug Trends 2000, UNDCP DELTA

SEIZURES OF CANNABIS RESIN BY REGION, IN KILOGRAMS, 1994-1998
In descending order from largest seizures, 1998

	1994	1995	1996	1997	1998
Western Europe	506,857	456,072	445,371	548,779	733,816
Near and Middle East/ South-West Asia	244,303	381,362	213,966	120,467	83,595
North Africa	100,259	113,363	66,036	72,530	58,644
Central Asia and Transcaucasian countries	1,252	2,044	1,654	4,416	22,571
North America	37,195	68,483	62,869	7,366	15,926
South Asia	514	5,764	19,472	3,299	12,692
Eastern Europe	1,546	10,565	15,375	3,401	9,161
Caribbean	30	995	242	2,018	2,852
East and South-East Asia	7,237	1,122	179	192	617
East Africa		5,711	19,640	7	68
Southern Africa	27	3,245	17	12,046	44
South America	76	19	29	21	6
Oceania	6,522	18	9	539	4
West and Central Africa	2	0	987	4,651	0
World total	905,820	1,048,764	845,846	779,734	939,996

Source: UNDCP Global Illicit Drug Trends 2000, UNDCP DELTA

SEIZURES OF CANNABIS RESIN BY COUNTRY, IN KILOGRAMS, 1994-1998
In descending order from largest seizures, 1998, for first 15 countries

	1994	1995	1996	1997	1998
Spain	219,176	197,024	247,745	315,328	428,236
United Kingdom	51,430	44,607	66,937	118,849	85,818
Netherlands	43,299	79,985	11,378	70,696	
Pakistan	189,252	357,691	192,837	107,000	65,909
Portugal	40,393	6,334	5,324	9,621	55,748
Morocco	97,048	110,245	64,769	71,887	55,520
France	55,890	39,203	35,576	51,664	52,176
Turkmenistan	1,000				22,249
Canada	36,369	40,369	24,655	6,178	15,925
Italy	18,128	14,922	5,940	14,741	15,412
Iran (Islamic Republic of)	7,618	15,854	13,063	11,096	14,376
India		3,629	6,520	3,281	10,106
Turkey	31,218	17,360	12,294	10,439	9,434
Ukraine	208	51	21	10	6,150
Germany	4,033	3,809	3,247	7,328	6,110

Source: UNDCP Global Illicit Drug Trends 2000, UNDCP DELTA

SEIZURES OF STIMULANTS BY REGION, IN KILOGRAMS, 1994-1998
In descending order from largest seizures, 1998

	1994	1995	1996	1997	1998
East and South-East Asia	1,493	2,428	3,640	4,507	5,488
Western Europe	2,132	1,622	3,245	4,466	4,805
North America	2,184	1,494	1,642	1,592	2,197
Oceania	629	619	340	203	184
Eastern Europe	69	26	71	240	155
Near and Middle East/ South-West Asia	94	67	85	162	36
North Africa	65	41	5	1	16
Southern Africa	0	282	0	0	16
South America	1	0.4	0.2	1	0.1
West and Central Africa	105	70	13	312	0.1
Caribbean			0.3	0.2	0.04
Central Asia and Transcaucasian countries			7	0.5	
East Africa	1				
World total	**6,774**	**6,649**	**9,049**	**11,484**	**12,897**

Source: UNDCP Global Illicit Drug Trends 2000, UNDCP DELTA

SEIZURES OF STIMULANTS BY COUNTRY, IN KILOGRAMS, 1994-1998
In descending order from largest seizures, 1998, for first 15 countries

	1994	1995	1996	1997	1998
Thailand	812	561	442	2,136	2,828
United States	1,918	998	1,469	1,551	2,044
United Kingdom	1,305	819	2,625	3,296	1,803
China	123	1,303	1,599	1,334	1,608
Netherlands	318	46			1,452
Japan	315	89	652	176	550
Belgium	28	77	26	77	448
Germany	120	138	160	234	310
China (Hong Kong SAR)	123	15	47	74	233
Norway	13	53	30	93	208
Australia	629	619	340	203	182
Spain	32	35	53	120	177
France	80	106	131	196	177
Myanmar			59	50	160
Sweden	210	277	164	188	135

Source: UNDCP Global Illicit Drug Trends 2000, UNDCP DELTA
Remark: The seizures reported to UNDCP by Governments under the category of "Stimulants" include mainly amphetamine and methamphetamine. Although some governments also include Ecstasy-type substances in stimulants, others, in accordance with the current reporting system, include them under the category of hallucinogens (along with substances such as LSD, PCP, DOB, mescaline and DMT). As a result, it is difficult to produce reliable statistics on ecstasy-type substances, a problem which UNDCP is presently trying to correct.